INNER-CITY KIDS

QUALITATIVE STUDIES IN PSYCHOLOGY

This series showcases the power and possibility of qualitative work in psychology. Books feature detailed and vivid accounts of qualitative psychology research using a variety of methods, including participant observation and field work, discursive and textual analyses, and critical cultural history. They probe vital issues of theory, implementation, representation, and ethics that qualitative workers confront. The series mission is to enlarge and refine the repertoire of qualitative approaches to psychology.

GENERAL EDITORS
Michelle Fine and Jeanne Marecek

Everyday Courage:
The Lives and Stories of Urban Teenagers
by Niobe Way

Negotiating Consent in Psychotherapy
by Patrick O'Neill

Voted Out:
The Psychological Consequences of Anti-Gay Politics
by Glenda M. Russell

Inner-City Kids:
Adolescents Confront Life and Violence in an Urban Community
by Alice McIntyre

INNER-CITY KIDS

Adolescents Confront Life and Violence
in an Urban Community

ALICE McINTYRE

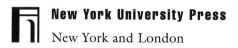
New York University Press
New York and London

NEW YORK UNIVERSITY PRESS
New York and London

© 2000 by New York University

Library of Congress Cataloging-in-Publication Data
McIntyre, Alice, 1956–
Inner-city kids : adolescents confront life and violence in an urban
community / Alice McIntyre.
p.   cm. — (Qualitative studies in psychology)
Includes bibliographical references and index.
ISBN 0-8147-5635-2 (cloth : alk. paper) —
ISBN 0-8147-5636-0 (pbk. : alk. paper)
1. Urban youth—United States—Attitudes. 2. Inner cities—United
States. 3. Social work with youth—United States. 4. Children and
violence—United States. I. Title. II. Series.
HQ796 .M237 2000
305.235'0973'091732—dc21   00-010317

New York University Press books are printed on acid-free paper,
and their binding materials are chosen for strength and durability.

Manufactured in the United States of America

10 9 8 7 6 5 4 3 2 1

■　　■　　■　　■　　■　　■　　■　　■　　■

This book is dedicated to
Clara Beatrice Lawton

May you grow up in a just society
where your dreams will not be deferred
due to the color of your skin.
Where you can live freely and
unafraid.
Where you can walk the streets and
know,
believe,
and be assured that
Black
is
truly beautiful.

■ ■ ■ ■ ■ ■ ■ ■ ■

"It isn't funny. . . . Take it back. Call that story back," said the audience by the end of the story, but the witch answered: "It's already loose/It's already coming./It can't be called back." A story is *not* just a story. Once the forces have been aroused and set into motion, they can't simply be stopped at someone's request. Once told, the story is bound to circulate; humanized, it may have a temporary end, but its effects linger on and its end is never truly an end.

—T. T. Minh-Ha, *Woman, Native, Other: Writing Postcoloniality and Feminism*

Contents

■   ■   ■   ■

Acknowledgments

Some of the young people the reader will meet in this book are considered "at-risk" youth by many educators and psychologists. I think about that often because if the term "at-risk" had been around when I was twelve and thirteen years old, I am sure that I would have been defined in much the same way. Therefore I am deeply appreciative of the grace of the Universe and some very insightful, courageous people who helped me navigate my adolescence and who continue to accompany me through my "at-risk" adulthood.

Let me first thank the people who cleared the way for this particular manuscript. Jeanne Marecek, Michelle Fine, and Jennifer Hammer provided me with what I needed most while I was writing this book: they made me stop. Touché to all of you for interrupting my urge to defend participatory action research, myself, the kids, and every decision that was made in this ongoing process. I'd also to thank Patricia Maguire and two anonymous reviewers for their questions, comments, and suggestions. To the many graduate students who participated in and contributed to this work, my gratitude. I hope you continue to avail yourselves of the many opportunities you have to generate social change in your classrooms, schools, and communities.

Second, I'd like to thank two people who, a decade ago, cleared the way for my journey into academia. Mary Brabeck and Brinton Lykes continue to challenge me to think, to listen, to take risks, and to stand in my own truth. Learning with and from them has transformed my life in profound ways. For countless cups of java on the first floor, and for "the intellectual debates" that took place in Room 201A, my deepest appreciation.

The third round of thank-yous goes to my family, friends, and day-at-a-timers who have cleared the way for me to live, learn, succeed, fail, win, lose, fight, make peace—the people who simply live their lives with determination, humor, faith, and a joy of living that steadfastly guides me as I attempt to do the same. I must also thank the offspring in the family who, like the young people in this book, remind me of the power of creativity, imagination, and love.

Finally, and most importantly, I want to thank the young people who are the "stars" of this manuscript. To Mariah, Risha, Jason, Bart, Michael, Collin, Boo, Alex, Veronica, Neaka, Bill, William, Rebecca, Yolly, Tina, Troy, Chesterfield, Mase, Senor, Jo-Anne, Monique, Tee, Blood, Janine, Flanango, Jeter, Tonesha, Puffy, Nadia, Mikey, and Melinda—thank you for allowing me to "chill" with you for the last few years. Your trust in me, your confidence in yourselves, and your commitment to "making things better around here" speak loudly to the power of collaboration that can happen between and among diverse groups of people. You're the best and the brightest. And since you are also the greatest lovers of food, the next time we go out for pizza, it's on me.

Proceeds from this book will benefit the continuation of the youth-initiated projects described herein.

Introduction

I WAS INTRODUCED to the principal of the Blair School,[1] an inner-city public school located in the northeast region of the United States, in September 1997. A community activist I had met when I relocated to the area encouraged me to speak with the principal about my ideas of developing a participatory action research (PAR) project with a group of middle-school students aimed at exploring how they negotiate their daily lives within an inner-city community. Mrs. Lawton, an energetic African American principal, was receptive to my ideas and within minutes, introduced me to Mrs. Leslie, an African American science teacher at the Blair School. At the time, Mrs. Leslie was also the homeroom teacher for the students in Homeroom 211. Like Mrs. Lawton, Susan (Mrs. Leslie) was very interested in a collaborative project and invited me outside to meet "her babies." We stood outside in the school garden—a contained space of soil and seed that is cared for by the sixth-grade students. Susan had spearheaded the creation of the garden many years ago and each year there is a new group of students who rake, plant, weed, and learn the dos and don'ts of growing vegetables, flowers, and other mysterious living matter that appears every season. As we stood near the garden, Susan invited the students to listen to my proposal, reminding me that the decision was up to the students—if they wanted to participate, she and they would commit to every facet of the project. But if they decided not to participate, she would respect their decision and I would need to investigate other possibilities.

I told the young people a little bit about myself: my experiences growing up and teaching in an inner-city middle school in Boston; my journey from teaching in a public school to teaching in a university; and my desire to collaborate with a group of young people in exploring community issues that were important to them. I also informed the students that I had recently moved to Ellsworth and that as director of a teaching program at a nearby university, I wanted to develop linkages between the students attending the university and the young people at the Blair School.

My "pitch" was successful—and so began our collaboration. Using a feminist (PAR) approach,[2] creative techniques (for example, collage making, storytelling), community resource inventories, and community photography, we began a participatory process of investigation and action in the hope of addressing community issues that were of most concern to the young people involved in this project.

This book describes that process—a process that has resulted in what Kohl (1995) refers to as a "radical story." By that he means a story with the following characteristics:

- the major force of the story is the community or social group;
- collective action is involved;
- there is an intentional effort to show opposing forces involved in social struggle and to represent the numerous complexities that get played out in people's lives;
- the story illustrates the comradeship as well as the tensions that are created when groups are engaged in some form of community-building or struggle or collective endeavor;
- lastly, a radical story has "no compulsory happy ending. . . . There are many defeats and regroupings, partial victories, new and larger problems to tackle and a decent world to sustain or build. What characterizes all the stories, however, is a projection of hope and possibility." (1995:68)

This book tells a radical story about struggle and possibility, hope and despair, frustration and enthusiasm, victory and defeat with the explicit intention of better understanding the experiences of a group of adolescents living in an inner-city community and, in response to those experiences, developing action programs to support and foster youth-initiated strategies for individual and community well-being.

The story of how a group of young adolescents of Color living in an inner-city community moves from dialoguing about issues that concern them to acting on those issues is fraught with confusions, complications, and a host of distractions, all of which can mobilize and/or paralyze a collaborative process. Traditional methods of social science research would not be able to contain the push and pull of conflicting and competing agendas that are inherent in a participatory process. Nor would conventional research paradigms provide a framework for addressing the researcher-participant relationship. Similarly, there would be little room for codeveloping the research process, and positioning activism and consciousness raising within the research experience.

Participatory action research *does* provide opportunities for codeveloping processes *with* people rather than *for* people. It is a counterhegemonic paradigm that emphasizes among other things the promotion of critical self-awareness about one's lived experiences, building alliances between researchers and participants, a commitment to just social change, the coconstruction of knowledge, and "the notion of action as a legitimate mode of knowing, thereby taking the realm of knowledge into the field of practice" (Tandon 1996:21). Although not widely employed by feminists and other researchers in and from the United States (for exceptions, see Brydon-Miller 1993; Lykes 1997, 1994; Maguire 1987, 1993), I chose to explore the idea of developing a project within the context of PAR because it provides opportunities for making important connections between urban youth's daily lives, their schooling, and the creation of healthy communities. As important, PAR has the potential to create public spaces where researchers and participants can reshape our understandings of how the political, educational, social, economic, and familial contexts that exist in many low-income, inner-city communities mediate the experience of adolescence.

Reframing Urban Youth

I watch the young people participating in the research project described in this book engage their lives like many other adolescents in the United States, with humor, intelligence, introspection, fear, anxiety, a determination to "be somebody," and bodies and minds full of energy, creativity, and hope. I also watch them struggle with the multiple issues that are particular to youth of Color living in inner cities and attending inner-city public schools: drug use and abuse, teen pregnancy, violence, "too much trash," poor housing, lack of resources, and other interlocking systems that marginalize and isolate large segments of young people who are already "losing ground, people whose lives are being determined largely by their inherited place in [the] system" (Finnegan 1998:xix). The system these young people have inherited erects barriers around their lives that often appear insurmountable. Tonesha carries a knife because "there's crazy people in the world . . . so you have to protect yourself." Tina doesn't go out at night "'cause in the summertime like if I went out at night, like they start shooting and stuff outside so I have to go in and I can't go back out." Bart "runs in the other direction" when he sees gangs walking down the street because "I ain't gettin' shot." Rebecca is "sick of lookin' at trash. Everywhere we look there is a piece of trash. . . . I see it every day when I go bike riding, driving in a car, or when I take the bus home." Veronica tries "not to get that many friends 'cause I know I'm about to move, 'cause I moved like six places in three years."

The challenges these young people face as they negotiate their lives are daunting. Yet it is difficult to dismiss their fate as a foregone conclusion. Although many urban youth live in and with instability, isolation, and various forms of discrimination, the young people described in this book also live with hopes, dreams, the everydayness of school, boys, girls, friends, sex, television, music, and other factors that make up the lives of teenagers. Their stories about life in an inner-city community reveal the various ways in which young people resist, rebel, and recast the constraints of race, social class, and gender—or to be more specific, racism, classism, and sexism.

The participants' engagement in this PAR project also reveals disturbing information about why and how young urban adolescents *resist* productive change. Given their history of isolation and marginalization from white, European American society, it is not surprising that young adolescents of Color are cynical about change and, at times, decide to invest their energy into defending themselves against what they perceive as further alienation. On many occasions during the PAR project various participants lost interest, lost hope, switched gears, skipped a session, came back, decided that "hangin' out" was more attractive than staying after school to work on a project, and for a host of other reasons "checked out" of the research process. One day, Blood stopped by a group meeting and told me that he couldn't stay because his mother needed him at home. Five minutes later, Mase told me to look out of the window. "Check him out, Ms. Mac. He ain't goin' home to his mama. He's playin' basketball." Another day, we had a very important meeting that required everyone's attendance. Thirty minutes into the meeting, Tonesha and Monique strolled into the gymnasium drinking sodas, eating chips, and wondering why the rest of us were upset with them. "We were hungry, y'all. And then we was just talkin' to people on the way."

There were just as many times when the participants came to the table with energy, hope, enthusiasm, a host of ideas, and concrete plans for how we were going to get from "here" to "there." Mase grabbed a broom every week and cleaned the classroom in which we had our meetings so that we could "enjoy ourselves and not have to look at junk." Monique took time out of her day to create fliers on the computer and generated enthusiasm among her peers when she took to the floor with her singing and dancing. Janine was a conscientious secretary, taking notes and keeping us informed on a weekly basis about what we needed to do and when we needed to do it.

It has been my experience working with this group of young people that both their active participation in the PAR process and their determined resistance to various activities were essential to the ongoing processes of reflection and action that characterized this project. When I and the other members of the research team accepted those dynamics and viewed the participants as multifaceted partners in processes of change, great things happened. The "great" things the participants in this project accomplished did not unsettle systems of power and privilege. Nor did their actions dismantle the status quo in any significant way. Yet what the young people *did* accomplish represents a form of activism and agency that not only contributed to their personal growth but also proved to them, their peers, and the rest of the community that persistent collective effort can lead to change. This change may not shift the social and political landscape in ways that remedy the multiple problems that urban communities confront. Nonetheless, the limited changes that did occur cohered with the participants' aims and were useful to and for them within the context of the overall research experience.

A Story of Struggle and Possibility

It is important at this juncture to state what this book is *not*. It is not about university-school-community partnerships, although it clearly reflects how a collaborative relationship might be initiated between interested groups. Nor is it about the intricate relationships that exist between public policy, economic trends, and educational reform, although certainly some parts of the book would suggest that major reforms are needed and necessary, and long overdue. Nor is the book about how schools of education can be more effective in preparing a large number of prospective teachers, counselors, and psychologists, the majority of whom are white and middle class, to work with young people of Color living in inner cities, although there are particular project methods that may be of assistance in that endeavor. Finally, the book is not about how "we" can help "them"—something that too often frames collaborative research projects where university people (outsiders) enter communities to "help" local residents (insiders).[3]

Instead, this book has two distinct yet interrelated and intertwining aims. The first is to create a space for a group of young adolescents of Color to narrate a story about themselves and their community—a story that presents urban youth as friendly, anxious, hopeful, enthusiastic, resistant, multifaceted people "without erasing the essential features of the complex story that constitutes urban life" (Fine and Weis 1998a:31). I agree with Fine and Weis when they argue that:

> Simple stories of discrimination and victimization, with no evidence of resistance, resilience, or agency, are seriously flawed and deceptively partial, and they deny the rich subjectivities of persons surviving amid horrific social circumstances. Equally dreary, however, are the increasingly popular stories of individual heroes who thrive despite the obstacles, denying the burdens of surviving amid such circumstances. (1998a:31)

The second aim of the book is to instill into psychology and education a commitment to activism as a core aspect of participating in research with urban youth. As Pastor, McCormick, and Fine suggest, "Critical insights without opportunities for [people] to reconstruct a world rich in the wonders of race, culture, gender, and social justice may wound a sense of possibility" (1996:29). Urban youth need to be celebrated, showcased, and presented in ways that are representative of their lives. Equally important, psychologists, educators, and researchers who work with young people in processes of change, need to link our representations, theories, and research to transformative actions that improve the social contexts in which they live. In so doing, we contribute to the well-being of inner-city youth as well as to the elimination of the potholes, detours, barriers, and impediments that inhibit them from gaining access to and being actively engaged in societal opportunities. As Kelley argues, if we really "believe that our [youth] are worth saving and the world is worth remaking," we must be ready to "look in different places with new eyes" (1997:13). The young people described in this book invite educators, psychologists, and other professionals to read the multidimensional worlds of inner-city youth with "new eyes." In so doing, we are also invited to move away from a focus on urban youths' needs, deficiencies, and problems, and to apply our psychological theories and research methodologies to an examination of urban adolescents' assets, skills, and talents for individual and collective mobilization and resistance.

The book is organized into eight chapters. In chapter 1, I describe PAR, emphasizing the contribution of feminism to PAR's underlying tenets of investigation, knowledge construction, and action. Given the paucity of literature concerning feminist PAR in education and psychology, and hoping that would-be practitioners will find this book helpful, I thread a detailed description of what constitutes this particular feminist PAR project throughout the manuscript.

In chapter 2, I introduce the research team and the participants, briefly describing the school and the community where the project is taking place. In addition, I describe the information-gathering phase of the project. Participatory action research takes many forms and it is therefore difficult to define the exact parameters of "information gathering." Similarly, collective investigation, education, and action occur both sequentially and simultaneously within participatory action research. Therefore, although I began with a draft outline of possible phases of the project, events and activities overlapped and did not always occur as planned. I provide examples of how the research team and the participants gathered and constructed information while also developing levels of trust with one another, learning how to participate in decision-making processes, and befriending each other outside the school environment.

The most salient issues that emerged during the first year of the project were the participants' concerns about violence. In chapter 3, I present their experiences with the multidimensionality of interpersonal violence within the school and community. As the data reveal, the participants' "discourse of violence . . . sits within a powerful, incisive, and painful social critique" (Fine and Weis 1998b:447). The structural systems the participants have inherited are significant impediments to the efforts to reduce the violence that exists in their environment. Their stories of violence are points of entry into how they—and we—can better understand the impact of violence on young people and, with that understanding, develop realistic strategies for insuring that urban youth can live in a safe environment, succeed in life, and thrive as creative, productive human beings.

The violence the participants describe and experience in their school and community goes beyond the more generally accepted definition of violence as "rough or injurious physical force, action, or treatment" (*Webster's College Dictionary* 1996). There is also a preponderance of environmental violence characterized by trash, pollution, graffiti, abandoned houses, and drug paraphernalia in the streets. The participants repeatedly voiced their displeasure about the "trashy way this community looks." Their descriptions of trash, pollution, and abandoned houses, and their feelings of disappointment, frustration, and resignation over the inability to clean up their neighborhood are examined in chapter 4. I pay particular attention to the community photography aspect of the project that assisted us in broadening our conceptualization of violence to include violations of and to the environment, which, as the participants reveal, have powerful implications for and in their community.

In chapter 5, I move from foregrounding the interpersonal and environmental violence that exists in the participants' community to highlighting educational violence. I describe the participants' preoccupation with what it means to "be somebody." I argue that the participants' ideas about what it means to "be somebody" is mediated by what Ponder refers to as "educational apartheid"—a system of education that is "supported by covert political and social policies . . . which enact separate developmental expectations for certain groups of students" (1994:1). I embed the discussion of "becoming somebody" in the context of a society that promises young people one thing—an equal education and an opportunity to live the American dream—and delivers another. Although urban environments may produce heroism in some children as they negotiate difficult terrain, the majority of young people living in inner cities and attending urban public schools are too often "rendered invisible" (Tarpley 1995:3). The reality for many young people of Color, particularly those living in low-income communities, is that the American dream is, as Langston Hughes suggested, "a dream deferred" (1951:62). It is a dream that does not exist for the majority of people of Color, economically deprived whites, and other socially marginalized groups.

In chapters 6 and 7, the book shifts from exploring the worlds of a small group of young adolescents to a description of how we (the members of the research team and the participants) formulated action plans to address the information we had gathered during the first year of the project. Chapter 6 focuses on how we developed a short-term career exploration program to assist the participants in exploring educational and occupational goals that were of interest to them. In chapter 7, I describe the process by which we developed a long-term project called One STEP—Save the Earth Program, which was and is aimed at cleaning up the school and the community. How we arrived at those points in the research process and negotiated the challenge of implementing the action phases of the project are described in both chapters.

Finally, chapter 8 provides a glimpse of where we are today in relationship to the overall research project. I explore the contested spaces of participation and action and discuss the implications of PAR for productive social change. I suggest that PAR can bring about a new way of thinking about what life is like for young people of Color living in an inner-city community. I further argue that it is up to professional educators, community leaders, psychologists, and researchers to act on the insights gleaned from PAR and to take responsibility for initiating new, effective, and transformative ways to engage teaching, learning, and research. As a feminist psychologist and educator, I believe we contribute to feminist psychology, education, and research by engaging in a PAR project that highlights young people's assets, that refuses to study young people of Color from a deficit model approach, that participates with young people in developing strategies for individual and collective well-being, and that advocates for social change.

(Extra)Ordinary Youth

It is clear from the data that there are "biggg problems" in the participants' community and that much needs to be done to improve the environment in which they live. At the same time, it is important to support the more positive experiences the participants engage in as they live their daily lives within an inner-city community. The young people play sports with one another, visit relatives both inside and outside the community, hang out at the mall, go to the movies, listen to music, attend parties, participate in after-school programs, fall in and out of "like" with each other, and generally wrestle with the unpredictability of adolescence. Those experiences, although significant, are not the core foci of this book. One reason for this is because this book is a story about how PAR helped a group of young people address issues and problems that were and are of concern to them. Thus, the majority of our conversations, time, and energy were spent gathering information and taking action about significant aspects of the community that troubled them the most.

The second reason the book focuses on the problematic issues of the participants' lives is that many white people in this country believe that racial discrimination is no longer a serious problem in the United States and that all young people, regardless of their social positions, have equal access to societal resources. As Hacker suggests, "Most White Americans will say that, all things considered, things aren't so bad for black people in the United States. . . . Some have even been heard to muse that it's better to be black, since affirmative action policies make it a disadvantage to be white" (1995:35). This myth that Blacks and other people of Color have it better than whites in our society, or that young people of Color have as many opportunities as young white people do, dismisses the real-life effects of racism, discrimination, poor schools, and lack of societal resources on urban youth. Highlighting stories about how young people play basketball in the courtyard, dance in the school yard, ride bikes to McDonald's, and stand in line for movie tickets, makes it easier for many white people who do not live in low-income urban communities to think that these young people are unaffected by the disturbing social contexts in which they live.

One night, a group of us went out for pizza at a neighborhood restaurant. We were having a great time, laughing, playing a game called "Name the Capitals of the United States," and discussing who had the best pizza, the coldest drinks, and the most delicious desserts in the city of Ellsworth. In the midst of multiple across-the-table conversations, Blood looked over at me and softly said, "I wish I could stay here all night and just eat pizza. That way, I wouldn't have to walk through the drug dealers on my way into my building." I told him he could eat pizza as long as he liked and that I would make sure he arrived home safely.

I enjoy spending time with the participants at an amusement park, the university, eating pizza at a restaurant, taking a walk to McDonald's, and going to a basketball game. Those experiences are important to me, and to them, and have been invaluable in our efforts to learn to trust one another. Yet, in order to create spaces for addressing problematic issues so as to effect change it is equally important that we spend time identifying aspects of urban life that interfere with the participants' ability to relax, enjoy their adolescence, and be free from worry and fear.

Michelle Fine (1998a) argues that it is not enough for those of us with varying degrees of power and access to gain access for others. She argues that we need to, and must, transform structures, communities, schools, and other contexts as well. The young people described in this book help us to think about how we can expand theories, rethink methodologies, and as important, transform environments. They also challenge us to "step into the complicated maze of experience that renders 'ordinary' folks so extraordinarily multifaceted, diverse, and complicated" (Kelley 1994:4).

1

■　■　■　■　■　■　■　■　■

Participatory Action Research

PARTICIPATORY ACTION RESEARCH emerged during the 1960s and
1970s as a social, educational, and political movement aimed at transforming the daily realities of people living in developing countries (Fals-
Borda and Rahman 1991). Its roots can be traced back to Latin America
where, in the 1960s, social scientists were engaged in collaborative
processes of investigation, education, and action with poor and oppressed
groups with the ultimate goal of transforming societal structures so as to
improve the lives of those involved (Hall 1981).

Over the next two decades, PAR projects were conducted in various
parts of the world, for example, in Tanzania by Swantz (1982a), Mduma
(1982), and Mbilinyi (1982); in Botswana by Kidd (see Kraai, MacKenzie,
and Youngman 1982); in Colombia by Fals-Borda (1985, 1987); in
Venezuela by Vio Grossi (1980); in Peru by de Wit and Gianotten (1980);
and in India by Tandon (1981) and Kanhare (1980). In these and other
countries, researchers collaborated with local people in the development of
programs that addressed issues such as literacy, agriculture, technology,
water supply and sanitation, grain storage, migration, and economic reform (Jackson, Conchelos, and Vigoda 1980).

In North America, educators and researchers were also engaged in
PAR, as evidenced in and through multiple projects designed to address a

number of social and community issues (see, for example, Chataway 1997; Forester, Pitt, and Welsh 1993; Gaventa 1988; Gaventa and Horton 1981; Hall 1977, 1993; Horton 1981; Maguire 1987; McIntyre 1997; Park, Brydon-Miller, Hall, and Jackson 1993). Additionally, scholars and researchers in the health field developed multiply diverse research projects throughout the world, employing PAR to examine mental health in the context of state-sponsored violence (Lykes 1994, 1997), women's health in India (Khanna 1996), AIDS intervention in South Africa (Preston-Whyte and Dalrymple 1996), and methodological issues in the study of sexuality in Bombay, India (George 1996).

Practitioners of PAR draw from a variety of theoretical perspectives. Marx and Engels, both of whom engaged in participatory approaches to social class struggles, have contributed to looking at people themselves as catalysts for change—a hallmark of participatory action research (Hall 1981). Similarly, Gramsci's participation in class struggles and his identification of workers as "organic intellectuals" resonates with an underlying tenet of PAR, which posits that people have the potential to be community organizers and create knowledge that leads to action (Selener 1997). In addition, Paulo Freire's (1970, 1973, 1985) emphasis on thematic investigation within the teaching-learning process, his theory of conscientization, and his belief in critical reflection as essential for individual and social change have contributed significantly to the development of participatory action research. Feminist theories have also informed the field of PAR with perspectives that have evolved out of a refusal to accept theory, research, and ethical perspectives that embody firmly entrenched double standards for men and women. Accounting for the multiple positionalities of women makes a significant contribution to the field of PAR where much of the literature continues to retain a largely androcentric analytic framework in which women and gender issues are not always central. Finally, critical theory, which grapples "with the central questions facing groups of people differently placed in specific political, social, and historical contexts characterized by injustice" (Collins 1998:xiv) has contributed significantly to the way practitioners of PAR think about people and their lived experiences.

A wide range of research practices and an equally wide range of political ideologies frame PAR projects. However, there are some underlying tenets that are specific to PAR and that distinguish it from other research approaches: first, a collective commitment to investigate an issue or problem; second, a desire to engage in self- and collective reflection in order gain clarity about the issue under investigation; and third, a joint decision to engage in individual and/or collective action that leads to a useful solution which benefits the people involved. These aims are achieved through a cyclical process of exploration, knowledge construction, and action at different moments throughout the research process. When all these elements are working in tandem and when the participants believe they have a stake in the overall project, PAR becomes a living dialectical process which changes the researcher, the participants, and the situations in which they act (McTaggart 1997).

The members of the research team and the young people participating in this project engaged in a dialectical consciousness-raising experience which was characterized by investigation, education, reflection, and action. By that I do not mean that the participants were lacking a conscience, or that they were waiting for us to come along and "raise" their awareness about their lives. What the PAR process did was to provide spaces for both the participants and the participant-researchers to engage our collective consciousness in ways that challenged us to rethink what we knew—or thought we knew—about the multiple issues that framed this project.

For instance, the participants "knew" they weren't allowed to chew gum or eat candy in school, yet decided for themselves that "this project isn't school." I informed them on more than one occasion that even though the project wasn't "school," it was taking place *in* school and therefore we needed to honor school rules. They did not agree with my perspective and furthermore they thought I was "bein' cruel 'cause we come here first period and we just got here and most of us haven't even eaten breakfast yet." They also informed me that I "worried too much."

I did worry too much—both about the participants' eating habits and about "breaking the rules." As a guest in the Blair School, I felt it was important to follow the school's procedures. I did not want to compromise the project or to undermine school policy. Yet, after clashing with the participants multiple times about their choice of food in the morning, I decided to stop policing their eating habits. I found that arguing with them about what they were or were not eating for breakfast was not conducive to cultivating group participation. Similarly, by interrupting the group meetings every time I caught them sneaking candy or sipping a soda, I was wasting the limited amount of time we had together. Although I continued to discourage them from "candy breakfasts" and strongly urged them to explore more substantial early morning meals, I told them that it was not productive for us to expend our energies on an issue that "felt" intractable to both parties. I also told them that controlling their food intake was not the role I wanted to assume in the project.

By stepping out of an authoritarian role, space was created for me to more fully experience being a participant-researcher and for the participants to take more responsibility for how, when, and what they ate for breakfast. Over time, a number of them came to the morning meetings and told me that they had decided to eat breakfast *before* they came to school. Neaka came to one session and said, "I decided you were right. I should be eatin' good stuff so I had some toast and cereal this mornin'. It wasn't bad." Tee, who came to meetings with boxes of cookies in his knapsack, told me he didn't feel "bad about eatin' cookies in the mornin' anymore 'cause I decided to eat breakfast first. I had some juice and some eggs. Cookies will taste better now." On occasion, I also brought juice, donuts, and bagels to the meetings, something the participants enjoyed mainly because, as Tonesha remarked, "Now we get to keep our candy for later!"

This story may sound simplistic in terms of thinking about the notion of consciousness-raising. Yet it is in people's daily practices that knowledge is constructed, built upon, and used to organize life. I "knew" the participants should eat well and follow the school rules. The participants "knew" that they were hungry and that the rules did not apply to them when they were engaged in the PAR project. I realized that the PAR project was not in danger of being ousted by the principal because the participants ate candy while they were working in it. The participants realized that eating breakfast at home was not "all that bad." In addition, they recognized that by not expending their energies sneaking food into the meetings, they participated more fully in project-related activities.

Processes of consciousness-raising, reflection, and action are mediated by the desires, commitments, and resourcefulness of the participants and the researchers. When those factors are attended to in a PAR process, possibilities are opened up for researchers to see and appreciate the nuances of participants' daily lives. Equally important, researchers come to "appreciate how individuals can both accommodate and undermine, both placate and rebuff, both obey and challenge" (Cushman 1998:xx–xxi) while engaging in a process of change.

Negotiating Shared Decision-Making Processes within PAR

There is enormous variation in the way decision making is played out within a PAR process, just as there are multiple definitions of what constitutes "shared decision making." For example, how "shared" is decision making when the group making the decisions consists of twelve- and thirteen-year-old inner-city adolescents of Color and one white, forty-three-year-old white female university professor-researcher, along with a shifting population of predominantly white graduate students who enter and reenter the process at various times? Can there be shared decision making when there are contested points of view among the participants which are not always settled through consensus or majority vote, but rather by shows of resistance, apathy, and/or who happened to be at the meeting that day? Similarly, how do issues of race, class, gender, age, ability, and other individual and collective identities frame decision-making processes while complicating, frustrating, and enlivening the overall research experience? Can adults and young people, who are located in different positions of power and authority, engage in decision-making processes that lead to change? With confidence, I answer "yes" to the latter question. As for the former questions, I offer this book and invite the reader to decide.

The decisions we grappled with throughout the project varied enormously: Who wants to glue the picture on the collage? Who wants to draw the picture? What color pencils should we order for the assembly? What design should we have on our T-shirts? Who is going to meet with the principal and set up a schedule for our group meetings? What kind of logo do we want? What color should it be? Should we do a dance and a skit in the assembly or just a skit? What is the letter to the mayor going to say? Who should present our project to the faculty members at the university? What should we say in our presentation? Who is going to write to the funders of the project and thank them for their generosity? Should we go to City Hall and present our project to the City Council members?

Within that continuum of questions were hundreds of others that, when linked together, led the participants to either act on an issue, decide something was not important enough to take action on, or simply ignore it and hope it would go away, fix itself, or reappear in a form that was easier for them to address later on in the project. For example, one of the things the participants wanted to accomplish in the project was the creation of a photo-text book which they wanted to publish and disseminate inside and outside the community. The photo-text book would include some of the photographs the participants took of their community (see chapter 4). Therefore, I asked a friend of mine, who is a graphic designer, to assist us in the initial steps of developing a book. It was impossible to arrange meetings between the participants and my friend due to the fact that the request came at the beginning of July when school was not in session and many of the participants were out of town. Therefore I acted as an intermediary and met with the participants prior to the closing of school to discuss how they might organize a photo-text book. Then I presented their ideas to my friend, who created a draft of what such a book might look like. She did so with the understanding that it was only a template and that when we decided to tackle the project in the coming months, we would start anew with the active involvement of the participants in the creation of the final product.

I arrived at school the following September with a first draft of a well-designed, colorful, inviting book that I felt captured the essence of what the participants were "saying" about the community through their photographs. The participants agreed that it was "cool." They also agreed that some of the photographs needed to be changed because "I don't like that one any more. I want to use a different one." "I think we should have lots of pictures on one page and then a page of writing and do it like that." "I like it this way except I think we should put the names on the bottom only." We also decided that the participants should write an introduction for the book—which Janine and Melinda immediately volunteered to do.

"Immediately" came a lot later than we had originally planned. Although the participants were eager to create a photo-text book, they had also decided at the end of the previous year to engage in two other projects which are described in chapters 6 and 7. First, they were interested in exploring "what they want to be when they grow up." Second, they wanted to develop a cleanup project aimed at improving "the trashy way the community looks."

Initially, the participants were confident that they could work on all three projects during the school year. However, as the process evolved, they realized it was not plausible or possible to focus on three projects simultaneously. As Maguire posits, "one of the most underrated limitations on participatory research is simply time" (1987:46). The participants came to the same conclusion. At one of the sessions Tonesha stated, "We don't have enough time to work on everything. So, let's put the book away until we finish the other projects. Everyone who agrees, raise your hand." All the young people raised their hands.

As the above story reveals, the participants came to some project-related decisions easily. But others were more difficult to realize, due in part to our respective roles and to people's unique personalities. Some participants jumped into decision-making processes immediately with a heightened sense of curiosity and enthusiasm. Others were less eager to participate in decision making and entered into the activities related to that experience somewhat hesitantly. Some participants contributed silently. Others loudly. Some engaged the project passively. Others did so aggressively. Some of the participants were proactive, assertive, and tended to "take charge." Others preferred to remain on the sidelines, speaking up or taking action only when they felt it was right for them.

The same was true for me and for the members of the research team. Some team members were enthusiastically involved in the project and eager to "get their hands dirty." Others were more cautious, taking time to observe, reflect, and think through issues before engaging in discussions and activities.

Ultimately, the decisions the participants made during the PAR project were doable and realizable when adults created spaces for them to voice their concerns, frame their circumstances, and articulate their thoughts and feelings about issues that were and are of concern to them. Similarly, as the data reveal, when the participants were able to develop strategies for decision making by working *with* one another in finding solutions to community problems, they gave each other necessary support, hope, and encouragement.

The Contribution of Feminism to PAR

As suggested earlier, PAR is counterhegemonic and attempts to create new spaces in social science research for investigating how people examine their realities in order to transform them. Yet, in seeking to "break the positivist monopoly on knowledge creation" (Maguire 1987:50) that exists in traditional research paradigms, practitioners of PAR are in danger of replicating the very practices they purport to change by ignoring and or dismissing the voices and concerns of women and children in PAR projects (for exceptions, see Kanhare 1980; Maguire 1987; Mduma 1982; and Swantz 1982b).

As Maguire argues, women have been relegated to the periphery of PAR through the use of male-centered language, the nonparticipation of women in PAR projects, unequal access to the benefits of a PAR project, exclusion of gender issues by a male-determined agenda, and an "absence of feminism in the theoretical debates on participatory research" (1987:52). A feminist PAR, Maguire continues, would be built on a critique of the positivist and androcentric underpinnings of dominant research, question who benefits from the project and in what ways, attend to the way language is used, problematize the composition of the research team in terms of race, class, gender, ethnicity, culture, and division of labor, foreground gender as central to every aspect of a PAR process, and track all projects in terms of their response to gender issues.

These concerns are not new to the field of feminist research. Rather, they are core issues in feminist theories, ethics, practices, and research methodologies and have been studied extensively by feminist scholars across a number of disciplines (see, for example, Behar and Gordon 1995; Collins 1991; Franz and Stewart 1994; hooks 1984; Luke 1996; Maguire 1987; Spelman 1988). These scholars have raised questions within social science research about epistemology, phenomenology, representation, and power—questions that are fundamental to the formulation of feminist principles, theories, and practices. These and other scholars have contributed to the development of theories and methodologies for and about women that problematize the multiple contexts that shape, constrain, and facilitate women's lives.

A Framework for Feminist Participatory Action Research

The framework I developed for the project outlined in this book stems from an orientation to feminist PAR that is characterized by: (1) an emphasis on the lived experiences of *all* participants, particularly urban youth; (2) a commitment to look for what has been left out of traditional theorizing about gender, social class, age, and other social positions; (3) the activist stance of the researcher; (4) an emphasis on social change which brings about new, emancipatory relationships among all people; and (5) a commitment to researcher-reflexivity.

The first characteristic includes the development of critical self- and collective consciousness and the importance of the participants' lived experiences within a feminist PAR project. This consciousness-raising experience is created when participants are given opportunities to share their experiences, beliefs, assumptions, questions, and confusions during the research process. Thus, the participants of the PAR project described in this book were expected to be researchers about their daily lives, to pose questions that arose from their life experiences, and to find strategic responses to their concerns as adolescents living in an inner city. Feminist PAR and the Freirean philosophy emphasize that this raising of consciousness occurs when spaces are created wherein "inquiry is pried open" (Fine 1992a:220). Within a context of dialogue and shared risk taking, we "critique what seems natural, spin images of what's possible, and engage in questions of how to move from here to there" (1992a:220).

This is not to imply that dialogue and risk taking, in and of themselves, become catalysts for increased consciousness about particular issues. The participants and the research team have spent three years engaging in dialogue about multiple issues ranging from rap music to politics, from violence to sports, from the latest dance craze to what we want to be when we grow up. Whether the participants' or researchers' consciousness are being raised, expanded, or enlightened in the course of a particular dialogue is difficult to say. It has been my experience in this project, and in other research I have conducted (McIntyre 1997), that critical, dialectical consciousness-raising, if and when it occurs, is usually the result of providing people with enough time to reflect on what has been brought to light and after such reflection, giving them the opportunity to revisit the knowledge that has been generated at various moments during the research process. By revisiting the ideas, stories, and questions that emerge in the course of disparate conversations, as well as through various stages of analysis and interpretation, participants are able to "see" themselves and their concerns from new and different perspectives. Once they have reviewed, revisited, and perceived issues with a new lens, they can make decisions about whether they will—or will not—act on this renewed body of knowledge. By acting on it, participants then embark on some type of transformative experience. When decisions were made to act on specific issues generated in this project, new possibilities emerged for me as the researcher, and for us as participants, in constructing knowledge about what to do next. The question then became: How do we now transform the dialogue into action? This question is explored in detail in chapters 6 and 7.

A number of feminist scholars have succeeded in moving the study of women "from the margins closer to the center of social science disciplines" (Stewart 1994:13). Stewart suggests that what has emerged from feminist theorizing over the last two decades is a number of strategies that can serve as guides for better understanding "what has been overlooked, unconceptualized, and not noticed" in the lives of women, men, and children. One of those strategies is to "look for what's been left out" (1994:13)—the second characteristic of this research project.

What has been left out of much of the PAR literature is how gender, age, and other less visible identities are embedded within multiple systems of privilege and oppression that, as Patricia Hill Collins suggests, form "an interlocking matrix of relationships" (1990:20). In this feminist PAR research project, I explore a matrix of relationships that both conceal and illuminate the significance of social positions within U.S. society, in particular the social positions of a group of young people of Color. Using the lens of feminism, I explore young people's relationships with one another, with adults, with their community, and with the larger society—relationships that are marked by gender, race, social class, and age, and are nestled within systems of power and privilege. In so doing, I hope to generate knowledge that will assist educators, psychologists, and researchers in our efforts to improve existing social conditions for urban youth.

Equally important, I attend to the formation of the research team—another issue left out of much of the PAR literature. In many accounts of PAR, the relationships between researchers and participants are discussed in theoretical or unidimensional terms with scant attention given to the actual ways in which race, class, age, ability, and ethnicity mediate a PAR project. By failing to problematize—both in theory and in practice—the researcher-participant relationship, practitioners of PAR run the risk of becoming oblivious to our complicity in a structural arrangement that may reproduce the very practices we seek to challenge. Feminists' commitment to problematize the layers of power, intimacy, and struggle that characterize many research relationships makes a valuable contribution to similar discussions that need to take place within the field of participatory action research.

Equally important, the members of the research team and I are members of multiple communities (Rosaldo 1989). We brought these varied memberships to the project in ways that both facilitated and constrained our collaboration with one another and our participation in this research process. I bring particular interests and concerns to this project that have shifted over many years of being a union activist and educator. In particular, my interest in engaging in this project has its genesis in my adolescent years growing up in Boston. During that time, a law was passed to desegregate the Boston public schools—a law that evoked hatred, fear, political instability, and violence throughout the city. The busing crisis that ensued was a catalyst for me in terms of how I wanted to be in the world—both personally, as a white female, and professionally, as a white teacher. My commitment to addressing issues of racism, educational inequity, systematic abuse of power, and most recently, the system of whiteness began then and continues for me now as I collaborate with the team members and the participants in the development of this project. In addition, my personality has largely been shaped by the complex interplay of my gender, working-class background, and whiteness. Being a white, Irish, working-class female brought up in a large Catholic family, I respond to teaching, learning, research, authority, power, and "the university" with a mixture of enthusiasm, cynicism, humor, and determination—all of which can lead to great success or, as we used to say in my neighborhood, to "dukin' it out" with people to prove my point.

For example, there were times when the combination of my personality traits worked against building trusting relationships with the participants of the project. One day, in a moment of exasperation at Blood's disruptive behavior, I told him that if he didn't "straighten out" he wasn't going to come to the amusement park with us. I immediately realized that I had made a mistake by threatening Blood with the idea of not being allowed to join us on the trip to the amusement park. By giving him an ultimatum, I had forced him into the metaphorical corner, a strategy I knew to be unproductive and one that would simply not work with Blood or with many of the other participants. It also never worked with me. Yet, I occasionally succumbed to coercion in my years as a classroom teacher. I didn't like it when I resorted to that type of behavior when I was teaching. I liked it even less when I did so while participating in a collaborative research project.

Blood stomped out of the cafeteria and said, "I don't care if I go or not. You think I care about this? I don't. I don't care at all." I tried to coax him back to the meeting but he was adamant about not returning. He refused to speak to me that day and did not return to the group the following day. When I called him at his home his mother told me he was at the park playing basketball. I drove to the park but he was not there. Nor was he at the cove, the school, or the corner where he hung out with friends. I finally tracked him down the next morning and apologized for the way I had reacted to his behavior. I explained that my threat to exclude him from the trip to the amusement park was a result of my frustration at his disruptive behavior in some of the group meetings, which resulted in discord among the participants and was not contributing to the development of the program. I told him that there were other ways I could address that issue without banishing him from the group when he wasn't doing what I wanted him to do. Initially, Blood stood silently and refused to look at me. After a bit of prodding from me, he finally acknowledged what I had said and told me that he did "fool around too much" and that he would "participate better from now on." He also gave me his permission slip for the amusement park.

Although there were times like this when I reacted without thinking about the consequences of my actions, at other times the combination of my class background, humor, cynicism, and determination contributed positively to the project and allowed me to relate to the participants in humanizing ways. Melinda was interviewed by a reporter from Beaconsville, a wealthy town adjoining Ellsworth, about the overall project and told us about the experience during a group session.

> *Melinda:* She just asked me a whole bunch of questions. What we're gonna do next year, what we've been doing for the past two years. Um, she also asked how we relate to you, how does it feel to be with a different color person.
>
> *Alice:* What did you say?

Melinda: Said it's fine! Far as I know it's the same. No difference 'cause you're white.

Alice: It's interesting that she would ask you that since she also interviewed me but she didn't talk to me about that.

Melinda: Oh, and she asked me how do I like Dr. McIntyre.

Mase: And what did you say?

[laughter]

Monique: I love Miss McIntyre!

[laughter]

Melinda: I said, I like you.

Tonesha: I would have been like, I like Miss McIntyre but she got an attitude.

Alice: She what?

Tonesha: She's great.

[laughter]

Alice: I have an attitude?

Tonesha: No, I was just saying that like

Alice: You don't have to take it back. You're right. I do have an attitude. Sometimes.

Tonesha: Yeah, you do.

Tee: Who told you that?

Tonesha: Well, c'mon. She does. Sometimes. But that's cool. I like your attitude. Even when you get me mad. (June 21, 1999)[1]

I did create opportunities for the participants to get mad at me during the PAR project. I did the same for the research team. I even got mad at myself on occasion. Therefore, it was important for me to be cognizant of my feelings and attend to the way my emotions and personality informed my engagement in the overall process. Equally important, I needed to be self-conscious about the ways in which I negotiated issues of authority, power, and control so that I could contribute to building equitable, trusting, and respectful relationships with the participants and with the members of the research team.

The members of the research team, who are identified in chapter 2, have their own histories that informed their engagement in the PAR project. Many of them joined the project in an attempt to learn more about inner-city communities and the young people who live there. Since they were students in credentialing programs, they recognized the need to expand their knowledge base regarding "diversity" and hoped that being involved in the PAR project would provide them with that opportunity. In addition, they wanted to be able to engage in research—an opportunity not afforded to the majority of masters' students attending the university where I teach.

The contradictions and the complexities that emerged for me and for the members of the research team were not resolved within this research project. We experienced many challenging moments when we came face-to-face with our own assumptions, biases, and human limitations. Similarly, we experienced a tug-of-war when issues of authority, power, and control highlighted the hierarchical relationships we were negotiating. We acknowledged and attended to those moments throughout the experience, and as revealed in the remainder of the book, they surely influenced the direction of this work.

Being an activist researcher is the third characteristic that informed this research. Maguire (1993) argues that being a practitioner of PAR requires that we not only examine the dilemmas and contradictions of participatory research, but also consider the dilemmas and contradictions of our life choices. In her own experience of engaging in a PAR project with battered women, she states: "I was forced to question my part in the social construction and maintenance of the larger social structures, systems, and relationships. And relentlessly, I found myself asking, How am I choosing to be in the world?" (1993:175) I found myself doing much the same thing, as I questioned my level of activism not just in the research process but in other areas of my life as well. Like Maguire, I am "often disappointed in myself" (1993:175) when I am unable to fit the square pegs into the round holes. I am constantly humbled by the slow progress I seem to make in the PAR project, in my administrative work, in teaching white students about whiteness, and in engaging white colleagues and administrators in a purposeful discourse about individual, institutional, and societal injustice. Nonetheless, I recognize that activist work, and activist research, is "not an event. It is a process that we are living through, creating as we go" (1993:176). The question for me isn't *should* I engage that process? The question is *how* and *when* will I do so?

The fourth characteristic which informs the research is an emphasis on social change. Social change requires not simply that we restructure institutions, systems, and gender, race, and social class relationships. It requires that we do so with the intention of forming *new* ways of relating, *new* ways of constructing knowledge, *new* ways of confronting privilege, *new* criteria for what is valued in society, and *new* directions for implementing democratic processes that lead to just social change. As importantly, engaging in feminist PAR is about working toward the radical transformation of social reality and improvement in the lives of the people involved regardless of gender, age, or social status.

The final characteristic that guides this project is the role of reflexivity in feminist participatory action research. As Reay suggests, "Reflexivity is about giving as full and honest an account of the research process as possible, in particular explicating the position of the researcher in relation to the researched" (1996:443). I am most effective explicating my position as a reflexive participant-researcher when I engage myself, the participants, and critical friends in the process of meaning making. First, I have to attend to my own history and to the factors in my life that profoundly influence how I listen, question, synthesize, analyze, and interpret knowledge. Second, I have to pay close attention to the way the participants construct meanings about themselves and their lives and respond to those constructions in ways that facilitate joint understanding. Last, I am challenged to be a reflexive researcher by the input of critical friends, and by colleagues who accompany me in the process of better understanding self and other. For me, researcher reflexivity is best practiced when those three aspects oppose and relate—when they are held together in creative tension rather than separated into distinct categories.

When I push the boundaries of reflexivity away from the concept of "the solo researcher" within a PAR project, I more fully capture what Patti Lather (1997) refers to as the "rigorous messiness" of research. That's probably a good place to be in because it is a messiness born out of competing and colliding narratives of self and other that challenge me to move a muscle, change a thought, shift a perspective, and ultimately, take an action that will hopefully lead to the construction of a story that best represents those who told it to me in the first place.

Participatory Action Research and the University

Distinctive challenges emerge out of and through actual PAR experiences. Thus, researchers and communities who engage in PAR refine the approach to the PAR process according to their particular circumstances, contexts, and collective need. Similarly, PAR projects are assessed and judged not in relation to preexisting criteria, but in terms of whether or not they served the specific and real interests of the people involved (Hall 1981). These issues have particular significance for those of us who engage in PAR from university settings where the role of PAR is highly contested (see, for example, Heaney 1993; Maguire 1993; McIntyre 1997; McIntyre and Lykes 1998; McTaggart 1997; Wolf 1996). Issues of collaboration, knowledge, power, decision making, privilege, and dialogue (to name only six) complicate a research process that is inherently counterhegemonic and was developed in opposition to dominant research paradigms, many of which are created, maintained, and sustained in and by university structures. Heaney argues that universities are systems in "which official knowledge is promulgated and the given order maintained" (1993:46). Thus, he posits, faculty can become invested in a PAR process by collaborating with others for change, but "by reason of their expertise and credentials" cannot assume a "special or guiding role as 'participatory researchers'" (1993:46).

I concur with Heaney when he asserts that universities devalue popular knowledge and retain a "monopolistic hold on the production and legitimatization of useful knowledge" (1993:42). But, I disagree with the premise that PAR and "the university" cannot share similar space. For certain, the space is messy, conflictual, contradictory, complex, and controversial. Yet this space can also provide university-based researchers with opportunities to link research with academic and community practices. By positioning ourselves as both participatory action researchers and members of a university community, we can bring to bear *inside* the university what we are attempting to bring to bear *outside* it: namely, institutional and social change, the formation of alliances with others so as to undo systems of injustice, the creation of new ways of thinking and being, and an intentionality about collaborating with others in order to produce and construct knowledge that benefits *all* people. How we engage those practices within the university depends on our various positionalities (for example, gender, race, age, social class, ability, and academic rank), as well as the types of institutions in which we labor. Thus there is no universal framework for linking one's engagement with PAR *outside* the university to one's engagement with the underlying tenets of PAR *inside* the university.

As an untenured assistant professor, I am conscious of the ways in which

I am both constrained and privileged by the positions I hold within the institution in which I am employed, the graduate school where I invest most of my time and energy, and the particular department to which I belong. These public spaces of teaching and learning are not free of and from conflict. Nor do I believe they should be. These contested spaces are rich sites for those of us who want to cross educational and cultural borders and challenge existing "ways of doing things." These spaces also benefit me in multiple ways. Thus, I find myself quite often "needing to challenge the very social systems to which [I] belong and by which [I am] . . . privileged in many ways" (Bell 1993:20).

In order to integrate notions of participation, reflection, agency, and critical analysis of existing forms of knowledge into the teacher preparation program that I direct, I require that students conduct their full-time student teaching practicum in a high priority school with a racially diverse student body. This is also a requirement for the fieldwork the students must do in some of their methods courses. Because I am very concerned that teaching in racially diverse environments can reify stereotypes rather than eliminate them, I make sure that the course work and the fieldwork are tightly interwoven throughout the program.

As important, I invite students to engage in the PAR project outlined in this book—an invitation that allows them to engage in a process that can potentially reformulate the way they think about children, teaching, learning, and how knowledge is constructed, valued, and used to inform their teaching practices. The opportunity to engage in PAR also contributes to further understanding the impact of urban life on children and adolescents and the way schools can function as agents of change in the lives of young people.

Audrey, a member of the research team and a student in the elementary education program, expressed the importance to her as an educator of participating in the PAR project as follows:

> I had no idea what PAR was or what it involved, but I was intrigued with the prospect of participating with people in the community. There was one thing preventing me from committing to the project and that was Ellsworth. I worked there for two years and had some experiences that left me with ill feelings. I think I left my job with the same stereotypes and perceptions I had when I first got there. I thought it just doesn't get much worse than Ellsworth.

After wrestling with these thoughts, I decided to see if I could contribute something to the project and to get over my reservations about working in Ellsworth and face it head-on. I knew that I had a lot to contribute but I also found out very quickly that I had much to learn. . . . The opportunity I had to actively participate in the project has been invaluable to me. (May 1998)

Sarah was also a member of the research team and a student in the elementary education program. Her reflections also suggest that by engaging in PAR, she and the other participating students had the opportunity to "stop and think about their views of people who live in Ellsworth."

I grew up in an affluent white community that borders Ellsworth. I learned growing up that Ellsworth was a dangerous place and had some "seedy" sections which were to be avoided at all costs. My views changed as . . . I became involved in the PAR project.

My comfort level in Ellsworth grew as I interviewed different people and visited various businesses [as part of the PAR project]. At the same time, I felt uncomfortable sometimes, especially talking to people who lived in the nicer section of Ellsworth and sent their children to private schools. As one woman told me, "I send my kids to private schools because kids going to the public schools here are mostly Black." Then she asked me not to write that down. That remark triggered a host of emotions for me. First, I thought it was a racist comment. Then I thought some more and asked myself, "If I lived here, would my kids go to public school or private school?" I knew immediately the answer would be a private school. The private school has more resources. I felt ashamed admitting that. . . . How can the schools expect to improve if all the parents, like me, take their resources elsewhere? I learned more than I thought I would about Ellsworth, and myself, and know that I have to work hard to eliminate my fears and work with others to do away with the division between the races, particularly in schools. (May 1998)

Vonnie "felt drawn to the group" because she had grown up in Ellsworth. She was eager to collaborate in a participatory process with a group of young people who lived in the same community in which she had once lived.

There is a stigma associated with living in, or coming from, Ellsworth. It is common knowledge that people from the neighboring towns (and I know because I now live in one) look down upon Ellsworth because of problems caused by poverty, drugs, and crime. Many people strive to "escape" this city, and after doing so, dissociate themselves with Ellsworth. So when I observed the Blair School students talking to us [at a presentation held at the university] about how outsiders negatively perceive them and their community, I made my decision to participate in the Blair School PAR project.

This project also appeared to be unusual in that it had a goal of enabling the participants to develop self-esteem and be more skilled at problem-solving. Most urban projects that I was familiar with in Ellsworth did not emphasize such long-term positive effects on the participants.

I was really impressed that adolescents from the inner city were motivated enough, through their group efforts, to take action to tackle the trash problem! This is a problem that plagues inner cities and typically, residents view trash as a condition that is part of city life. Littering is as widespread as crime is in this city and my own family felt helpless to do anything about it. I shared my own experiences with trash around my family's house in Ellsworth and the kids knew exactly where I was coming from. (July 1999)

Jennifer and Nicole, two students enrolled in the school psychology program, shared similar reflections about how their histories growing up white, privileged, and "with little or no contact with people of Color," influenced their engagement in the PAR project. A more detailed account of their participation in the project is presented in chapter 6.

As these reflections reveal, participating in PAR provides opportunities for prospective teachers and psychologists to engage in a process of reflexive research that contributes significantly to the way they view themselves, urban youth, and the multiple social issues that characterize urban communities. In addition, participating in PAR gives students an insight into the power of creativity and personal expression within educational and psychological discourses, and assists them in developing new ways of dialoguing with *their* students about issues that concern them.

Integrating the underlying principles of PAR into an existing university structure can be challenging, frustrating, and at times somewhat discouraging. One reason is that "PAR is a philosophy of life as much as a method, a sentiment as much as a conviction" (Fals-Borda 1997:111). It appears that if one is committed to the underlying principles of PAR, one must also be willing to engage in processes where those principles are problematized by practice—processes that are difficult to set in motion, much less sustain, in many university settings.

Yet, fully engaging in a process aimed at creating spaces for more just and participatory ways of teaching, learning, and conducting research can be exciting and educative. As important, it contributes to the development of "pedagog[ies] of possibility" (Luke and Gore 1992:x) within university settings. From a PAR frame of reference, such a contribution can change the perception that universities are exclusive spaces for thinking and theorizing, to one which sees them as sites of critique, and of teaching, learning, and research as tools for social justice.

Visual Stories by Inner-City Youth

Complementing the feminist PAR approach described above is community photography. Community photography is a methodology that (1) enables people to record aspects of their daily lives from their own perspectives; (2) provides people opportunities to increase their knowledge about the issues that most affect their community; and (3) gives people a way of informing policymakers, and other people who control resources, about "community issues that are of greatest concern and pride" (Wang 1995:1). Photovoice (Wang 1995, 1999) has been used to develop collaborative experiences with homeless children (Hubbard 1991, 1996), children living in the Guatemalan City garbage dump (Franklin and McGirr 1995), children of Appalachia and India (Ewald 1985, 1996), children of poverty and affluence in Mexico (Ziller, Vern, and de Santoya 1988), women in rural China (Wu, Li, Wang, Zhan, Xian, Yang, and Wang 1995) and Guatemala (Lykes 2000), and the Kayapo in Brazil (Ruby 1991) so as to facilitate social change. By putting cameras in the hands of young people, we hoped to enrich our understanding of how they perceived their lives within the community. As important, the camera provided resources that enabled young people to tell "visual stories" about themselves and their communities, thus giving them the opportunity to engage in reflexivity and to express themselves in their own images, words, and reflections. In turn, these images, along with other activities the participants engaged in, became points of entry into exploring solutions for community development purposes. The participants' multiple photographic stories were powerful tools for illuminating the lives of young people who do not always have a forum in which to express themselves. These stories are outlined in detail in chapter 4.

Concluding Reflections

There is a paucity of literature that addresses PAR with young people living in inner cities (see Alder and Sandor 1990, and Atweh, Christensen, and Dornan 1998 for examples of action research projects conducted in Australia). Therefore, the participants' experiences with this project are significant contributions to the field of participatory action research. In addition, the participants' engagement with PAR suggests that educators, psychologists, and researchers "take up the call" and expand our understanding of urban youth in the United States by joining them in participatory processes of change. We can do so by learning with and from feminist researchers like M. Brinton Lykes (1989, 1994, 1997), Mary Brydon-Miller (1993, 1997), and Patricia Maguire (1987, 1993, 1996), to name a few, who have courageously engaged in PAR for many years and have developed frameworks for PAR that are at the intersection of research and action. Their commitment to recreating new ways of knowing and being, and their continued pursuit of social justice through their teaching and research, guides me as I attempt to do the same.

2

■　　■　　■　　■　　■　　■　　■　　■　　■

Exploring Community

A RECURRING QUESTION in the PAR literature is whether the researcher needs to be approached as a resource by a community or group,
or whether she or he can determine that a problem exists within a particular context and initiate a conversation with a group to explore it (see, for
example, Bryceson and Mustafa 1982; Maguire 1987; McIntyre 1997;
McTaggart 1997). I chose the latter approach, entering this process with
a preexisting question for study: How does a group of young adolescents
living in an inner city make meaning of their community?

Once I had established a relationship with Susan and the participants, I
developed an initial set of activities that would assist us in exploring the
above question, using collages, storytelling, community resource inventories, and community photography, among other things. I presented my
ideas to Susan and the participants, and invited them to contribute ideas,
activities, and other strategies that might assist us in uncovering and examining community issues. As the process evolved, the participants and
the research team codeveloped a number of additional activities such as
role-playing exercises, neighborhood inventory walks, and field trips which
also contributed to the development of a more kaleidoscopic view of how
the participants experienced their community.

Overall, the PAR project had three objectives: (1) to gather information about the community; (2) engage with young people in creative and interactive activities that would contribute to further understanding how they made meaning of their community; and (3) to cocreate youth-initiated intervention or action programs that would address the participants' concerns and promote individual and community well-being. In this chapter, I describe the evolution of that cogenerative research process, paying particular attention to the design and objectives of the project, the formation of the research team, and the context in which the project took place.

Design of the Project

Developing a predetermined program for working with participants in a PAR project runs the risk of constraining the emergence of the participants' experiences. Nonetheless, at the outset of the project I felt a need to develop a preliminary framework from which to proceed in my efforts to begin a process of dialogue with and among the teachers, participants, community members, and colleagues and students about how we might explore community issues with a group of young people. I describe that draft framework below. I do so in detail because there is a dearth of detailed descriptions in the educational and psychological literature about how we as university researchers initiate PAR projects, involve graduate students in those projects, make direct links between theory and practice, integrate course work and field experiences, and remain grounded in, and flexible with, the tenets of feminist participatory action research. I introduce all the university-based team members in this section, although they appear at different intervals throughout the research project. This will give the reader an overview of the research team and a better understanding of how this particular team was formed and reformed throughout the research process.

The Research Team

At the beginning of each semester, I asked some of my colleagues to inform the graduate students in their classes that I was looking for people interested in participating in a long-term PAR project. I invited students in my classes to get involved in the project as well, offering course credit for participation in one particular course I teach. In addition, I asked faculty members to join with me in thinking of ways to incorporate participation in the project with the students' course requirements.

Thus far, fourteen graduate students have participated in the project. Eleven of them were females, and all identified as middle or upper-middle class. Nine of those students also identified as white. One female student identified as Puerto Rican; one identified as Portuguese. The three male students all identified as white middle class. Ten of the students were enrolled in teacher preparation programs. The remaining four were enrolled in a school psychology program. Some of the students participated in the project for one semester. Others remained with the project for one year. Still others have participated in the project in a host of different ways for well over two years.[1]

All the members of the research team met regularly to review not only the research project but also to discuss our own personal responses to the multiple experiences we had encountered in the project both individually and as a group. These meetings were essential for us as we continued to build trust with one another. Similarly, the team meetings provided a space for us to ask questions, clarify ideas, and work out some of the complicated issues that arose in the course of the research.

We kept detailed field notes as well as personal journals to record our observations and our personal reactions to the various aspects of the research process. These documents assisted us in reflecting upon our own experiences during the project. The field notes and the personal journals also guided us in the process of remembering events and experiences, describing and interpreting situations, developing (and redeveloping) ideas, questions, and goals, and reminding ourselves that our subjectivity—and positions within this project—were important factors in the PAR process.

The Participants

The majority of the participants live within walking distance of the school. The remainder are bused to the school from other sections of Ellsworth. The initial group of twenty-four students we collaborated with ranged in age from eleven to thirteen. Eleven identify as African American (six females, five males), four as Puerto Rican (one female and three males), and two females identify as Haitian. One male and two females identify as Jamaican. One male identifies as Dominican, and one as Colombian. One male and one female identify as biracial (both have Puerto Rican fathers and white European American mothers)

Eleven students live with their biological mothers and all but one of them also live with siblings. One student lives with her biological father and grandmother; her siblings live elsewhere in the city. Two of the students live with their biological mother and her boyfriend or husband. Seven students live with both biological parents as well as with siblings. The remaining three live with relatives (brother, cousin, great-grandmother, and grandmother) and two of the three also live with siblings. English is the primary language spoken in the home of eighteen of the students. Although they all speak English in school, six of them speak Spanish or French Creole at home.

There were many young people who participated in and contributed to the project described in this book. Throughout the book, the reader will "meet" many of the participants and research team members, some of whom will be heard more than others, depending on which phase of the project they were involved in and in what ways their presence and participation intersected with the overall experience. Regardless of where and how they appear in this book, all the participants and team members contributed to the formation and development of this collaborative process.

When we first began the research process in early October 1997, there were seventeen sixth-grade students in Homeroom 211. Due to overcrowded classrooms in nearby schools, there were twenty six students by November 1997. Three new students arrived in late December and early January 1998, and two more arrived in February and March. Between March and June of that year, seven students moved out of the area or were transferred to other classes. By the end of the school year, there were twenty-four students in the class: twelve girls and twelve boys. These twenty-four students were the core participants during the first year of the project. Since the end of August 1998, thirteen of the original twenty-four students have moved, been expelled, or been transferred to other schools and classrooms, some leaving before school began in September, others leaving between October 1998 and September 1999.

The School

The Blair School serves an average of 645 prekindergarten through kindergarten and grades three to eight students in a low-income community in Ellsworth, an urban city located in the northeast region of the United States. Due to space constraints, students in grades one and two attend another public school located nearby. According to the 1997–98 Blair School profile, the enrollment was as follows: 382 Black, 224 Hispanic, 29 white, 6 Asian American, and 3 American Indian. The school also provides after-school, weekend, and summer programs for children, parents, and other local residents. There is a staff of forty nine (thirty nine teachers, two administrators, and seven additional staff members), with 46.2 percent of the faculty being faculty of Color. All scores for the state mastery tests in reading, writing, and mathematics, which are taken in grades four, six, and eight each year, are consistently below the state averages. Yet in the past few years students have been demonstrating positive gains, albeit small, in reading, writing, and mathematics. Sixty-five percent of the students received free or reduced-priced meals during the 1997–98 academic year.

Data Analysis: (Re)Constructing Knowledge

By engaging in dialogue, self- and collective reflection, and participating in a wide range of problem-posing activities the participants were given opportunities to engage in constructing new forms of knowledge. The creation of knowledge generated questions, themes, concepts, and interrelated patterns that became units of analysis within the overall project. Although I had initial questions that informed the analysis, these questions existed in the abstract and were only concretized as the project evolved. How did the participants define community? What did it mean for them to live in their particular community? What did they think about violence, education, and other issues salient to young adolescents? What has changed, or is changing, in the way they think about life opportunities, personal responsibility, and community well-being? These were some of the questions that emerged and became points of entry into the overall analysis.

The participants were the informed insiders in this project—a group of young people who came together, discussed their concerns, revisited their discussions, and decided to develop strategies to make changes in their lives. In the process, they changed their minds, decided they didn't really care about changing anything, changed their minds again, and revisited what they had said and decided they meant something else. I did much the same thing. I interpreted, reinterpreted, analyzed, and reanalyzed data. I went back and forth to the participants endless times to clarify, verify, confirm, and "get permission to" write this or state that, always conscious of the need to be reflexive, always hoping to capture their lives as authentically as I could. Given their age and academic abilities, it was impractical to give them drafts of the chapters of this book for review, or drafts of articles I had written, or papers I had presented at national conferences. But I did explain each article, presentation, and chapter to them and invite them to comment on the examples I had used, the interpretations I had developed, and the connections I was making between and among various concepts.

I questioned the participants repeatedly about various things I had said or written, asking them if they would like to add or clarify certain things. I invited them to choose the photographs, collages, and stories they thought would best represent the ideas and themes that were outlined in the article I was writing or the presentation I was giving. They were usually very responsive to my request for feedback, as long as they didn't "have to write anything." Overall, they listened to my explanations and interpretations and, for the most part, nodded in approval and agreed with whatever I had written.

I was not always comfortable about the "ease" with which we came to joint conclusions about the themes I was highlighting in the dissemination phases of the project. I wanted them to challenge my interpretations, disagree with my examples, and choose photographs that would require me to rethink my analysis. As I saw it, if they didn't challenge my interpretations and analyses, they either weren't listening or they weren't taking the research seriously. In retrospect, I think I was right on both counts. But only sometimes. Sometimes they simply weren't listening. Sometimes they didn't take the research seriously (or so I thought). But only sometimes. Other times, they were very quick to remind me of things they had said that I had misinterpreted. Specifically, they would recall with amazing clarity who had initiated what ideas and who was responsible for making *that* phone call, or writing *that* letter, or creating *that* flier. When they disagreed about who had said what or who did what, they would refer to the audiotapes, requesting that we listen to the tapes again and "find out the real deal."

The audiotapes and transcripts of the sessions were always available for the participants to listen to, read, and comment on. Initially they were eager to hear themselves and each other on tape. Listening to themselves talk to one another did help them clarify some of the content of the sessions. But the novelty of hearing their own voices wore off within a few weeks. They became proficient at setting up the tape recorder, making sure the red light was on, and informing me and the other team members when a tape had ended. Their familiarity and comfortability with being audiotaped was an asset to the project. But it failed to entice them to pursue a more critical reflection of their conversations. Instead, they considered listening to themselves a "chore," reminding us that we were the ones who "needed to listen and transcribe so you can tell us what we say." As Tonesha remarked to me one day, "We trust you, Ms. Mac. If we say somethin' important, we know you'll tell us."

As I was completing the draft of an article that focused on various aspects of the project for an educational journal, a colleague suggested that I review the overall themes of the paper with the participants and then invite them to write what *they* would like to say to the readers of this particular journal. Although the majority of the participants "hated writing," they told me that they would tell the readers about the programs they were developing. Here is some of what they said:

> For the past year, me and my fellow classmates have discussed big issues like drugs, violence, and the garbage in our community. We got cameras so we could photograph some of the highlights of our neighborhood, too. We also talked about what we were going to do about all this garbage. Now, instead of talking about it, we are going to do something about it. We have two different programs: the Clean Up Project, a.k.a., STEP (Save the Earth Program) and Career Exploration. To sum it all up, we have done a lot. In my mind, I don't think the meaning of the programs will ever end. (Melinda)

> I think this cleanup project will do good because we are working hard and we want the people to know that we are serious and not playing around. We hope we get to talk to the mayor because we want people to clean up and

not pollute our community. This community will get far because of the effort we put into it. (Tee)

As far as the career exploration program, I think it should stick with us because when we graduate from high school, we need to have something to do. I really think we should continue the cleanup group, too, because I am sick and tired of seeing trash. (Tonesha)

I think the programs will come out great. I am really expecting a good job on these programs. Also, what I think we should do for this program is to go to a higher step. We can invite the mayor, the school, family, community, and more. These programs can help us with many things and can even help us in college and I would like to continue these programs until I leave for college. I would like to finish these programs with something to look back on in the future. (Janine) (November 10, 1998)

I appreciated the participants' enthusiasm about the projects, but felt that they had failed to capture the multiple ups and downs we had experienced throughout the research process, and/or their "real" feelings about the project. I felt they had succumbed to the traditional response to a teacher asking them to write about their recent field trip to a museum or what they liked about the curriculum unit they had just completed on the environment. I interpreted their responses as being linked to and mediated by their experiences as students within a public school environment that, like many other school environments, requires students to follow the rules, conform to authority, and toe the party line. The participants were not accustomed to disagreeing with authority figures, and although I tried to dispel the notion that I was an authority figure who was an extension of the Blair School staff, it took them considerable time to trust that it was safe to disagree with me. It also took them considerable time to learn how to accept responsibility for particular aspects of the project and make decisions for themselves without worrying about whether or not they had my approval.

After the writing exercise, and after I had told the participants that I thought their responses were not exactly representative of the previous year we had spent together in the PAR project, they said, "But, we *do* like everything about this project, except maybe some things." Although they didn't feel the need to write about the more challenging aspects of the project, they did talk about some of them in an ensuing discussion. They discussed how difficult it was for them to attend meetings after school, how hard it was to get together and plan activities unless an adult from the team was present, and how slow they were to finish writing letters, creating logos, or scripting a skit for an assembly. They talked about not always wanting to work together as a group, how difficult it was to attend a session when "we're missin' cookin' class and today, we're makin' chocolate chip cookies," and how nerve-racking it was to present their work to their peers and to adults from both inside and outside the community. They openly discussed the nitty-gritty details of the day-to-day life of a youth-directed PAR project, but did not feel called upon to reflect on those discussions in their written responses. As Tee stated: "If we say all that, we'll have to write for longer. We just wanted to say the facts, not be tellin' them about how we can't decide between a blue logo or a green one. Thing is, we like the project, Ms. Mac."

Social Constructionist Grounded Theory

I used social constructionist grounded theory method to analyze the information gathered from the participants' written reflections, audiotaped group discussions, and the community resource inventories (see, for example, Charmaz 1990; McIntyre 1997; Orona 1990; Strauss and Corbin 1990, 1998). This method of analysis fosters the development of analytic and conceptual constructions of data. It also stresses the active stance and positionality of the researcher as crucial to the interpretation of the data.

I made conscious choices about how to include myself and the research team in the data analysis. Although the discourse produced in the sessions was cocreated by the participants and team members, the research questions focused on how the *participants* made meaning of the myriad issues that were generated throughout the project. Although the research team's contributions to the group discussions informed and influenced the direction of the talk, I chose to situate the data analysis in the participants' meaning making, specifically in terms of how they constructed meanings about violence, community life, and "becoming somebody." Notwithstanding that decision, I highlight the participatory dimension of my role and that of the other team members in various sections of the book by including data from our field notes, team meetings, and our participation in the group sessions. I do so in the hope that it will assist the reader in gaining a better understanding of how all of us contributed to the group discussions and to the construction of the data.

Notwithstanding the measures I employed to include the participants in the final analysis, and notwithstanding the extent to which the team members contributed their own interpretations of the data, I remain the authoritative interpreter in this work of the participants' lives and the research team's involvement in the project. By virtue of my role in the university and in the project, I take full responsibility for the analysis, the representation of the project, and the contents of this book.

Year One

During the first few months of the project, the initial research team—which consisted of me, Sarah, Kayla, Audrey, Daniel, and Carmen—established relationships with businesspeople, churches, local residents, teachers, parents, other school personnel, and university-based participants. For instance, Sarah decided to investigate the role of businesses in the neighborhood. She also contacted a number of local residents to interview them about their views about the community. Kayla chose to visit and attend services at three main churches in the community, interviewing the pastors about the relationship between parishioners, local residents, and the local houses of worship. For many years, Audrey had been actively involved in the area as an HIV educator. Her knowledge about the relationship between social service agencies and the surrounding community facilitated her exploration of the role of the former in the Blair School area. Daniel joined her in that exploration. Carmen's focus was parental involvement. One of the ways Carmen established relationships with parents was by being a regular participant at the weekly parents' volleyball games held at the school during the first year of the project.

While the team was establishing these various relationships, we remained focused on the original group of sixth-grade students for two reasons: first, because early adolescence is a formative period in human development when young people are "in transition," making crucial choices in their academic and personal lives, and second, because young people in urban areas are often marginalized from larger societal discussions and from public policy decisions that deeply affect their lives.

Audrey, Kayla, and I "hung out" in the sixth grade from October 1997, until June 1998, visiting the classroom on a weekly basis, observing students, participating in class activities, and engaging in the important work of developing levels of trust and communication. We participated in the participants' Thanksgiving feast, accompanied them on field trips to a science museum, a newly opened local community center, and the movies. We also invited the students to the university where they "buddied up" with a group of undergraduate students who escorted them around the campus of the university, showing them what "a day in the life of a college student" was like. In addition, as part of the community photography aspect of the research project, the participants attended a photography class on campus and were instructed in how to develop and enlarge photographs. During the first year of the project, we also conducted community resource inventories with them and engaged them in activities aimed at examining their ideas and feelings about the meaning of community. The activities included collages, storytelling, and community photography.

Community Resource Inventories

The community resource inventory (CRI) is a tool for gathering information about people, identifying community concerns, and generating knowledge about how individual and collective assets can be tapped and utilized within schools and communities (Kretzmann and McKnight 1993). After reviewing a wide variety of what Kretzmann and McKnight (1997) call capacity inventories, I developed specific community resource inventories tailored to the various groups we were and are collaborating with in the project such as parents, local residents, businesses, social service agencies, churches, and young people. (The CRI we used with the participants can be found in Appendix B.)

The CRIs were instrumental in gathering information for two important reasons. First, using the CRI provided team members with the opportunity to speak one-on-one with the participants, an opportunity not always afforded at other points during the research process. Subsequently, we were able to talk about a number of things that came up spontaneously in our conversations with them, things that may or may not have been related to the exact questions outlined in the inventory. This in turn became an effective tool for initiating trust and building relationships. Second, the

CRIs assisted us in developing a more holistic assessment of the community as perceived by the participants. Conducting the CRIs allowed us to gather information about the community from individual participants which was later supported by, elaborated on, and/or refuted in the group discussions.

Collages

Collages[2] were just one of the tools we used for better understanding how the participants defined and represented their community. Combining visual as well as oral representations of the issues raised in the discussions about the community provided different entry points into the research experience. The participants created visual images that were reflected back at them, both individually and as a group, thereby eliciting a number of ideas and realizations about their perceptions of the community that would not have surfaced in the verbal exchanges.

During our first brainstorming activity, we asked the participants to tell us what they thought about when they heard the word "community." They generated a list of items that ranged from "where you live," "family," and "school," to "where you clean," "drug cars," and "violence." Following the brainstorming activity, Susan prearranged the participants into small groups. Using magazines that the research team and Susan had brought to class (for example, *Jet, Hispanic, People, Sports Illustrated, Hispanic Business,* and *Latina*), we invited them to create group collages that represented their community. They were asked to bring in magazines as well but either forgot to do so or didn't have any magazines at home to contribute to the exercise. The participants were given approximately forty five minutes to complete the exercise. Over the next few days, they presented their various creations to the rest of the class, interpreted each other's collages, and engaged in a number of discussions that emerged from the images presented on the collages. There were a number of images that spoke to the participants' representations of their community, including sports, guns, drugs, career possibilities, music, education, and the environment. The ensuing discussions ranged from the community being "full of drugs, guns, and violence," to the "community is a junkyard and should be cleaned up," to the "community is a place where there are friendships, where we play sports, and where there are nice people." The collage activity became a significant point of entry into a yearlong process of information gathering and reflection, and is discussed in more detail in later chapters.

Drawing and Storytelling

Another activity we invited the participants to engage in during the first year of the project was storytelling. As a tool for representation, storytelling creates an outlet for reflection, fantasy, and imagination, while also providing an opportunity for people to mirror, alter, and/or shift their realities.[3] By engaging in storytelling exercises the participants were provided with opportunities to collaborate with one another in developing stories which spoke to issues and conflicts salient to them.

In this particular research experience, we decided to link the storytelling exercise to science, the subject the students were studying in Susan's class. Susan organized them into groups, and once formed, we asked them to write a story that began with the following prompt: "A scientist came to visit our community and. . . ." We told them that they could write any kind of story they liked, including, horror, mystery, fantasy, realistic, and/or humorous. The participants were also invited to illustrate their stories.

In the first storytelling exercise we engaged in, four of the six stories generated among the small working groups included themes that resonated with the issues that were already emerging in the collage exercise, in the CRIs, and in our group discussions: namely, violence, drugs, and the environment. For example, Michael, Nadia, Puffy, and Neaka wrote and illustrated the following story:

> A scientist came to our community and he looked around and he smiled. Then the scientist said, "What a great community!" Then we told him why it was a great community. He reported how great our community was. The scientist said the community was great because it has a lot of people and it is a clean place. (We wish it was.)
>
> The scientist talked about how better our community would have been if all the drugs and all of the violence will stop. We have a great community but it's just something that messes it up. Like people shooting everybody and all the violence.

The storytelling exercises generated multiple discussions about the community, the majority of which focused on violence, health, drugs, and the fact that, as Puffy stated: "We want lots of people to visit here, not just scientists. But we gotta clean it up a bit so they'll come."

Community Photography

Throughout the research process, we met in large and small groups, sometimes in mixed-sex groups, other times in same-sex groups. The grouping was usually based on who was available at any particular moment. Other times, it had to do with how the participating teachers and/or members of the research team randomly grouped the young people together for an activity. Sometimes the participants created their own groups. Through the large and small group discussions, visual representations of the community via the collages, storytelling exercises, CRIs, and hours of participant-observation and one-on-one conversations, both the participants and the team members felt that we had developed a better understanding of which issues were most salient and of greatest concern to the participants. Wanting to further those understandings, we decided to implement the community photography aspect of the project in March 1998.

As discussed in chapter 1, community photography provided a resource to enable the participants to tell "visual stories" about themselves and their communities, thus creating an opportunity for them to express themselves in their own images, words, and reflections. The participants took over six hundred and fifty photographs of their community. They then spent months reflecting upon their developed prints. They deciphered multiple images that emerged in their photographs, comparing and contrasting their varied perspectives about what constitutes community. They discovered that although there were some positive aspects about their community, the negative aspects were far more significant and needed further attention. Like the collages, the photographs were significant entry points into a long-term process of information gathering, reflection, and action. The majority of the photographs the participants decided to reflect on depicted a community significantly affected by multiple forms of violence. This will be discussed in detail throughout this book.

Building Relationships within Transient Populations

We began this project with a core group of twenty-four participants. As of this writing, that number has decreased to eleven. It is difficult to assess the impact, both on the team members and the participants, and on the research process as a whole, of participants leaving, coming back, being here one day and gone the next. The unpredictability about who will participate and who won't is a constant thread and disruption in this particular community. We have young people who have participated in the project since its inception. But we have just as many young people who were integral participants of the project at one time or another but are no longer present.

During a team meeting in December 1998, Jen, Nicole, and Amy told me that Tee had not shown up that day for one of the group sessions because he had moved to Georgia over the weekend. Tee is a young, handsome African American male who I met the first day I came to the Blair School. Tee has beautiful dark skin, a fabulous smile, "dresses cool," and has just enough charm to keep him from being labeled "a troublemaker." He is also very bright, articulate, fun, engaging, and popular among his peers. Tee's mother was shot and killed when he was six years old. She went to a party one evening in Ellsworth and never returned. His father has been in prison for over seven years. Tee has been living with his grandmother and/or his aunt since his mother died. He also has relatives living in Georgia.

Tee was one of a small group of participants who formulated the initial plans for the development of the cleanup program discussed in chapter 7. As we collaborated in the development of that program, Tee and I spent a lot of time together talking about life, boys, girls, sex, school, racism, homophobia, television, sports, politics, movies, and a host of other issues that Tee was always eager to discuss.

One day as I was driving Tee home from a research session, I asked him if it would be OK with him if I met his grandmother, Marion. Tee had often told me stories about how much trouble he got into at home and in school and how angry his grandmother was with him for disobeying her and for "foolin' around too much." Although I was and am always in touch with the participants' parents and caregivers through letter writing, informal notes, regular telephone calls, and one-on-one meetings, the participants have resisted a collective meeting between the team, themselves, and their parents and caregivers. They "refuse to have our parents all comin' together and stuff. That's just not cool." I have chosen to respect their decision and therefore I only meet members of their families face-to-face when our paths cross at school, during school-related activities, or when I bring the participants home from project-related events.

As I stood in Marion's parlor and watched her watch me, I kept thinking of a remark that an African American staff member at the Blair School had made when I had first visited the school. As she was introducing me to a community resident, she referred to me as "the nice white lady from the university." So there I stood thinking of that remark and wondering if Tee's grandmother, Marion, felt the same way—that I was a nice white lady from the university. I wanted her to know that I wasn't all that sure I was all that nice, but I *was* sure that what Tee was doing in the project was important and that I enjoyed collaborating with him in developing strategies for addressing community issues. I also wanted to thank her for her support of Tee's participation in the project, even though she had deep reservations about his involvement in any activity that kept him away from home.

On one occasion, I arranged for Tee and four other participants to present aspects of the PAR project to faculty and graduate students at a research symposium to be held at the university. Prior to the event, I arranged for the five participants to visit the university so they would have the opportunity to practice their presentation in the auditorium. When Barbara went to the Blair School to pick up the group for one of those visits, Tee informed her that he had to go straight home because he was being punished for not coming home on time the previous day. After Barbara explained Tee's absence to me, I contacted him at home and we talked about how his actions at home and in school were having an impact on his participation in the project. He assured me that he was going to "stay out of trouble" and that it was just a misunderstanding between him and his grandmother. I also spoke to Marion on the telephone and she told me that she was "not going to put up with his stuff anymore" and if he wanted to be in the project, he needed to "stop his nonsense." I agreed and told her that I would do my best to accompany Tee in that process.

A week later, Tee telephoned me at my office. It was the Wednesday evening before the Thursday afternoon presentation at the university. He informed me that he would not be able to attend the presentation because he had received a detention in school that day and would have to stay after school on Thursday until 5:00 P.M., thus missing the 4:00 P.M. research symposium. His aunt took the phone from Tee and made it very clear to me that she was "sick of him playing games in school and that he would go nowhere if he kept up his nonsense." I asked her if Tee could fulfill the detention requirement on another day. She said even if he could, he was still not going to the presentation, because "he fools around too much in school and he is supposed to be an honor student."

Marion got on the phone next and explained that she had to go to the Blair School the following morning to speak with the teacher who had given Tee the detention. She told me that she would make her final decision about whether Tee could attend the presentation after that meeting. I spoke to Tee once again, stressing that he might want to "stop his nonsense" for a host of reasons, the most immediate one being that we simply did not want him to miss out on an opportunity to speak to faculty members and graduate students about the research project. He had been an active participant in the project over the previous year and a half and this was a chance for him to articulate his experiences to members of a community who, I would argue, are in dire need of hearing the life experiences of urban youth.

I called Marion on Thursday morning. She had gone to the school and straightened things out with the teacher who had given Tee the detention. Marion gave me permission to pick Tee up after school and bring him to the university for the presentation. She also reminded me that if Tee managed to get himself into trouble during the day, he would have to come right home and he would not be permitted to join us at the university.

The team members had arranged to pick the participants up after school, bring them home so that they could, as Mase said, "change into their church clothes" and then drive them to the university. I decided to pick Tee up twenty minutes earlier than planned in order to keep him from getting into any trouble during the closing minutes of school.

As Tee and I drove back to the university, I asked him why he had received the aforementioned detention. He told me that the teacher had called his name and rather than sit in his chair and respond to her, he had stood up and walked over to her desk. "She got mad because the last time someone walked up to her desk, they stole her credit card when she wasn't looking." According to Tee, "whoever stole it racked up a thousand dollars on the card before she knew it was gone." School personnel had not found the person who did it, but Tee said that "lots of kids know who it is; it's just that there are kids from The Courts [a housing project near the school where many of the students from the Blair School live] in the class and if they find out that someone told, they will hurt the person." He also told me during that ride to the university that he was definitely moving to Georgia in a few weeks and that he wasn't coming back.

A number of participants had left the school, the project, and the community by the time Tee informed me about his upcoming move to Georgia. Given that I experience a range of unsettling emotions as a result of their departures, I decided that I would simply ignore the reality that the next person to leave would be Tee. However, I was only able to ignore that reality for a short period of time.

When I arrived at the Blair School after hearing that Tee had moved, I immediately asked the participants if they had seen Tee before he left for Georgia. They said they saw him in school on Friday and that he had moved on Saturday but they didn't "say good-bye or anything." I told them that I was really sad that he had moved and wished that I had been given an opportunity to say good-bye and give him some project-related items that he might want to take with him. The young people appeared disinterested in my disclosure of sadness or in my desire to remain connected to Tee. When I saw the blank looks on their faces, I asked if any of them missed Tee. They all shrugged their shoulders and said, "No."

Later that day I was walking down the hall with some of the participants when I mentioned to Mase and Blood, two of Tee's closest friends in school, that I was going to send Tee a package of photographs and an update of what we had done thus far with the cleanup project Tee had been instrumental in developing. I asked them if they would like me to include anything in particular from them. They both gave me their "you gotta be kiddin' me" looks and Mase said, "I ain't sendin' him nothin'." I looked at him and said, "You mean to tell me that you don't miss Tee at all?" "Not at all," he said. I told him that I didn't believe him and kept walking, at which point he saddled up beside me and whispered, "OK. I do miss him. But only a little."

Mase's comment reminded me of a conversation I had had with a small group of female participants months prior to this interaction, regarding the young people's friendships in the Blair School community.

Veronica: Some people go to the school over here because some people don't like schools over there [the other side of Ellsworth].

Jeter: See, I like the schools there better.

Alice: Why?

Veronica: I do, too.

[ct]

Jeter: Yeah, I went to a school there from kindergarten to fourth grade and I had friends there.

Alice: Oh, so that's hard. You had your friends there and then you came here?

Jeter: No, then I went to a private school. Then I came over here and now I'm gonna move to another school 'cause I'm gonna move from my house.

Alice: That's tough to move, huh? Because you develop friendships with people and then you have to leave them[

Veronica: That's why I try not to get that much friends because I know if I'm about to move, 'cause I moved like six places in three years.

Alice: So you try not to make friends?

Veronica: Yeah, because what's the use? You gonna move at least in that year but now I'm livin' over here for like maybe until my mom, she says she wants to buy a house.

Janine: Yeah, 'cause of the shootin' that is goin' on. All the kids doin' drugs, um, the violence and everything. (November 17, 1997)

Jeter moved out of the neighborhood in February 1998. Veronica moved to another area of Ellsworth at the beginning of September 1999. I didn't get a chance to say good-bye to either of them. Neither did their peers. I sent both of them notes to update them on the project, as I do with all the participants who have moved and left the project. Sometimes the letters come back to me "address unknown." Other times, the letters aren't returned and I can only hope that they arrived and that the participants realize how much they are missed and how important they were to the project.

I was deeply saddened by Tee's departure. I called him a few times in Georgia to update him on the project and to see how he was faring. He told me that he was impressed that he had a Black teacher who "dates a white guy." He also told me that his teacher always reminded the class that "no one is better than anyone else—no matter what color your skin is." He told me that school was sort of boring, but that he had "three friends I hang out with and so far, I've stayed out of trouble. I'm only in trouble at home 'cause I only do a half-job on my chores." He missed being part of the program and hoped to come back to Ellsworth soon.

I write about Tee and the other participants who have relocated during this project for two reasons. One has to do with the way we gather information in a long-term PAR project, and once gathered, what we do with it. The information and indigenous knowledge that becomes "known" through cocreating experiences where stories can be told, heard, and acted upon by research participants becomes the fodder for whatever changes may take place within a community or group. Thus, when participants who have contributed to the construction of that knowledge and to the overall information-gathering process, are no longer present, there is an interruption, a pause, a question mark as to what to do with that information. When a person who contributed important information to a project is no longer present, the cyclical process of investigation, reflection, and action is to some extent disrupted. Thus, the departure of participants from PAR projects raises questions about the meanings we attach to "participation," "research," and "action." Similarly, it calls into question methodological and epistemological issues about representation, analysis, interpretation, and how we integrate a missing participant's information into our interpretations and into the action phases of a PAR project.

The loss of participants within a PAR project does not necessarily indicate that the project will fail and or that the generated knowledge that has been collected both individually and collectively is no longer useful. What it does indicate is that if the participants of a PAR project are "residentially unstable" (Newman 1999:162), the PAR process needs to be flexible enough to handle the strain that results. Equally important, if the PAR project is to remain viable, there must be a core group of committed, available participants willing to sustain the research process in the midst of an ever-shifting participant population.

The second reason I write about the effects of residential instability on urban youth is because I feel it is important to learn with and from young people about what it means to address loss and how that loss affects young people's ability to develop trust in themselves and in other people. In listening to a group of urban youth talk about friendships, Niobe Way (1998) discovered a pervasive sense of mistrust between and among urban males and females. She concluded that a number of factors contributed to the high levels of mistrust among the adolescents she came to know: cultural and social expectations for males and females, the environments in which the young people lived, the school they attended, the young people's relationships with their parents, and "the poverty, violence, racism, and homophobia that shapes and pervades these adolescents' lives" (1998:140–41).

My experience suggests that having friends and classmates moving from place to place and from school to school on a regular basis has a profound effect on adolescents' ability to trust and develop a constellation of friends.[4] Being in this constant state of uncertainty, not knowing whether they will be the ones to leave or the ones to be left, results in a heightened sense of self-protection which is potentially harmful to the development of intimate relationships so essential for the well-being of young people. Equally important are the roles of parents and caregivers in the lives of the participants, for they are their primary role models for the way relationships are developed and maintained over time.

The present research does not attempt to make judgments about the participants' relationships with their parents and caregivers. Nor does it attempt to make judgments about the stability and/or instability of those relationships. Yet the research does raise questions about how child-parent/caregiver relationships inform the way urban youth negotiate their own relationships with peers and other adults. Further, it challenges professionals and policymakers to address the systemic structures that make it necessary for many people living in inner cities in the United States to always "be on the move," putting a strain on children, adolescents, schools, families, and communities. It also makes it extremely difficult to develop supportive networks of friends and neighbors, which are integral aspects to building safe and trusting communities.

An Addendum

At a meeting in June 1999, I informed the group that I was sending Tee a videotape of the two schoolwide assemblies they had organized the previous month, in which they had presented aspects of the PAR project to the Blair School community. Very nonchalantly Blood looked over at me and said, "Why are you sending it? He's back." I was stunned. "He's BACK?" I exclaimed. "Yeah," replied Blood. "We were playin' basketball with him the other day." "Yeah," Monique continued. "And he wants to come to Coasterland with us this week." (We had organized a day trip to an amusement park.) When I asked the participants if he was living in the house he used to live in, they said he was and that he intended to stay there and return to the Blair School in September 1999.

I returned to my office later that day and immediately called Tee to reconnect with him and to let him know that I was thrilled that he had returned to Ellsworth and that he could definitely come with us to Coasterland. He was happy to hear from me and asked if I had received the two letters he had sent me from Georgia. Unfortunately I had not, but I assured him that he could fill me in on the contents of the letters when we met for our trip to Coasterland.

I was delighted to see Tee and eager to hear about his life in Georgia. He informed me that when he arrived in Georgia, he had been required to take a test to determine if he needed to remain in the seventh grade or be enrolled in an eighth-grade class. After reviewing Tee's score on the test, the school in Georgia decided to enroll him in the eighth grade. Thus when he returned to Ellsworth, the school system was unsure of where he would be placed the following year. Tee told me that he didn't mind skipping eighth grade at the Blair School because he knew "some of the people at the high school and that'll be cool." He said his only reservation about leaving the Blair School was that he would miss being part of the PAR project. He asked me three times in the span of an hour if we were seriously going to continue with the project the following year. I, and the participants, repeatedly informed him that, yes, we were definitely continuing with the project. We told him that we had decided to develop a photo-text book, and also continue to work on the cleanup project we had developed. By the end of the hour, Tee decided that he didn't really want to attend high school in September and that he preferred to "stay here at

Blair. I don't want to miss the project anymore. So, I'm just going to tell them that I don't want to move on."

I explained to Tee that I did not think the decision was up to him—that those decisions were made by teachers and administrators in the Ellsworth public school system. I also assured him that no matter where he attended school in September, he would always be a participant in the program and that we would make arrangements so that he could remain an active member of the group.

Months have passed since that conversation. Tee is still an active participant in the project. As it turned out, the Ellsworth public school system decided that Tee's test scores from Georgia did not warrant him attending high school. Therefore, he joined the rest of the participants as a student at the Blair School.

I continue to be concerned about how urban youth develop, maintain, and sustain friendships when those friendships—and here I would add other significant relationships as well—are mediated by instability and uncertainty. At the same time, I am encouraged by the possibilities that arise in a PAR process for creating spaces to initiate and cultivate interpersonal relationships between and among adults and urban youth that are supportive, build confidence, and allow young people to feel purposeful about addressing some of the complex issues in their lives.

Concluding Reflections

By the end of the first year of the project, we gained a substantial amount of knowledge about the participants and how they experience living in their community. We moved between moments of investigation, education, interpretation, and analysis, foregrounding the participants' feelings, beliefs, and personal experiences as vital elements in constructing knowledge about their lives. We engaged in a dynamic process of self- and collective reflection that ultimately led to the next phases of the project: developing and implementing strategies for building a cleaner, safer community.

The continued dialogue between the team members and the participants was critical to the PAR process and supported a climate of openness, trust, and cooperation. At the same time, the dialogue raised issues that provoked deep, sometimes painful, emotional responses from participants and team members. Negotiating those dialectics and allowing various elements to act in relation to each other resulted in increased consciousness for those involved. With probing dialogue, a critical questioning of reality, and an exploration of their own environments the participants gained new perspectives about themselves and their community. They became more aware of the connection between knowing and doing. Furthermore, they realized that they knew more than they thought they knew and that what they knew could be used to alter their conditions—if only slightly. "I know the community has some nice things about it," Melinda said, "and I wish people would pay more attention to the good things, like what we are doing in this project, than concentrating on the bad things all the time." Risha stated that "I know now that we are dedicated people and that it doesn't matter if City Hall wants to help us or not. We already did some good stuff and we can do even more." Tee said, "The cleanup project is great 'cause it shows people that we care and that we can do something positive to help the community. And sometimes, people think kids can't do it but we are showin' them that they are wrong."

In the next three chapters, I describe some of the most salient information we gleaned during the first year of the project. I lay the groundwork for a discussion of how the participants then took this information, reflected on it, and decided to take action to address issues that concerned them. In so doing, I illustrate the participants' determination to show people that "they are wrong" and that if given a chance, urban youth can and will "create the material and political conditions necessary to sustain [a] common project" (Grundy 1997:127) aimed at individual and collective change.

3

■　■　■　■　■　■　■　■　■

Constructing Meaning about Violence

FOUR TYPES OF VIOLENCE—interpersonal, educational, structural, and environmental—framed the participants' ongoing discussions about how they experience their lives within their community. Interpersonal violence is the one they experience, engage in, observe, and talk about the most. It is also the kind of violence regularly focused on by politicians, the public, and the mainstream media (see, for example, Barrett 1993; Chasin 1998; Garbarino 1999; Heide 1999; McCord 1997). The second type of violence that shapes the participants' lives and which they "feel" on two fronts is systemic violence. This is the direct or indirect result of decisions made by "elite" groups of people working within and through economic, political, and other societal systems in the United States (Chasin 1998). Those decisions affect the participants in two ways: they attend underfunded schools (educational violence) and live in underresourced communities (structural violence). Finally, the participants suffer from environmental violence, which results in many poor people and people of Color living in the most polluted communities in the United States.[1]

In the next three chapters, I describe how the various types of violence mentioned above shape and inform the participants' lives. I do so in the hopes that educators will pause, listen, and be stimulated by the young people's stories to engage in critical conversations about how we can better understand the multidimensionality of violence and its impact on young people. I also hope this discussion generates new ideas for building bridges to schools and communities that will enable urban youth to succeed and thrive.[2]

The Multidimensionality of Violence in an Urban School-Community

In 1992, two students were gunned down outside the Blair School. One of them was killed in full view of students and teachers. Mrs. Lawton told me that when she had arrived at the school eight years ago, it was the "worst school in Ellsworth. . . . I said I wouldn't come here unless they put bulletproof glass in the kindergarten rooms as the windows had bullet holes in them. See, those kindergarten rooms faced [a building] which has since been torn down, where all the drug dealing took place, normally between 11 A.M. and 1 P.M." (Field notes, November 3, 1997)

Mrs. Lawton went on to tell me that the kindergarten students were taught how to get down and crawl out of the room when they heard the gunshots. She said that things had "gotten better" since then. There was still violence, guns, open-air drug dealing, and "too many issues for these kids to deal with, but in the midst of everything that they deal with in their lives, they STILL want to learn. I always say to people, 'Can you imagine if they lived in another environment what they could do?'"

The bulletproof glass in the Blair School's kindergarten rooms symbolizes one aspect of the violence that exists in the school-community. There are many others. In this chapter, I focus on three aspects of interpersonal violence that mediate the participants' lives: the normalcy of violence in their community; the sense of impending doom that they experience and live with on a daily basis; and the extent to which they themselves become both victims and perpetrators of violence. Below, I present dimensions of these themes, illustrating the obstacles the participants face and navigate as they experience the varied dimensions of violence within their school and community.

"It's a Shame I Gotta Carry a Knife"

During our first brainstorming activity, I asked the participants to tell us what they thought about when they thought of community. Some of the students said, "where you live," "family," "school," and "neighborhood." Many others said, "where you clean," "where you throw away guns and get like $100 for your gun," "drugs," "drug cars," and "violence." Thus from the outset of the research project, there has been a focus on the multiple forms of violence that exist in the community.

Following the brainstorming activity, we organized the participants into small groups of four and five and, using magazines that the research team and Susan had brought to class, invited them to create group collages that represented their community. They presented their various creations, interpreted each other's collages, and engaged in a number of discussions that emerged from the images presented. There were a number of images that spoke to the young people's representations of their community: sports, guns, drugs, material things, career possibilities, music, education, and the environment. The ensuing discussions ranged from the community being "full of drugs, guns, and violence," to the "community is a junkyard and should be cleaned up," to the "community is a place where there are friendships, where we play sports, and where there are nice people." But overall, and throughout the entire research project, one of the main foci of the participants' discussions about their community has been violence.

During the course of a large group discussion following the collage presentations, Puffy mentioned the word "kidnapping." When I asked him to elaborate, he told us a story about a girl who had been in his class the year before. (At the time, Puffy was attending another school in the district.)

> *Puffy:* She like never came back. 'Cause she died. Because somebody kidnaped her 'cause her mother owed them money. . . . He told her he had toys for her. So, she knew she wasn't supposed to go. . . . She walked him to her house and he killed her. He stabbed her and he was smashing her head into the doorbell.
>
> *Monique:* That's her cousin [pointing to Tonesha].
>
> *Tonesha:* That's my cousin.
>
> *Monique:* And you got the story wrong.
>
> *Puffy:* No, she was in my class. And no, I don't got the story wrong 'cause her brother came into the school and told the teacher what happened.
>
> *Tonesha:* Can I tell you what happened? You, you on the right track but you a little bit off. This is what happened. Her, her mother was out. She [the

mother, Tonesha's aunt] was working 'cause she had a part-time job at night. She had a boyfriend . . . and he said that um, he'd be right back 'cause he was going to the store to get some groceries and stuff. So, um, Evelyn was left in the house to watch her sisters and brothers. So then James came to the door and he said, "Come here, Evelyn. We gonna go get some toys." And Evelyn's brother, he came to the door. He said, "Can I come?" and James was saying, "No." And then because James was mad 'cause something just happened to him, he took her next door to his back-yard. And he stabbed her up in her neck and stuff and then he threw her in the yard. And he didn't slam her fingers in the door. He cut off her fingers. And then um, the neighbors they saw him. And then they found her on top of the gate. They knew it was him 'cause he threw, he threw his dirty clothes in the pantry of his house. And they had blood and all this stuff on it. (November 10, 1997)

Immediately following Tonesha's story, other participants rushed to tell their own stories of violence and horror: a baby who died because her mother left her alone in the carriage and the baby choked on her own blood; a seven-month-old baby who drowned in a bathtub while the mother was on the telephone: "She went to jail and the little brother um, went to foster care." And the little girl who found a gun under the couch and shot her little sister by mistake. There was no pausing between stories, no questioning of the storyteller, and no visible emotions expressed by the participants. As soon as one person had finished a story, another would follow up with another. It was as if there was one continuous story that had numerous character changes, though the plot remained the same. At one point, Tonesha reentered the discussion and continued with her earlier narrative:

Hello. Can I talk? We was like talking about violence. Like four or five years ago my uncle he um, he picked up a gun and didn't know if it was loaded or not and he was just playing with it and shot himself in the head. But he didn't die. He had to go to the hospital and get treatment and stuff. But like a year after that he came out and um, his friend shot him in the head. The same spot. (November 10, 1997)

The storytelling had a sense of urgency about it, but was also marked by a sense of normalcy. Although the young people sat quietly, somewhat in suspense, as Tonesha told the story of her cousin, who was fifteen years old at the time of her murder, they quickly moved out of that space when she had finished. Like many adolescents who are in the midst of multiple transitions—some occurring almost simultaneously—the participants quickly gained control of the discourse and began a kind of tit-for-tat storytelling which consisted of telling violent vignettes filled with stabbings, kidnapping, motherless children, and murder. Through my experience working with and teaching adolescents, I have learned that asking particular questions of the storyteller can uncover exaggerations and clarify incidents that may get distorted as a story travels from one source to the next and back again. Some of the stories the participants have told me over the years have been garnered from television, movies, street-corner gossip, and a desire to capture my—and other people's—attention. On the other hand, way too many of their stories are based in reality. Tonesha's cousin *was* murdered. A little girl *did* shoot her sister by mistake. The mother of one of the third graders at the Blair School *was* stabbed to death by her boyfriend last year—in front of her children. Some of the participants who live in The Courts *did* see a "crackhead" shot to death last year (and others before him). Thus, there is always a violent story and/or event placed alongside and compared to another violent story and/or event. The recurrence of violent acts becomes habitual and the matter-of-fact, unaffected responses by participants become normal.

A few weeks after the collage exercise, I was sitting talking with Tonesha and she said, "Sure is a shame I gotta carry a knife." There was a lot of noise in the background, so I was not sure I had heard her correctly. What I thought she had said was, "Sure is a shame I can't go out at night." That would have made sense to me, as many of the participants can't go out at night. Their parents and caregivers are frightened for their safety and do not want them getting into trouble. (Blood, one of the young boys who lives in The Courts, told me he puts the radio on in his bedroom loud enough so his mother will think he is in there and then he sneaks out the window. He climbs back in later on when he thinks he won't get caught.) I turned to her and said, "What did you say, Tonesha?" And she replied, "It's a shame I gotta carry a knife." She went on to tell me that after her cousin was murdered, her mother gave her and her sister pocketknives which they were to carry with them at all times.

See, there's crazy people in the world. They kill you. And so you have to protect yourself. My mother told us that if you see someone walkin' towards
you, or if they're grabbin' you, stab him and run. Or he'll rape you and kill
you. Psychos out there. But my neighborhood's pretty good I guess. There
are drugs and used crack pipes on the ground and that drives me nuts. It's a
shame, but that's the way it is. (Field notes, November 24, 1998)

Tonesha is outgoing, friendly, and, as she would say, "kind of tall, thin,
with dark hair that has brown tips. I also have black skin 'cause I'm Afro-
American. I say Afro-American because it's shorter to write." Tonesha is
also smart, motivated, engaged in her academic work, and wants "to grow
up and go to college and get a degree and be like a lawyer because I would
like to, for all the violence and stuff out there, I'd like to help the innocent
people." Throughout the project, Tonesha has repeatedly mentioned that
"kids have to get good grades and help the community." Tonesha also has
strong views about what young people need to do in order to stay out of
trouble—"stay in school and don't be stupid"—and appears to want very
much to contribute to creating a healthier and cleaner environment. She is
not alone in her zeal to "make life better around here." Yet, accompanying Tonesha's zeal to improve life in her community is a sense of resignation about the way things are there. This is evident in her comment: "It's
a shame, but that's the way it is, I guess"—a feeling shared by many of the
young people participating in this project.

Yet, along with their feelings of resignation about aspects of the community that are not conducive to healthy living, the participants also believe that there are positive aspects about their community that are worth
saving. They have friends, acquaintances, favorite hangouts, and public
spaces where they can ride bikes, play basketball, dance, listen to loud
music, and go to the movies. They know the people they can hang around
with and those they are supposed to stay away from. They know the police, the truant officers, the security guards at school, and they will readily
tell you who the "mean" store owners are as opposed to the ones they consider "cool." In many respects, the participants engage in the same daily
practices as many other young people in the United States do: eating,
sleeping, attending school, studying, watching television, listening to the
radio, and playing sports. Yet, the daily practices they engage in are lived

out and embedded in contexts of violence, racism, poverty, and other forms of inequality that have profound consequences for the way these young people organize their lives.

In response to living in a violence-prone community, the participants have developed a set of strategies for organizing—and normalizing—their lives, to the extent that that is possible. One of the strategies they use to organize their lives is to "be ready for anything"—a protective stance that takes its toll on these young people and distracts them from engaging in other aspects of adolescent life. It is to that sense of "distraction"—that sense of "being ready for anything"—that I turn in the next section.

"Suppose I'm Waiting on the Bus": Anticipating the Worst

A recurrent theme in the participants' narratives is the anticipation of violence—the "what if this happens? What if that happens? What would I do?" questions that become a familiar refrain as the participants negotiate their daily lives. This way of being in the world resonates with Martín-Baró's description of "normal abnormality" (1994:125) and results from engaging in the dailiness of life with a sixth sense that one is never really completely safe and that violence is the organizing principle of one's life.[3]

The following conversation is representative of many others we had over the course of the project and highlights how the participants negotiate their day-to-day activities, cognizant all the while of the dangers that are ever-present in their environment.

> *Veronica:* You can't go on [the main] street like by yourself because you never know what happens 'cause there's two bars over there and they got go-go dancers there, strippers. And um, every Friday like at least somethin' happened at [the bar]. Cops always be there every Friday. Like one time this man fell out. I saw him. He got drunk and everybody thought he was dead. Everybody thought he got shot. But he was drunk and he fell out. It was like ten cop cars.
>
> *Jeter:* And every night you go out or come back from a place you see like, how do you call it? Um, drug dealers. Um, not go-gos, um, prostitutes. You see prostitutes lookin' for men and you see men lookin' for prostitutes lookin' in the cars for where they at.

Tina: Around where I live, it's like dangerous. You have to keep your doors locked at all times because like at my house when the doors weren't locked, criminals came in my house and the police came in and got them and some of them had guns and stuff and one time, around where I live, this um, girl she was going to the car. She . . . owed this man money and stuff and this twelve-year-old boy was in the car with the man and when she bent down to talk to the man, the twelve-year-old boy shot her in the head and she had to go to the hospital where she's still alive.

Alice: So what do the people in your neighborhood do to[

Tina: Um, we have like a neighborhood watch . . . and when people see someone doing something bad they call the office and the office calls the police so they can do something about it.

Alice: Does that make you feel safer?

Tina: Yeah, but I don't go out at night 'cause in the summertime like if I went out at night, like they start shooting and stuff outside so I have to go in and I can't go back out.

Alice: Uh-huh. What do you do in the house?

Tina: Um, I watch TV and I play video games. I work on stuff and I study over the summer.

Janine: I'm not home in the summer. The whole summer, I be down South with my family. [When I'm here] I play with my sisters or my cousins when they come over but when it's time to leave for them to go home, their father will come pick them up. We play games like hide-and-go-seek in the house.

Veronica: I don't go out ever in my neighborhood. I go out around my aunt's neighborhood 'cause I go to her house 'cause she baby-sits me when my Mom goes to work. I don't like, like you cannot go outside and expect not to see cops ride by or cops goin' with sirens. You expect and sometimes, it be so much, it just be so much noise that you just wanna go in your house and not come back out because what's the use? If you, 'cause like one day I saw these men runnin' from some cops. And it was three men and one hopped the fence and he was goin' in a house, well, he wasn't goin' in the house. He was goin' in the yard and these kids have to run in the house because they didn't know if he was gonna hit them or not 'cause he was just runnin'.

Jeter: The only thing, the only two bad things that happened, no, three bad things. They um, stole in my house. They broke into my house when my mother was in the hospital when she had my little baby brother. And um, when this guy with a stolen car, he came and broke our fence. And they stole two of our bikes in front of my house.

Tina: Like one time criminals ran through where I live and like I got scared because the police was pointing guns and then they tell us that these people have guns on them so they could do all this violence in my neighborhood. Everything that's bad is violence and drugs . . .

[ct]

Mariah: I'm scared. Um, suppose I'm waiting on the bus to go to school and like, I hear gunshots and I don't know what I'd do. I would just stand there . . . because I would panic. (November 11, 1997).

Immediately following Mariah's reference to her panic, the conversation quickly moved to violence in Jamaica (where two of the participants have relatives), followed by a conversation about swimming in the ocean, doing cannonballs in a swimming pool, sports, Michael Jordan, and rap singers. The discussion about rap singers led Puffy to pull a song out of his pocket that he and his cousin had written over the weekend. Within minutes, he and Neaka—along with the rest of us—began "writing" the music (by drumming on the table) to accompany the words he and his cousin had crafted:

Just come clean with me. I'm not begging.

Baby, the way you treat me. The way that you talk to me and the things that you say to me is something about love. I don't need nothing else but you.

Baby, what you do to me. I'm not happy without you. But what is wrong with you and me?

Baby, our relationship is over. I never meant to hurt you, but I gotta let you go.

The bell rang to change classes and on that particular day, we never did return to Mariah's panic. Nonetheless, a low-level sense of panic—somewhat quiet and controlled among some of the participants, loud and explosive in others—is an ever-present, palpable factor in their lives.

The participants also anticipate the worst when outsiders enter specific areas in their community. This was demonstrated to me one day as I drove

Blood and Tee home from the university. Both Tee and Blood had failed to give me permission slips that would allow them to join the research team and the other participants at a pizza party we were organizing at a local restaurant the following week. Therefore, as we drove along I suggested that when I dropped them off at their houses, they run in, get their signed permission slips, and bring them back to me in the car. Blood, who lives in The Courts, immediately said, "Oh no. You don't want to do that, Miss. They'll [people who live in The Courts] think you want drugs and bug you in the car." I told him not to worry about that but Tee quickly agreed with Blood, saying, "No. He's right. You're white and the only time white people come into The Courts is to buy drugs. I went in The Courts with the elders [from his church] last week 'cause they are always trying to talk about our church to people and the people in The Courts, they kept followin' them and givin' them trouble."

I again reassured them that I would be fine and mentioned to Blood that when I dropped him off, I could say hello to his mother whom I had met at the Blair School on a previous occasion. Blood replied,

I don't think that's a good idea. She never comes out. She's afraid. She don't even like it that I go out. Especially 'cause of what happened Wednesday night. [A gang] came to The Courts and The Courts gang and [the other gang] don't get along. So [the gang] was visitin' someone in the building and when they come down the stairs, someone shot one of them dead. So you see? You shouldn't drive in there right now. (Field notes, November 30, 1998)

I drive around and through The Courts quite often. Yet, as Blood and Tee reminded me, "That's during the day, Ms. Mac. It's dark out now so it's a different story." I explained to Tee and Blood that I appreciated their concern for my safety. I also reminded them of the multiple discussions the research team and the participants had engaged in over the course of the research process about the stereotypes that many people who live *outside* The Courts have about the people who live *inside* The Courts. Hadn't we discussed the fact that not all the people who live in The Courts are drug dealers? Hadn't the participants told me many times that some of the people living in The Courts are nice people "who don't want no trouble?" Hadn't we walked through The Courts together and met a number of their neighbors and friends who were happy to see that they were involved in a school-community project? They agreed that those conversations had taken place and they also acknowledged that most of the people who lived in The Courts were "cool." Nevertheless, Tee and Blood couldn't quite shake the feeling that "something bad might happen" if I drove them inside The Courts. We finally agreed that I would drive up to Blood's building but I would forgo saying hello to his mother. Instead, Blood jumped out of the car, ran into his house, and said, "I swear, Ms. Mac, in seconds, I'll have that slip back here." As Tee and I waited for Blood to retrieve his permission slip, Tee looked over at me and said, "Even though I don't live in here, I come over here a lot, but I don't like it in here. You just never know what's gonna happen in here. You just never know."

This idea of "never knowing what's going to happen," and the themes of "unpredictability and cautious realism" (Way 1998:167), were repeatedly expressed by the participants. These themes are both limiting and necessary. The strategies the participants and their parents and caregivers develop may protect the participants from harm. Yet they also enclose them in socially constructed areas that limit their opportunities to expand their worlds. Within those boundaried spaces, the participants learn to live in a state of "just never knowing," negotiating unpredictable social contexts while also negotiating school, peer, and familial relationships, as well as the everydayness of being adolescents.

"Every Day I Walk Home from School I Throw a Rock at Him"

Adolescents living in urban areas are not only victims of violence but are perpetrators as well (see, for example, Fine and Weis 1998b; Garbarino 1999; MacLeod 1995; Sullivan 1989). If we conceptualize violence as including littering, stealing, graffiti, and physical assault ranging from intentionally pushing and shoving each other inside and outside school to serious infliction of physical injury, then most of the participants in this research have been perpetrators. Only recently have the participants reconceptualized violence as involving more than *serious* physical harm, which is the way they appeared to understand it at the beginning of the project. Since then, many of them have made a connection between what they consider the more serious types of violence that occur in their community, such as murder, armed robbery, and physical assaults requiring hospitalization, with less serious, though no less disruptive and alienating to and in the community types of violence, such as trash, peer-on-peer physical fighting, graffiti, pollution, and verbal assaults.

The physical violence, both serious and "not-so-serious" (the latter being characterized by fist fights and "givin' each other a beatin'"), that occurs in the community is most often perpetrated by boys and young men. That is not to say that girls in the community, and some of the girls participating in the project, practice nonviolence. Over a period of two months during the second year of the project, I witnessed four physical altercations that involved girls. In one of those incidents, I was standing inside a classroom speaking to a teacher when, within seconds, two seventh graders—one boy and one girl—jumped up from their desks and started assaulting each other. They flipped each other on the floor, at which point I grabbed the girl and the teacher grabbed the boy, an action that resulted in the teacher being kicked and thrown to the floor.

This incident was not unique. Nor are incidents of girls pushing and shoving each other, pushing and shoving boys, and/or vice versa. Yet girls and boys do not see these incidents as violent. Instead, they view them as a way of jostling for position. The physicality is usually accompanied by sarcasm and verbal taunts aimed at getting a laugh and/or forcing the other person to "shut up" and "get outta my face." Although some of that behavior is characteristic of many adolescents, both white and of Color, both rich and poor, the interpersonal violence experienced in this community is, as Tonesha once said, "just the way it is here." Further, many young people in the school and community expect, and to some degree sanction, the ways in which conflicts are addressed—or not—both inside and outside the school environment.

Adolescents as initiators, accomplices, and/or perpetrators of violent acts aimed at physically harming another person was the theme of a discussion I had with a group of four boys one day in late November 1997. Our conversation was representative of many of the narratives about violence that are commonplace among young males in this community and foregrounds the normality of violence in the everyday lives of these boys, and in their daily adolescent banter. It began as Boo made reference to an announcement that Mrs. Lawton had made that morning on the public-address system about a fourteen-year-old boy who had attended another school in the neighborhood. The fourteen-year-old boy had left school the previous day, walked into a neighborhood store, and tried to rob the owner. In the scuffle that ensued the owner shot and killed the young boy. Many of the participants knew the student.

Boo: Mrs. Lawton announced over the loud speaker that some kid got killed 'cause he was skippin' school, and then he went to some store and he tried to steal and then a man shot him up. That was messed up.

Mikey: I saw the one on Good Friday this year, ya know. I didn't see when the guy got capped but I was passin' by on my church bus. I saw the dude layin' down there and the cops pickin' him up.

Senor: Also, I saw some dude in back of The Courts, out layin' there for four days. This guy, this bum layin' there for four days. Every day I walk home from school I throw a rock at him, me and Benny and them and he wouldn't get up.

Alice: Why did you throw a rock at him?

Boo: Because he be botherin' people.

Senor: And late at night he be pacin' around.

Boo: Be quiet, be quiet. He be jumpin' in people's houses and robbin' people.

Senor: I saw that too one night, 'cause he said um, one time he asked me for a dollar and I ran and he started chasin' after me.

[laughter]

Blood: There's a lot of bums be in The Courts. Then there be a lot of crack-heads.

Mikey: They sometimes, ya know, I don't wanna dis' no one up in The Courts because I don't wanna lose my life or nothin', but, ya know what I'm sayin'? A lot of people be comin' up there for crack, ya know? They be just standin' up in the middle of the road just crackin'.

Senor: And sometimes they say people in The Courts get so high they steal they own furniture out their own house and go sell it.

[laughter]

Mikey: I live in The Courts, too! Last year, they shot at the windows in the [school] lunchroom [from The Courts]. But it's lucky that the um, windows was bulletproof. Because you could still see the bullet prints in there. . . . But the part where I live. It's not so bad. I go out freely. I don't go down to where it's, ya know, where they're dealin' the drugs and killin' people, 'cause trust me, they got this one spot . . . they be killin' people there in that same spot like nothin'. One time they had killed somebody there and put a box where the dude had got shot.

Blood: Um, with some candles. And then the box, where the box was there was a big heart and a lot of tags in the floor. 'Cause this is my building [where the killing took place]. Sometimes I be hangin' with my friends, but sometimes my mother doesn't let me go outside 'cause she scared, like there be a lot of shootin'. She scared I get shot or somethin', but I still go outside. I jump out the window.

Mikey: What's the dilly with that? Ya know what I'm sayin'? You could get capped like that.

[ct]

Senor: See, these little boys right, we, they be goin' to go steal cars. And they be thinkin' it's funny and stuff. And they be crashin' and cops be takin' their sneakers and throwin' them in the water and everything. They be throwin' them in the car and beatin' them up. One time, we was in a stolen car, we was going real fast, real fast. And they stopped, and I bust my head open because my head hit on the windshield. That's when we ran. That's when we ran out and the cops chased me. That's when um, they caught my boy. That's when they threw my friend in the back of the car and they took his sneakers off.

[ct]

Alice: Is that what you said, you were hanging out with kids from The Courts and then you stole the car?

Senor: I didn't steal no car! They stole it. I was gonna go get gas and um[

Alice: They stole it and you just got in it?

Senor: Yeah.

Alice: Did you know it was stolen?

Senor: Nope. I thought it was their uncle's car 'cause their uncle got one just like that.

Boo: Man, no you didn't.

A long conversation ensued about how Mikey and Senor used to live in Philadelphia and the kinds of trouble they used to get into while living there. Boo felt upstaged and after interrupting the group repeatedly, managed to get their attention:

Alice: Boo, go ahead. You were with your friends and[

[boys keep interrupting Boo]

Boo: [to the boys] Your mom.

Senor: Oh, you be hangin' out with her.

Boo: It was like, they went to this um, corner store, and then they was throwin' eggs.

Alice: You and your friends?

Boo: I wasn't throwin' eggs. I ain't gettin' shot. I was just mindin' my business. I was just talkin' to a few girls. My big brother's friends, girls. And then they threw some eggs out the window. And you know spark plugs, like the little pieces that heat up?

Blood: Yeah, I done that.

Boo: They threw it and the whole window shattered. It was like, a whole bunch of cracks in it. The dude came out. He opened the door, he had this like[

Blood: 9 mm?

Boo: With the sound effects.

Mikey: A 45?

Boo: No. Millimeter.

Blood: A 9 millimeter?

Boo: Shut up. God.

Mikey: All right. Give him his turn. Give him his turn.

Boo: You know that movie with the big gun?

Senor: A Tommy?

Boo: Shut up!

Mikey: Like the old cowboys' one?

Boo: Yo' man, I ain't playin'. I'm about to smack one of y'all. Um, and then he came out with one of those guns, you know like on HBO, one of those guns, they all black? They ain't no Tommy guns, they ain't no western guns. It had like a little, like a big, long thing, with like a big barrel. And then he started shootin', then he shot this, he shot my friend.

Alice: And what did you do?

Boo: Like everybody would do, I ran. My friend wasn't dead. He got shot in the arm. (November 24, 1997)

The conversation turned to a discussion of the mob, the Mafia, and how people had to be careful about what they said because "you never know who might be listenin' to you." The boys also talked about what they thought the community could do to rid itself of guns. They discussed buyback programs that the community could organize, but that discussion was aborted when Senor started laughing at Mikey about a fight that Mikey had engaged in earlier that month with someone who called him "bubba lips."

> *Mikey:* See, I'm a person that I don't like people talkin' about me because, I like, I mean, I react. First of all, Miss McIntyre let me tell you, one time Blood started, he was callin' me bubba lips. So I got, I got mad. I was like Benny, his little punk friend that he be hangin' out with was like talkin' about bubba lips, too. I said, "Come over here and say bubba lips to my face and I'll smack you." So he came over here and he was like, "Bubba lips." He said, "I don't see ya doin' nothin'." So I said, "Hit me if you bad." Then he hit me. He didn't punch me or nothin'. He like, brushed me on the arm, and I got up[
>
> *Senor:* Who won?
>
> *Mikey:* and I pushed him into the wall. First of all, the point is, I won.
>
> *Blood:* Who was bleedin'? Who was bleedin'?
>
> *Mikey:* Me and Benny was bleedin'. That doesn't even matter.
>
> *Blood: You* was.
>
> *Mikey:* Me and Benny was bleedin'. Because he hit me in my mouth. And I hit him in the nose. (November 24, 1997)

The discussion ended with the boys laughing over the fight and the school bell ringing, signifying that the time was up and the boys were needed elsewhere.

Although this bantering among the boys is commonplace and this excerpt is representative of numerous conversations I had with both girls and boys, it would be misleading to suggest that this is the *only* conversation that takes place among the young male and/or female participants. There were other conversations that revolved around sports, school, trips down South or to their native countries, parties, families, sex, teachers, clothes, music, television, movies, amusement parks, and other topics particular to young adolescents. What is disturbing to me is that the emotions elicited by conversations about the violence they experience via the media and the violence they experience in their own communities do not appear all that different from the emotions elicited when they discuss the newest dance, or the latest CD, or the basketball game they watched last night. These young adolescents discuss types of guns, seeing someone arrested the previous night, and a shooting in the housing projects in the middle of conversations about what they are having for lunch, someone's new dirt bike, and what they will study for their science projects. There is a seamless thread that connects these disparate topics—normalizing violence and desensitizing the participants (and us) to the power of violence to disrupt, organize, and structure young people's lives both within the community and within the confines of the Blair School.

"That's Just the Way It Is"

The young people who live in the Ellsworth community often perceive the adolescent bantering described above as harmless, humorous, and a natural means of relating to one another. In many respects, it is through such bantering that they learn to test the boundaries of interpersonal relationships while making sure that they are perceived as "phat" by their peers. (When I inquired as to the origins of "phat," Tonesha told me that "I'd learn that if I was on the streets" and that it means "pretty high at temptin'"—in other words, one's "pose" is tempting to others and personifies the height of "cool.") Rather than "be gay," which means responding to bullying, teasing, name-calling, and other forms of verbal violence with compassion for the victim, the participants contribute to the culture of violence by implicitly and sometimes explicitly supporting a range of violent acts. Rarely do they demand that the perpetrator of the violence stop whatever she or he is doing that is causing someone harm. They believe, like many urban youth, that if they do not respond violently—in other words, in a way that hurts the other person, either physically, psychologically, or emotionally—they will "be taken advantage [of] in the future, lose their status in the community, and be viewed as a 'nobody'" (Elikann 1999:167).

Although the sarcasm, name-calling, and jostling for position are accepted as normal behavior and usually go no further than the situation at hand, there are times when the "hangin'" (making fun of someone to get a laugh) leads to physical altercations. In those instances, young people pay little attention to the consequences of the violent acts that ensue. The adolescents' impulsiveness and their predisposition to react violently to what they perceive as a personal threat or insult is immediate, automatic, and seen as normal. The following incident, which occurred in the course of the project, illustrates such behavior.

After almost two years of meeting together, the participants were ready to present some of their research to the students and staff at the Blair School (see chapter 7 for details). In preparation for those events, they visited every classroom in the school to ensure that the teachers and students had completed the activities that framed the assemblies that they, the participants, had organized. During a group session in which we decided who would go to which classrooms, a serious fight erupted between Blood and Jason. Jason had shaved his head during the previous weekend. Jason is also overweight and is constantly being harassed by his classmates about his physical appearance—something we addressed in the group sessions, but never resolved. It was Jason's shaved head that gave Blood ample ammunition for what Back calls "wind–ups . . . that is, the process of getting another person angry then ridiculing their anger by exposing its illegitimacy—'I was only joking'" (1996:74).

As Blood and Jason walked out of the cafeteria to visit their designated classrooms, Blood smacked Jason on the back of the head and said, "Ooooh, you got AIDS." (For a reason that Blood never made clear to me, he associated Jason's bald head with AIDS.) I did not see the smack but I did see Jason glare at Blood and yell, "Stop slappin' me." Blood slapped him again, and again Jason yelled, "Stop slappin' me."

Blood reacted angrily and within seconds, they were pushing and shoving each other, throwing fists, and screaming at one another. Blood is a good-looking Puerto Rican boy with a mischievous smile, a small wiry body, and a quickness about him that kept him from being hurt by Jason who is double his size in weight and height. I yelled over to them but knew they were unable to hear me. As I ran over to break them apart, the rest of the participants, who were still sitting at a table in the cafeteria, jumped up and started laughing and cheering them on. I stopped, turned around, and said, "This is not funny." I was furious at their response and yelled for Mase to come and help me separate Blood and Jason from each other. As we pulled the two of them apart, Jason let out a piercing, rage-filled scream.

I asked Vonnie to take care of Jason while I took Blood outside the cafeteria. Blood was shaking uncontrollably, his heart beating wildly as I held him. I spoke to him for a few minutes, made sure he was OK, and asked him to wait outside the cafeteria while I checked on Jason. I returned to the group and invited Jason to join me in a corner of the cafeteria. Jason was shaking, sweating, and complaining of "a terrible headache." As a result of the fight, Jason also had a long scratch on his neck and kept saying he wanted to call his mother and be taken home.

The policy at the Blair School is that if students are involved in a physical fight they are suspended for five days—no questions asked. The day the fight between Blood and Jason occurred happened to be the Monday prior to the assemblies we had scheduled for the upcoming Friday. Given that reality, I did not want to see either Jason or Blood suspended. Therefore, I told Blood and Jason that if we could resolve the argument among ourselves I would explain the altercation to their mothers and to Mr. Thomas, the assistant principal, in the hope that Mr. Thomas would not enforce the instant suspension rule with them.

Jason wanted nothing to do with Blood and didn't seem to care if he was suspended. Blood, on the other hand, did care about being suspended and was willing to do whatever was necessary to avoid a suspension. I told both Blood and Jason to think about what they wanted to do and once the rest of the participants had completed the activities we needed to attend to that morning for the upcoming assemblies, we would speak to Mr. Thomas.

Feeling frustrated and disappointed by the participants' collective response to the fight, I walked back over to the group.

Alice: You know the violence that we talk about all the time?

Rebecca: Yes.

Alice: Well, I don't know what disturbs me more. The fact that those two start whacking each other or that you all jump up and laugh. Especially since our conversation last week about violence! [The Littleton shootings had occurred the week before.] Not to mention all the other ones we have had for two years. How do you think more serious violence gets started? What have we talked about for almost two years?! It gets started by calling each other names. It goes from that to bootin' each other in the head. And then you laugh and jump up and down. It's like the day that Jo-Anne and Monique had a fight [described below] and I happened to be here. And everyone's jumping on the tables in here like it's a wrestling match!

Mase: [laughs]

Alice: That's not funny! And I think you need to think about how you react to what happened just now. It doesn't mean you have to jump in there if you think you might get hurt. But you don't have to jump up and laugh and contribute to the fact that people are beating up on each other. Unless I'm totally off base and I've got it all wrong. And you can certainly tell me if I do. Whenever we talk about violence or the way you treat each other or the way the students in this school act toward one another, you have the attitude: "That's the way this place is." Well, you said that about the trash, too, and look what you've done about that. You've done an excellent job developing the cleanup program and you've contributed in a positive way to the littering problem. So I think you might want to think about that as far as violence goes.

Tonesha: We're sorry. I think they need to give you an apology, too.

Alice: Well, it's not an apology to me I want. It's, I just want to see you contribute in a different way to what goes on around here in terms of violence. I think you could contribute in a positive way. If that's the way it is around here, change it! You changed the trash thing!

Mase: But these are fights. Ya can't change that.

Alice: You said you couldn't change the trash last year either and look what you've done.

Mase: Yeah, 'cause trash don't got hands and feet!

Alice: What's the difference? Do you hear him, what he's saying? You used to tell me there was nothing you could do about the trash. And look what you've done about that. So how can you say there's nothing you could do about the violence?

Mase: Nothing much you could do 'cause trash don't got feet and hands. They easy to clean up. But people do! They ain't gonna say, "No fightin', no more."

Alice: What could you have done just now? To not contribute to that?

Mase: Stopped it!

Tonesha: He never hit me, though, so why would I stop it?

Alice: OK, you may not want to stop it. But what could you have done differently right now?

Group: Not laugh. That's something. That changes something.

Mase: But I wasn't laughin'.

Tonesha: We need to make a resolution or a goal or something.

Mase: But right now we gotta get on track about the assemblies.

At that moment, we did need to "get on track about the assemblies." We managed to accomplish the various tasks that needed to be completed that day and partially resolved the conflict between Jason and Blood. They both agreed to "stay out of each other's face." They also agreed to speak to Mr. Thomas who listened as I, and we, explained what had occurred between Blood and Jason. I had conversations with Mr. Thomas, Jason, and later with Jason's mother, about how we could use existing resources to help Jason develop nonviolent strategies for dealing with the incessant name-calling he experienced from his peers. I had a similar conversation with Mr. Thomas, Blood, and Blood's mother regarding Blood's propensity to engage in "wind-ups" that often led to open conflict with his peers. During those conversations, I also explained that I didn't want Blood and Jason suspended due to their participation in the upcoming assemblies. Ultimately, neither Blood nor Jason were suspended and they resumed their participation in the project.

That afternoon, Tonesha looked over at me and said, "You lookin' rough today, Ms. Mac." I smiled and said, "Yeah, well I had a rough morning." She replied, "Yeah, I did too, 'cause I was disappointed in myself for being so disrespectful this morning. That goal we talked about this morning? Well, my goal is not to laugh any more at those fights."

"Not laughing at the fights" is an important step, albeit a small one, in the ongoing struggle of knowing how to address the various forms of violence that exist in the Blair School community. Yet it is a step that is doable and one that contributes to the participants' efforts to create nonviolent spaces within their school and community.

I have heard the participants repeatedly say, "Hey, that's just the way it is here," "Nothin' changes here," and "You have to fight back to take care of yourself." Their tendency to "fight back" in order to take care of themselves makes sense when one listens to their experiences with and of violence: Blood crouching down in front of a fence one night to avoid getting hit by a bullet. Tina always having "to keep your doors locked at all times because like at my house when the door wasn't locked, a lot of criminals went in my house through the years." Neaka ducking behind her couch as bullets ricocheted off the cars outside her window. "I was scared 'cause I had to call the police and the bullets was right there." Mase having a gun pulled on him as he rode his bike through the neighborhood. Mariah trying to sleep at night but being awakened by gunshots and police sirens. The participants have learned that in order to survive they have to "fight back" and that they are fighting not only the conditions of life around them but also what is going on inside their heads (Garbarino 1999).

Within this PAR process, we had multiple opportunities to hear about what was going on inside the participants' heads. Through collective dialogue and reflection we looked closely at some of their experiences of and with violence. From there we began a long, slow process of critically examining the various forms of violence that occur in the community and how we, as individuals and as a collective group, could both perpetuate and eliminate specific types of violent behavior. Some days, that process felt overwhelming. For example, my field notes reflect how I felt the day I left the school after the fight between Blood and Jason.

> I was really happy to leave that school today. I'm exhausted. And feel somewhat defeated by both my anger at the kids and their seeming inability to stop beating on each other. I don't like reacting so strongly to their behavior because I don't think it is effective. Yet, I hate listening to their explanations for why they continue to act violently. I understand them but I also want the kids to take some responsibility for how they act. Makes me crazy that they chalk it up to "that's the way it is here." I realize that there are many areas where they have little or no control over what happens to them or to their community (e.g., inferior schools, inadequate social services, racism, classism, sexism, lack of access to resources, and laws, policies, and practices that maintain the cycle of deprivation in which many of them live), but given that I have been hanging around with them for two years, I do know that they can control how they act in certain situations. At least I think I know. (Field notes, May 2, 1999)

There were other days when I left the school energized and content, when I believed that "not laughing anymore" was a start. As Freire suggests: "Let me put it this way: you never get *there* by starting from *there*, you get *there* by starting from some *here*. This means, ultimately, that the educator must not be ignorant of, underestimate, or reject any of the

'knowledge of living experience' with which the educands come to school"
(1994:58). By beginning "here" and by initiating a conversation about violence as it related to the participants' lived experiences, we *did* manage to
begin a process of unpacking the multiple meanings of violence that exist
in their lives with the explicit intention of developing strategies to promote
nonviolent behavior.

"I Ain't Takin' It No More"

As previously mentioned, boys are not the only ones who engage in violent behavior in the Blair School community. Some of the girls, much like
some of the boys, were quick to lash out and strike back in response to perceived insults, threats, and the belief that they were being disrespected.

I stopped by the school one day in January 1999, to say hello to the participants during their lunch period. I arrived at the cafeteria in time to hear
the assistant principal, Mr. Thomas, speaking loudly into a microphone
about the fighting that had been going on in the cafeteria and how it had
to stop. I saw Janine and Melinda sitting at a table with some other girls.
Just as I arrived at their table and was about to sit down, I saw Monica and
Jo-Anne, two other participants, jump out of their chairs and start punch-
ing each other. In an instant, they were flipping over chairs and tables, legs
and arms flailing, food and drinks being splattered about the area. The remaining students in the cafeteria began jumping up on tables and chairs,
cheering for Monica and Jo-Anne, screaming, clapping, laughing, and ignoring Mr. Thomas, his microphone, and anyone else (like me) who was
trying to contain the situation. A few of the students grabbed the two girls
separating them from each other just as Mr. Thomas arrived at the other
side of the room. He grabbed Monique and Jo-Anne, walked them to the
front of the cafeteria, put them face first against the wall, yelled into the
microphone that they were suspended for five days, and then told the rest
of the students that there would be no talking for the rest of the lunch period—something the students blatantly ignored. Janine looked over at me
and said, "There have been three fights in here this week. And you should
have seen the big food fight the other day. I got hit in the head with milk."

I looked over at Monique and Jo-Anne as they made faces at each other
and communicated with their peers through codes and gestures. It surprised me that Jo-Anne had engaged in a physical altercation with another

person. Jo-Anne is a quiet girl with shoulder-length brown hair, dark brown eyes, and is "too short for my age." She was born in Haiti, had moved to the United States in 1997, and in December of that year enrolled as a student in Susan's sixth-grade classroom. She was a regular participant during the first year of the project but had difficulty participating during the second year because she arrived late to school on most mornings and missed some of the sessions. I had never heard Jo-Anne make a disparaging remark about anyone. Nor had I ever seen her strike, or be struck by, another student.

Monique is Puerto Rican, also short for her age, with long dark hair and brown eyes that are always in motion, always "checkin' things out." Monique has a history of trouble inside and outside school: fights, tardiness, absenteeism, and poor academic performance. Susan helped Monique improve her academic standing when Monique was a student in her sixth-grade class by tapping into Monique's leadership skills and unofficially naming her the teacher's assistant. Although I watched Monique take that role to the limit at times, she was rarely late for school, stayed out of fights, missed less school than she had the previous year, and managed to pass all her courses without threat of being "kept back" in sixth grade.

Monique's seventh-grade year was not as successful. The transition from Susan's class to an all-female seventh-grade classroom had been a difficult one for her. She had countless verbal and physical fights with other students during the year. Her academic work suffered and she spent many hours in after-school detention for incomplete assignments. She was late for school quite often and, at one point during the year, stopped participating in extracurricular activities. Monique struggled not only with her academic work but in her relationships with people in authority as well. In addition, during her seventh-grade year, she moved out of The Courts into an apartment a few streets away from the Blair School. Although Monique told me that she would only feel safe "if we put a fence around The Courts and you can only get in if you have an ID 'cause it's a bad place," she was devastated to have to move away from there. "It's hard 'cause it's a place I been my whole life."

In the midst of negotiating the transitions in her life, Monique remained a steadfast and active participant in the project. She has a great deal of energy, lots of ideas, a keen memory, and a knowledge of the school and community that has made an important contribution to the project. That is not to say that Monique was always a productive member of the participant group. There were times during the project when she had little interest in developing the action plans that are discussed in chapters 6 and 7, and on a number of occasions disrupted activities the participants were engaged in. When I asked Monique about what was going on with her during particular moments in the research sessions, she gave me a range of responses. One day she told me that the substitute teacher had made her mad and that she was "sick of him and she wasn't gonna take it any more." Another time, Monique said that the reason she was "acting bad" was because Mr. Thomas was mean and she "wasn't gonna take it from him any more either." She also told me that she wasn't going to take it any more from any boy, girl, or teacher who "bothered" her. On another occasion, the research team took the participants to a university men's basketball game. When we arrived at the school to pick up the participants, Monique walked out of the gymnasium and informed me she wasn't going to join us because "I have a bad attitude. I got up on the wrong side of the bed and I don't want to take it out on everybody else." I reassured her that she could be in any kind of mood she chose—we really wanted her to join us. But she refused.

As I was leaving the school on the day Monique and Jo-Anne had their altercation, I met Monique in the hall. She had a big scratch on her face. I put my arm around her and asked her if she was doing all right. She said she was fine but continued with: "I'm not takin' it any more. I took it all last year and I'm just not takin' it no more." I asked her if there was something I could do or if she wanted to speak to someone about how she was feeling and she said, "There's nothin' goin' on with me. I'm just not takin' it no more."

The "it" that Monique consistently referred to goes well beyond a derogatory remark or action directed at her by someone else. Monique, and the other young people in the Blair community, do not always clearly articulate this "it." The "it," as I experience it, is a feeling that at any moment something is going to happen that will surprise, hurt, offend, alienate, or frighten the participants. It's Mr. Thomas screaming into the microphone during lunch. It's the incessant blowing of the whistle he wears around his neck while students eat, talk, gossip, sing, and try to be young people. It's the chaos that occurs when children and young adolescents physically attack each other. It's the constant teasing that some of the students have to endure—students who feel powerless to change the way they are treated by their peers and by particular teachers. It's the interruptions over the school intercom that remind students to dress appropriately, come straight to school so they won't get into trouble, and go straight home from school so they won't be abducted. It's the additional intercom reminders that intrude into so many teaching and learning moments, telling students to "report any strangers you see in the school building to the security office" and "stay off the streets because if you are not in school and you're getting in trouble, there is a good chance you'll be killed."

The "it" is a constellation of variables that makes it almost impossible for some young people to concentrate on their work, to focus their desires, and/or to learn new ways of being in the world. As I suggested earlier, some of the incidents described here are not unique to the Blair School or to other inner-city schools. As we have seen in the last decade, there are many white suburban schools where teasing, bullying, and feeling ostracized, coupled with feeling powerless over existing situations, have contributed to peer-on-peer violence. What is particular about the Blair School—and other inner-city schools—is that they exist in contexts quite unlike schools located in wealthy suburbs. The students at the Blair School experience the ravages of racism, classism, and poor schooling (to name a few) and are forced, on a daily basis, to negotiate the negative consequences of structural conditions that beget fear, anxiety, anger, and disillusionment. As many researchers and scholars have documented (see, for example, Anyon 1997; Children's Defense Fund 1999; Council of the Great City Schools 1994; *Education Week* 1998; McQuillan 1998), the way the educational system in this country has been constructed some groups of students are barely surviving, such as poor students, immigrants, and students of Color, many of whom live in urban areas and attend inner-city schools, while others continue to flourish, such as white middle- and upper-middle-class students who attend schools located in suburban areas.

In many ways, the participants of this project are "barely surviving." In other ways, they continue to prevail. In the midst of their anger, fear, resentment, resistance, acts of violence, and refusal to "take it any more," they have continued to show up for this project and in so doing, have proved to me, the research team, and more importantly to themselves that they can work together to generate positive alternatives to much of the negativity that surrounds them. They have not succeeded in dismantling systems of racial discrimination, nor have they succeeded in becoming 100 percent nonviolent. What they have done is engage in processes of change that have contributed to decreasing some of the violence in their lives—to the extent possible—thus working toward their aim of improving school and community life. This is most evident in their efforts to address environmental violence which is discussed in chapter seven.

An Addendum

By the time Monique had completed seventh grade, she had "settled down. I'm not as mad as I used to be and my grades improved and I made second honors." Monique also began attending after-school programs at a new community center located within walking distance of the Blair School. When I asked her if I could write about her fight with Jo-Anne in this book and discuss the difficulties she had experienced during the second year of the project, she said, "Yeah, I guess so. But I wasn't that bad. I mean don't say that I was mad all the time 'cause you got that wrong if you do. I mean I was mad but I got over it."

"I Don't Litter; I Don't Write on the Walls No More, and I Don't Fight Like I Used To"

As the second year of the PAR process began, I felt it was important to establish a framework as we engaged the next phase of the project, described in chapters 6 and 7. We were no longer "housed" in Susan's classroom. Therefore we needed to reconstitute community in a new space with a new agenda.

During the initial meetings that took place at the beginning of the second year of the project, we asked the participants to create a set of ground rules that would facilitate group discussions and assist us in following through on the activities we planned to engage in that year. As Tee suggested, "It's a good idea to have rules for everyone. That way we know what to do and what not to do." I expressed a desire to concentrate on developing ground rules to help us organize the next steps of the project, rather than concentrate on developing a set of dos and don'ts that would restrict the participants' individual and collective participation.

Alice: Since we are starting a new phase of the project and since our meetings are no longer in Mrs. Leslie's room, let's talk about how we can organize the meetings and share responsibility for the rest of the project? That's something we wanted to do. Are we ready to tackle that now?

Group: Yeah.

Tee: Yeah. First one: No hangin'.

Blood: Like no dissin'.

Tee: No disrespectin' another, your peers.

Bill: No disrespectin' others.

Alice: What do you mean by "no disrespecting others"?

Blood: Don't be like "Shut up you dog." Like no hangin' and no callin' names.

Bill: Um, no using profanity.

Tee: Ooh, I never knew you knew that word. That's a long word.

Melinda: That's, that's a hang right there, what you just said.

Blood: No standin' up. Raisin' your hand.

Jason: Nobody will fight because how are you gonna start a fight unless you don't do rule #1, disrespectin' others.

[ct]

Alice: OK. I appreciate your concern for how people behave in the group. I think it might help if we also talk about the positive things we can do.

Melinda: Yeah, a positive thing is to participate.

Group: Yeah, participate.

Blood: Talk, speak out.

[ct]

Blood: Raise your hand.

Tee: Say excuse me.

Blood: Don't stand up without raising your hand.

Tee: No foolin' around.

Mase: Well, some foolin' around.

Tee: No yellin'.

Melinda: Yeah, that's a good one.

Tee: No playin' like Blood there with grabbin' and snappin' people like you doin' right now.

Jason: No profanity. No fighting.

Blood: One person speaks at a time. No yellin'.

[ct]

Alice: Now the hardest part about ground rules isn't so much making the ground rules[

Melinda: It's followin' them.

Alice: Yeah, it's following them, because what's going to happen when for instance, somebody keeps disrespecting somebody by making fun of them? What if somebody keeps playing around? What is the group going to do? Maybe we could talk more about the helpful things we can do in the group.

Tee: Three strikes you're out!

Blood: Man, nobody has to do that.

Tee: Yeah, 'cause last year in the project, we were straight. We were good. I think we need a contract.

Melinda: Wait, wait, wait. I have a suggestion. We can have just like have this huge piece of paper and it has the rules on it. We could hang it there to remind us to follow the rules.

Blood: Like what if people are absent and miss the meetings? We should have a book or somethin' to write it down.

Alice: I have really nice notebooks for you as a matter of fact.

Blood: Like take attendance and when they like have three absences, they out.

[ct]

Jason: We should have a contract about following rules at all times and then write everybody's name down, whoever signs it has to do it.

Tee: And if somebody does somethin' wrong you give them a check or a star or whatever. We do somethin' about it.

Alice: What do you want to do about it?

Blood: Kick 'em out.

The discussion continued with the participants generating various strategies for developing an effective set of rules for the new phase of the project. I wrote the final set of rules on a large sheet of paper, reminding them that these were *their* rules and they could modify them at any time. Again, my initial desire was to have them think proactively about how we would organize the meetings so as to facilitate productive group sessions. That is not what materialized at the meeting. Instead of generating responses along the lines of "Let's participate," the participants focused on maintaining group cohesiveness by demanding certain behaviors from each other and imposing penalties if people did not adhere to the rules. Their response to developing rules for participating in the project was not surprising, given that their ideas about how to get along and work collaboratively were shaped largely by their experiences as students in an educational system that focuses on social coercion as a way to control young people's behavior.

Immediately after the brainstorming session, I handed notebooks to the participants so that they could copy down the rules they generated, take notes during the remainder of the meetings, write their reflections about issues that we were engaging in the project, and keep track of our individual and collective responsibilities. We also elected Janine as the group secretary.

The notebooks, which the participants "really liked," were rarely seen or used after that meeting. The participants took sporadic notes now and then during the remainder of the year but most often they forgot, misplaced, or lost their notebooks. They decided they really didn't need them anyway, as Janine was "doing such a good job being the secretary of the group meetings." In addition, we never did get the hang of following the ground rules by disciplining people, kicking people out, or taking notes on who was doing what so that we could reprimand them later. Almost immediately, the participants realized that some of the rules they had created were impractical. For example, if they had enforced the "three times, you're out" rule, most of them would have been excluded from the project. The participants also realized that working collaboratively takes practice and that it is counterproductive to force people to do something when they don't want to do it, particularly when those people are participating by choice.

Although we failed to follow the ground rules as written, the exercise of generating the rules proved significant in and of itself. For instance, it became evident that over the course of the research project the participants became more aware of how "respectin' one another" was linked to the way they spoke to one another, which in turn was linked to how successful they were at completing particular project-related tasks. For example, "shut up" was a common response in many of our group discussions. After many months of meeting with the participants, I counted how many times they told each other to "shut up" over a ninety-minute period of time. Some days they would say "shut up" to one another at least fifteen times in one session—and those were only the "shut ups" heard on audiotape. I informed them of how many times they said "shut up" to one another and asked them if they thought that telling someone to "shut up" was an effective way of engaging in a conversation, making a group decision, or getting information about something we needed to do in the project. They agreed that "shut up" was probably not necessary. Tonesha said, "So what does that leave us with, Ms. Mac? Are we supposed to say, 'Excuse me. I do not want to hear anything you are saying right now. Please be quiet.'" After a few minutes of hilarity over Tonesha's suggestion, we began to think of ways of communicating with one another that would create a space in which everyone felt they could say what they wanted to say as long it was not meant to hurt or offend someone, and as long as people did not feel put down by their peers for making a suggestion, telling a story, or voting a particular way about an issue raised in the group.

Throughout the group sessions, the participants referred to the meeting in which we had initially generated the ground rules, reminding each other that they were to respect one another, refrain from interrupting people when they were speaking, and avoid saying things that "get people spankin' mad." As a group, the participants stopped a number of conversations to attend to something that someone had said that was hurtful to someone else, or led to someone feeling they needed to respond in a physically violent manner. We averted many serious arguments and found different ways to address disagreements between two or more participants. We role-played various scenarios so we could practice new ways of responding to particular situations. We brainstormed how we could respond to language that some or all of us deemed inappropriate or hurtful to someone. In addition, we took individual and/or group "time-outs" to step back from incidents that had provoked people's anger and to assess how we wanted to address those incidents nonviolently.

I did not stop the participants every time they said something offensive or hurtful. Nor did I demand that they apologize or retract their statements. What I and the members of the research team *did* do was to invite them to reflect on the relationship between their verbal interactions and the extent to which they were contributing to a group process. Equally important, we invited the participants to reflect on how their verbal interactions related to the violence that existed in the school and community. This was not—and is not—always easy for the participants to grasp and required repeating, revisiting, and rethinking in a host of different ways.

Over time, many of the participants refrained from saying "shut up" to each other in the group sessions. There were and are far more incidents of "be quiet, please" evident in the transcripts. Similarly, attending to the overuse of the term "shut up" led to the highlighting of other derogatory phrases and terms that some of them used quite consistently during the group sessions, such as "stupid," "your momma," and "gonna slap you on the side of ya head."

During a review session of the previous two years the participants commented on what they had learned about violence and its connection with the way they interacted with each other and other people.

I learned not to say shut up but to say be quiet. (Mase)

The photography class, collages, the cleanup group have all helped me to think differently about myself and the community. They have helped me to stop littering and stop using violence. Like instead of fighting with my brother whenever he teases me, I could just ignore him now. I do think differently about working in a group. I learned that I can work in a group. (Rebecca)

I've learned a lot by working together and arguing and just learning to work together by building this group. (Risha)

Not to litter anymore, not to say shut up. I stopped the way I talked mean to people so that is how I stopped violence. (Mase)

I really learned how to work together with my peers. (Melinda)

I don't litter. I don't write on the walls no more. And I don't fight like I used to. (Monique)

It would be easy to discount the participants' attempts at self- and collective improvement as a response to me, a person they perceive as an authority figure and who is present with them during the group sessions. I disagree with that form of "adultism" and argue that the participants are solving real-life interpersonal issues that arise on a daily basis in their relationships with their peers. Similarly, they are dealing with taken-for-granted actions that shape their schooling and their lives. That is not to suggest that the participants have maintained some of their new behaviors both inside and outside the group sessions. My experience with them suggests that they are on "better behavior" when I am present—as is to be expected given their relationship with me. As Risha recently told me when I repeated my request that the participants call me Alice, "We can't call you that. You're older and we respect you." Out of respect, I assume that they work harder to live out the goals they develop for themselves in terms of intergroup relationships when I am present. Yet, I do not think that my presence is the *only* factor in their decision to make changes in their behavior. I give them more credit than that and suggest that they really *do* want to get along, act peacefully, and experience their school and community as safe places for living and learning.

Monique ran into a group session one day in late April 1999, proudly displaying a checklist she had created for the assemblies the participants organized and that I describe in chapter 7. She immediately instructed me to "have a seat 'cause you are gonna love this skit we came up with for the assembly." I did love the skit. More important, I loved seeing Monique and the others being enthusiastic about the actions they were taking to better their lives and their community. I do not think enthusiasm alone is sufficient to overcome "it," or to counterbalance the pervasive forms of violence that permeate the participants' lives. Yet I do believe that their enthusiasm, coupled with the accompaniment of adults who are committed to cocreating spaces for young people to develop a sense of purpose and agency, can be powerful deterrents to apathy, hopelessness, and the multiple forms of violence that characterize many urban communities.

Concluding Reflections

Many scholars would interpret the participants' responses to violence as survival strategies that are developed in order to stabilize one's sense of self and gain a sense of control over one's environment. Although that may be a realistic assessment, labeling young people's responses to violence, trauma, and ongoing discrimination as "survival strategies" does more to assist us in "treating" the individual than it does to alter the social conditions that contribute to the development of behaviors necessary to live and function in one's environment. I report the participants' conversations not to reify stereotypes about urban youth of Color but to suggest that when we individualize the effects of violence and see "the effects of [violence] as primarily or exclusively residing in the individual" (Lykes 1994:546), we run the risk of minimizing and/or failing to take into account the "social roots, in other words, the traumatogenic structures or social conditions" (Martín-Baró 1994:125) that contribute to sustained violence in urban areas. As important, by taking an individualistic perspective on violence within social science research, we contribute to the way young people think about violence as well. They too fall prey to individualizing violence within certain types of people (crackheads, gang members, people who live in The Courts). The participants mimic the dominant discourse that pervades U.S. society when they say: "He's a bum 'cause he's crackin' all the time." "He's a drug dealer and should go to jail forever." "That man is bad. He don't work and he don't do nothin' but stand on the corner and do drugs." "That lady I saw was a prostitute and she be doin' the wrong thing. She should be takin' off the street." Although it is important for the participants to recognize that individuals need to take responsibility for and accept the consequences of their actions, it is also important that they understand how social and cultural factors mediate the individual and collective violence that exists in the Ellsworth community. Therein lies one of the challenges in this PAR project—how to integrate the subjective realities of the participants with the larger socioeconomic conditions that mediate those realities in ways that are meaningful, understandable, and helpful for this group of young people.

By viewing violence as a *psychosocial* phenomenon, as a phenomenon that involves the individual within the context of her or his multiple environments, educators, psychologists, and researchers can focus the problem of violence within a system of social relations and institutional and societal infrastructures rather than strictly within individual young people. This has implications for the way we interact with and "treat" young people of Color living in urban communities.

This PAR project has afforded the participants opportunities to explore the intersection of individual responsibility and systemic forms of violence—to the extent that twelve- and thirteen-year-old adolescents can engage that intersection. The participants learned how to name certain types of violence and identify how they felt about them, which in turn opened up spaces for practicing new interpersonal behaviors and trying out new and different ways of engaging with each other. In so doing, the participants learned, and continue to learn, how to remain hopeful about their goals, maintain a sense of humor and realism about themselves, and in the midst of discord, misunderstandings, and peer-to-peer fighting, generate enough enthusiasm to keep the PAR process moving in a direction that most benefits them and their community.

4

■　■　■　■　■　■　■　■　■

Community Photography

Visual Stories by Inner-City Youth

AS NOTED IN CHAPTER 1, community photography is a tool for investigation that enables people to "reflect on photographs that mirror the everyday social and political realities that influence their lives" (Wang, Wu, Zhan, and Carovano 1998:80). With those photographs, people can increase their knowledge about the issues that most affect them and use that knowledge to initiate change. By putting cameras in the hands of the participants, we hoped to enrich our understanding of how this group of young people perceived their lives within their particular surroundings. We also hoped to provide the participants with an opportunity to express themselves in new and imaginative ways. In this PAR project, the use of photography complemented, and in many respects augmented, the previous activities we had engaged in and gave us an opportunity to gain a more kaleidoscopic view of the participants' community. Equally important, the use of photography as a tool for investigating that community helped us broaden our conceptions and definitions of violence to include violations to the environment. This reconceptualization created new knowledge about how to actualize plans aimed at individual and community well-being.

Getting Started

Initially, the participants learned the basic mechanical aspects of using a camera: the various parts of the camera, how to take care of it, how to focus, what kind of film to use, and how to insert and rewind the film. In addition, the research team took the participants to a photography class at the university where they were given an opportunity to see how film is developed, enlarged, and later made into prints. To assist us in formulating how we wanted to structure the photography project, we also reviewed the work of other researchers, educators, and activists who have conducted similar projects in other parts of the world.

In preparation for the photography project, the members of the research team discussed the ethical issues involved in community photography with the participants, developing shared understandings of when picture taking is appropriate, respecting people's choices about their inclusion in a photograph, and clarifying the reasons for taking particular photographs. We role-played various scenarios, highlighting some of the situations that may occur as the participants engaged this aspect of the project. We then generated a number of "rules" to guide the photography project and assist us in better understanding what we wanted to explore about the participants' community in relation to the environment, families, schooling, and themselves. For example,

1. Always explain the community photography project to someone whom you want to take a picture of. Remember that the idea is for you to create a "visual story" about your community. As we have discussed all year, your community includes all kinds of people, places, and things. Some of the things you like, some you don't like. All of what we have talked about (and maybe some things we haven't talked about yet) make up your community. So, be creative and have fun.

2. Always ask a person if she or he wants her or his picture taken. If the person says, "No," thank them anyway and make another choice.

3. If you want to take a picture of something belonging to someone else (e.g., car, store, radio), you still need to ask them for permission. If they say, "No," thank them anyway and make another choice.

4. Do not go to places that your parents and caregivers have told you not to

go to. If you want to take a picture of something that is in a place that your parents and caregivers would rather you not go to, ask them if they will accompany you there. If they say, "No," thank them anyway and make another choice.

5. Do not give your camera to anyone else unless you want a family member or a friend to take a picture of you doing something with them or by yourself.

Each participant was given a camera and two rolls of film (one color and one black and white) for a five-day period, Wednesday through Sunday. This enabled them to take pictures in school and at home on the weekend. Prior to giving the participants their cameras, we discussed their responsibilities for taking care of the camera, for keeping it in a safe place, and for making sure that no one else took photographs with the film that was designated for the photography project. Susan was a bit concerned that some of the participants would not take their responsibilities seriously. Therefore, in concert with Susan and the team members, I asked the participants to sign a contract stating that they understood that by receiving the camera they were taking full responsibility for it. The contract also stipulated that the camera was to be returned to the school on a specified date. Initially I resisted the idea of asking the participants to sign contracts. I was concerned that they would think that we perceived them as irresponsible. Trust is important in a PAR project and therefore I was apprehensive about instituting a formal agreement that might disrupt the relationships we were building. My concerns were quickly dispelled when Collin said, "Wow! We're like real professional photographers signing these contracts." The participants were so impressed with the documents that they requested that they be allowed to keep them after the project: "We get to keep the contracts so we can hang 'em on our bedroom walls."

Reflections on Being a Photographer

There was a high degree of energy and anticipation when the participants arrived at school after having spent the previous five days "being photographers." Each participant had a story to tell, a mishap to explain, and/or a one-of-a-kind photograph that they wanted to share with their peers and the research team. Susan was right about Puffy. She kept telling me that he wouldn't bring his camera back. He didn't. Neither did Tonesha. "I wasn't done taking pictures yet," she said. Flanango forgot her camera and one of her rolls of film. "I left it on the kitchen table so I would remember to take it to school and I forgot it anyway." Troy couldn't find one of his rolls of film. Blood ripped one of his rolls of film while taking it out of the camera. Collin did the same. Mase's camera had been stolen on Friday afternoon while he was in school. Unfortunately, he never told Susan or me. "She [Susan] would have killed me," he told me. "He's right," Susan told me later. "I am very upset with him. He's a classroom monitor and he should be a role model. He knows not to leave things out on his desk like that. And you have a soft spot giving him another camera. I wouldn't have."

I do have a soft spot for him. I knelt down and asked Mase why he hadn't telephoned me when he realized the camera was missing. He told me the reason he didn't call me was because his grandmother said he couldn't play around with the phone. "She said that I was at her house to help her with work not be talkin' on the telephone." I gave him another camera. I also gave Jason and Michael cameras as they had been absent the previous week and had been unable to pick up their cameras from Susan. Three of the participants were absent on the day the cameras were due back in school, which, along with other glitches that occurred, led us to modify the project schedule and give the participants more time to complete their picture taking.

In the midst of the minor glitches that are to be expected in a PAR process, the participants were eager to tell the research team and one another about some of their favorite "camera moments." Collin loved the way he surprised people with his camera. "I'd tell people to just be doin' what they doin' and then I'd yell, 'Hey!' And they'd turn around and I'd snap the photo." Rebecca loves her cat and was "very happy to have photographs of him in case he dies and then I can have something to remember him by." Michael got a new puppy during the weekend and he was thrilled to have had "a camera handy so I could take pictures of him sleeping, and looking around, and being in my house." Tee went to a birthday party and no one remembered to bring a camera, so he became the "party photographer." Puffy took his camera with him as he drove with his mother through the community. He wanted to see what photographs looked like if they were taken through the car window. Jo-

Anne "loves my little cousin and I had a really fun time taking pictures of him. He wanted to take pictures, too, but I wouldn't let him 'cause he is too little."

We spent a number of sessions reviewing the photographs, sharing stories, and listening to each other's experiences about what it felt like to document the community through photography. We also took time to reflect, in writing, about what it felt like for the participants to be photographers.

It was very fun because I went to a lot of different places to take pictures. I really wished we had more time 'cause it was a great project. I really like taking pictures of my community. (Collin)

It felt good to have the camera. Although I had to make sure that no one messed with it. No one said no to me at all. They didn't mind that I took a picture of them. It was sort of like being a photographer but a lot shorter. (Rebecca)

My experience with photography was fun. Having a camera was so exciting. I think I might want to become a real photographer some day. I think my favorite pictures are the pictures of my dolls and me, the picture of classroom 211, and our social studies teacher. I took pictures of kids in my community, too. Being a photographer was really fun and I hope we can do this again. I think photography is me. (Tina)

I liked this project. I took pictures about things that amuse me, things that make me happy, my neighborhood, and two of my friends and their family. (Chesterfield)

I think it was great to do this so we could show other people our community. Instead of us only seeing our community other people could see it and help our community, too. (Monique)

What I learned was that this community really needs to be cleaned up. All kinds of trash was in one area that I took pictures of. One thing that is certain is that this community, even though it has its problems, is underrated. This community has good people. Like the people who go to church, the kids on the playground, and the people who help out. That's what this project has brought to me. (Flanango)

I had a splendid, wonderful time and I loved it a whole lot and the camera did not mess up. I took the pictures and I loved it. I took a lot of them, too. I had a lot of fun doing this project. (Puffy)

Visual Storytelling

Prior to returning the processed prints to the participants, I reviewed, organized, and compiled the photographs to facilitate the dissemination process. As I previewed the photographs, I jotted down questions that came to mind, comments I had about particular photographs, reactions to certain prints, and any other thoughts or feelings that came to me as I poured over the participants' photographs. As I engaged in this process, I was particularly struck by Blood's photographs. As I looked through Blood's envelope of prints, I envisioned him standing in the middle of The Courts, camera in hand, turning slowly to the left, then to the right, and aiming, shooting, aiming again, shooting, but never moving from that one spot. There was a photograph of a stark brick building, then another brick building, then another, then a pigeon walking in front of a large graffiti-stained rock, then another brick building, and another, and then it appeared that he had raised his head and taken a magnificent shot of a seagull flying overhead (see photo 1). Then back to shooting the brick buildings in the project where he lives.

I was instantly drawn to the paradoxes I saw in Blood's photographs. There was the image of a seagull flying freely above a community that, although located on the water, defies the image of the "waterfront property" that is so coveted in the rest of the county where Ellsworth is located. In the upper right-hand corner of the seagull photograph, which Blood entitled: "Our Community," one can see the corner of a building—a building that houses a number of women, men, and children who do not experience the kind of freedom that the seagull represented to and for me.

For Blood, the camera also represented a type of freedom that he does not experience in school, a setting that emphasizes verbal skills and "using our words" to demonstrate knowledge, mastery of skills, and one's potential for success. Blood is a student many educators would label "at-risk"—a young Puerto Rican who lives in The Courts with his mother, who rarely leaves her building because "she is always afraid she is going to be killed." One of Blood's older brothers is in the Navy. Another brother attends a high school in Ellsworth. Blood's sister lives in another section of Ellsworth, as does his father. Blood refers to himself as "stupid," although he does consider himself quite good at math. He doesn't particularly like school, although he rarely misses it.

Photo 1. "Our Community" taken by Blood

I chose the seagull because that shows a seagull from my community. I liked this picture because that represents our community. The bird is chillin' and I know that because he was flyin' around all day. I took the picture at daytime in back of my building near my friend's house. (Blood)

That was not always the case. Prior to being a student in Susan's class, he was late to or absent from school quite often. One morning, Susan was taking attendance and asked the class if anyone had seen Blood. "Yeah," one of the kids said. "I saw him in The Courts. He says he isn't coming to school 'cause he doesn't feel good." Susan immediately walked over to her desk, took her handbag out of the drawer, retrieved her cell phone, and said, "OK. Someone give me Blood's phone number." One of the students yelled it out and within seconds Susan was speaking to Blood's mother. She told Blood's mother that she understood that Blood didn't feel well but that the school had an excellent nurse on staff and that she needed to send Blood over to the school right away. Susan assured her that Blood would be seen by the nurse as soon as possible. "We have to educate our children Mrs. ___ and we can't do that if they aren't here. So, I appreciate your support and we'll see Blood in five minutes." Susan never gave

Blood's mother the opportunity to disagree or refuse her request. She gently but firmly made it known that Blood needed to be in school and in school he was—five minutes later. As Susan said to her students when she hung up the phone: "We have to take care of each other and make sure that we are all here, all the time."

When the research team and I gave the photographs back to the participants the following week, we spent time talking to each of them, questioning them about certain photographs, and commenting on things and people we found interesting or provocative, humorous or disturbing. In speaking to Blood, I asked him if he had stood in one place while he took the majority of his photographs. He said, "Yeah. I just stood in front of a building and took things that were there. But I only did that for the pictures I took in The Courts. Not when I took some of my other pictures." I told him I particularly liked the seagull photograph and that although I was not a professional photographer, I thought he had quite a knack for photography.

About an hour later, Blood walked up to me, slipped something into my hand, and walked away. I looked down, and it was the photograph of the seagull—which now has a prominent place in my office. That was the first time in eight months that Blood had initiated any type of interaction with me. It was not to be the last time. Prior to the photography project, Blood had been a quiet participant-observer during the research project. Although he participated in most of the activities, he rarely spoke about his feelings, thoughts, or experiences as they related to whatever we were discussing. It wasn't until after the photography project that Blood became an active participant in just about every aspect of the project, questioning this issue, confronting that problem, and engaging in the group's decision-making processes. He participated more fully in group discussions and also contributed his thoughts on a one-on-one level. Blood also became the unofficial class photographer, documenting different aspects of the project with the classroom's camera. By December 1998, Blood was presenting aspects of the research project in front of an auditorium full of graduate students and professors at the university where I teach.

In addition, Blood experienced the challenge of being part of a democratic process. He did not always get what he wanted; nor did he always get to do what he wanted to do. And that sometimes resulted in a contest of wills—Blood's will against mine; Blood's will against the group's; and Blood's will against one of his peers which, on more than one occasion, resulted in verbal taunting and or physical altercations, as was described in chapter 3.

Blood's participation in the research process is not unique. All the participants have had their struggles working in and with a group, making decisions together, and taking responsibility for their actions (see chapter 7). What is unique about Blood's participation is that it is so closely linked with the photography project. Using the camera was a catalyst for many of the participants in terms of concretizing particular aspects of the project. For Blood, it was also a catalyst in that he subsequently participated more fully in the project and tapped into skills he never knew he had.

"Trash Is a Big Problem in Our Community"

We had some of our most poignant conversations about the community after the participants had completed their picture taking. These conversations helped link what had hitherto been thought about as unrelated aspects of the community into a more cohesive understanding of the multiple factors that contribute to or inhibit community life. As Wang and her colleagues argue, "Photographs alone considered outside the context of participants' own voices and stories would contradict the essence of photovoice" (1998:80). Thus, we encouraged the participants to tell stories about their photographs in order to define the meanings of their images, and in so doing, identify the assets and problems that characterized their environment.

The Blair School had organized a celebratory week at the culmination of the 1997–98 academic year to highlight students' achievements as well as to provide the students opportunities to participate in games, sports, music, and drama. The participants requested that they be given space within the school building to exhibit their photographs—a request that Susan immediately granted. Therefore, after reviewing and reflecting on hundreds of photographs, and after multiple individual and collective discussions about the prints the participants had developed, we decided that each participant would choose three photographs they felt best represented their community and their understanding of the issues we were

Photo 2. "Car" taken by Risha

I chose this picture of a car because it's not a drug car. Many people think that all fancy cars are drug cars. This man is in love with this car. This car costs a lot of money. The parts he puts in this car are ridiculous and it costs so much I can't believe him. I don't agree with what some people say because not all cars are drug cars in my neighborhood. (Risha)

addressing in the project. These photographs would be highlighted in the photography exhibit mentioned above.

These same photographs later became the centerpiece for what turned out to be three exhibits that were held over the next six months: one at the Blair School, one at the local community center, and one at the university. In addition, the participants provided titles for each photograph and wrote accompanying text to describe their pictures.

The participants' photographs represented multiple aspects of their community: families, neighborhood landmarks, personal belongings, teachers and schoolmates, cars, and play areas.

Although the participants represented their community in a variety of ways, the majority of the discussions generated by the photographs focused on how community life suffers from the state of the environment. Repeatedly, in one-on-one conversations, in small groups, and as a collective, the participants spoke about issues related to "the trashy way this

Photo 3. "The Courts" taken by Melinda

I chose the picture of The Courts because it shows the projects in our town. It also shows the place where children play. (Melinda)

Photo 4. "Getting Ready" taken by Neaka

This is a picture of the test we had to take. Everybody in our class has to take the test and there is no getting out of it. So we just have to get ready for it and then it is over after a couple of days. (Neaka)

Photo 5. "The Old Abandoned House" taken by Veronica

This house represents abandoned houses in our community. People throw garbage in abandoned houses and they bust the windows. I don't think people want to fix up this house. I don't think they care about that house any more. (Veronica)

community looks." Subsequently, the photographs that represented those discussions were the ones that many of the participants chose to include in the photography exhibit.

Below, I include lengthy conversations between and among the participants to illustrate how the photographs and the ensuing discussions led to numerous conversations about the trash problem, which then led to conversations about what we could do to solve it. The first example is a discussion that Janine, Flanango, Risha, Melinda, and Rebecca engaged in that focused on photographs they took which revealed the amount of trash and pollution that are "ruining our community."

Alice: So what do all these photographs tell you?
Risha: Trash.
Rebecca: Trash. Gosh, I mean we have a big problem with it in our community. You know?
Janine: Pollution and graffiti. That's the problem.

Alice: What do you think about the fact that most of you took pictures of trash, pollution, or graffiti?

Melinda: It shows that it is a really big problem but every time we even go out there [and clean] it just gets dirtier. So we're like, every time we clean up people get more careless. And they just keep on doing it. Every week we go out there it gets even worse.

Alice: Who's we?

Melinda: The whole class. We go out, the garden club, and we clean up the whole school, in the back and the front, the courtyard, and every time we go out there it just gets worse. And people just, they see us out there but they just get careless.

Rebecca: They think that we're gonna keep cleaning up after them and we're not. Because after the garden club is over the school is gonna get even dirtier because we won't be cleaning up after them anymore.

Photo 6. "A Messy Waste" taken by Mase

I don't like the way my community stays. That's why I am going to do something about it. I can help by using tools and the help from my parents and friends in my community. In my neighborhood I would like a swimming pool and a basketball court. In front of my house I would like a park for me and my friends. Beside my neighbor's house there is a lot of trash and I would like to clean it up. (Mase)

Photo 7. "Trash" taken by Monique

It is a good picture to show how our community is and what I see every day. (Monique)

Alice: Um hm. So it seems to me that you have been telling me about trash since October. I have heard about trash a lot.

[laughter]

Alice: Why do you think that issue is the one that most of you talk about?

Melinda: Because we can get sick [laughing]. I mean it piles up and it gets into the air and then we die. If we don't clean it up, we die. I guess we get sick. It's pollution. So it's a big deal. For me, that's why.

Janine: I feel the same.

Alice: If you look at it in terms of other issues that we have talked about[

All: Violence, violence. Drugs.

Alice: Yeah, violence, drugs.

All: Guns, drug dealers, drug cars.

Rebecca: Well, a lot of like the drugs and the guns they are found in the trash because people just dump it right there. They say, "Well there's a bunch of trash. Who's gonna see a gun and [unint.] drugs?"

Janine: Another problem is drug needles are found on the ground and little kids pick the needles up.

Melinda: It's dangerous.

Flanango: Um, I just think the trash in our community is not a place that kids can go out and play now for days and stuff like that.

Melinda: It also shows that people are lazy and they don't want to wait 'til

Photo 8. "The Trash in the Community" taken by Flanango

I am part of the community so I think that we should all clean it up. We could organize a group of adults and kids to clean up. The trash is getting worse and worse every day. If we don't start to clean up soon it might be too late. The picture shows tires, paper bags, and bottles that we could clean up. So that's why I think you should always clean up. (Flanango)

Photo 9. "Pollution" taken by Janine

I chose this picture because it shows a lot of trash, burned down things, and large logs. It also shows buildings that are releasing gas and oil into our environment. This is pollution that affects the neighborhood and the way animals and plants live. It has logs and wood that blocks and covers the creatures in the dirt and soil. I think that the community and myself should stop all this pollution and work together on doing it so we won't get sick. (Janine)

they see a garbage can. They just throw anything they like. Just like my cousin yesterday. I asked him to throw something out and he just threw it on the floor. It was outside and we came from the store and he just rolled up the bag and threw it over the fence.

Flanango: It makes good people seem like they're bad or something. Like, just 'cause it's dirty outside don't mean that their house would have to be dirty. They're not[

Rebecca: Dirty people.

Flanango: It's not like a suburb neighborhood or something like that.

Janine: Just like my neighborhood they throw anything on the ground. They throw bike parts, things from the house, trash, clothes, everything is out there on the ground.

Flanango: Um, you know it's not like when you know like some of the shows
   that you see on TV where all these people live in the suburbs and they have
   like these little problems like, my best friend won't talk to me or something.
   . . . And 'cause we live here, like they think, well, you can't just walk by a
   place and say, "Oh those people must be dirty and must have a whole bunch
   of rats and roaches in their house or something." We're not all like that.

Risha: Well, if you keep your neighborhood dirty they, you know, you have
   rats and roaches.

Flanango: Or you could just be lazy.

Alice: When you talked about the TV and they have little problems? What's a
   big problem to you?

Flanango: A big problem is something, I don't know. Like my sister's on
   drugs or something. I don't know. One of those talk show issues.

Photo 10. "Trash" taken by Rebecca

Trash is a big problem in our community. Everywhere we look there is a piece of
trash. It's all over the communities. Some people don't care where they throw their
trash. This picture represents what I see every day when I go bike riding, driving
in a car, or when I take the bus home. I don't like to see trash in my community.
The trash can make animals and people sick. Our community needs to form
cleanup groups to help remove the garbage. (Rebecca)

Alice: Do you think your neighborhood has more little problems or big problems?

Rebecca: Big problems, big, bigggg problems. (April 27, 1998)

The preceding discussion about "trash" was related to the other issues the participants were concerned about in their community. As we reflected on the photographs, the participants spoke about the interconnected relationship between violence, drugs, guns, and the environment. They reflected on how the outside community perceived them—"people think we're lazy and dirty"—recognizing that "some of the people here are and some aren't." Similarly, the students spoke to the reality that if their community was seen as a "junkyard," then people did not want to live there, visit the neighborhood, and/or teach at their school.

The conversation moved from a discussion about trash to the question of judging people by their "outsides." The girls talked about how people from outside the community perceived people who lived in "trashy communities" as "bad people." Their interpretations of how people outside the community perceive them illustrates the complexities of addressing environmental violence within the contexts of racism, classism, and societal neglect.

Flanango: That's why they don't want to live here.

Melinda: Well, they just don't want to come.

[ct]

Melinda: We went on a trip before I came to this school, and we went to Beaconsville and the teacher told us to behave ourselves because the people of Beaconsville think that we're disgusting crackheads and stuff like that and she was saying all this garbage [laugh] and she was saying that everyone thinks that Ellsworth is a bad place to live and blah, blah, blah. Because of all the drugs and violence.

Alice: Do you believe that?

Melinda: Not necessarily.

Flanango: In some parts.

Alice: Do you believe that people think that?

All: Yeah.

Alice: Do you believe it is true?

Janine: Yeah, because every time we try to get a substitute nobody will want to come to Ellsworth.

[ct]

Melinda: Because of our behavior and they just found knives and stuff and crack upstairs.

Janine: Three bags of drugs in the bathroom.

Melinda: So, see that just adds onto what they think. Now they're just gonna think even worse and they won't come. So, [I feel] really bad because we didn't do nothing.

Again, the conversation continued to focus on how people judged each other. The girls had a lively discussion about parental responsibility. Some of the girls thought it was entirely up to parents to keep their children polite and out of trouble while the rest of the girls suggested that parents could only do so much to keep their children "on the right path."

Melinda: Getting back to the garbage thing. I think why it becomes a big problem is that if they see one person, if someone sees one person do it then they feel, "Well, I can do that, too."

Alice: And how do you think people would think about you or your school if the community was cleaned up and it stayed clean? Do you think that that would[

Melinda: Well, probably we could get a substitute [laughter].

Rebecca: They would think that we are clean people. Like Melinda said we will be able to get a substitute once in a while.

Flanango: It's not only the trash though that stops substitutes from coming here.

Rebecca: It's the kids.

Melinda: Or it's the behavior.

Flanango: Like it's not just because they see trash and that stops them from coming here. It's part of it, but it is not the whole reason.

Alice: What else is it?

Flanango: I don't know. It's just drugs, how some kids act in the school.

Melinda: Our reputation.

Rebecca: They know that there is drugs in here and there's lethal weapons in here so why would they want to come? I mean why would they want to come to a school like that when they can go to a school when the kids can walk in a single line, their behavior is excellent, school is clean.

Melinda: So it's like they're judging us by what they heard but they haven't actually come here to see. (April 27, 1998)

This same message was heard from another group of students who struggled with living in a community they perceived as having been discarded.

Chesterfield: Well, we have to kind of clean up 'cause people, like say a person from New Jersey comes in and looks at our community and they want to move in. They might change their mind or say this place is bad and even like if they were going to do something in Ellsworth like a movie or something they see the trash and they say they would rather go to New York where it is cleaner. . . . .

Mase: It makes us feel bad and them feel bad 'cause suppose their state is dirty and "Oh let's go to a different state and see if theirs is clean" and they go there and they see it is dirty they say, "Let's get out of here and go to another one." Suppose Bill Clinton comes driving through our neighborhood and he sees all this trash. He gonna blast out. He is *not* going to stay here for a long time.

Chesterfield: It makes me feel like we have less opportunities than other states. Because Bill Clinton, well, I never heard of him staying here.

William: Yeah and nobody, almost nobody ever comes here. It's like a city that nobody cares about. It's just like a city in the state that is like apart. And then there is New York City and all the big cities that he [Clinton] has to take care of more than here. He doesn't really care about Ellsworth.

Mase: That's why many people don't live around here, they don't move around here.

Chesterfield: A lot of people make comments about Ellsworth, like "I don't want to go here. The school is bad and then inside looks like a mess."

William: And the taxes. . . . .

Chesterfield: I'm disappointed that people dissin' us and they don't believe that our community is good and . . . it's like saying that we don't have a chance to prove ourselves. (April 27, 1998)

As the data reveal, these discussions—and many others that occurred during the project—focused heavily on the environment. In addition, there was a preoccupation with the way the participants and people who lived in their community were perceived and treated by people from outside the community. On multiple occasions during the project, the participants spoke openly about how they were treated when they ventured outside the familiarity of Ellsworth. Tonesha recently told us that she had entered a card store in Beaconsville, a predominantly white, middle- to upper-middle-class town neighboring Ellsworth. She entered the store to purchase a card for her mother. No sooner had Tonesha opened the door than the saleswoman, who was white, asked her to leave.

Tonesha: And I went in there and um, I was lookin' for a card for my mother and she said, "What kind of card do you want?" I was like um[

Blood: A nice one.

Tonesha: Yeah, like a thank you card or whatever. And she's like, "We don't have those here." And I saw like a mother section and I was like, "They're right over there." And she's like, "I can't sell you those." I was like, "Why?" She's like, "Because you're Black and you can go in your own stores." And I was like, "What?"

Alice: She said that?

Tonesha: Oh, yeah. She just said it. I couldn't believe it myself. I know people think it but to say it, that had me really[

Mase: I would have yelled, "TOO BAD!"

[ct]

Tonesha: I'm tellin' ya, she thought I was tryin' to steal 'cause I'm Black.

Alice: So what did you do when she said she wouldn't sell you a card because you're Black?

Tonesha: I cursed her out! Then I was like "That don't got nothin' to do with it."

Monique: I would've taken it and walked out!

[laughter]

Tonesha: I had to walk out 'cause she threatened to call the police if I didn't leave.

During the project, other participants shared similar experiences of being discriminated against because of the color of their skin and/or because they lived in Ellsworth (also see chapter 6). Rebecca was asked to leave a game room in Beaconsville because the owner, who was white, told her there was no room for her and her friends. "There was lots of room for us," said Rebecca. "But he said we should go to the game place in Ellsworth instead. When we were leaving, a group of kids said, 'Get outta here, 'Ricans.' We turned around to say something to them and the owner told us we better leave or he would call the Beaconsville police." Monique told us a similar story about entering a store in Beaconsville with her class the year before and the owner, a white woman, telling her employees to watch the students in the store "because they come from Ellsworth."

The participants are aware that they face scrutiny because of their skin color, age, and the neighborhood in which they live. What store owners—and many other people who live outside their community—see when the participants walk in the door "is a black face, and they fill in the negative assumptions accordingly" (Newman 1999:155). Many people living outside inner-city Ellsworth have a set of beliefs about the people of Color who live there that are deeply racist, prejudicial, and make it increasingly difficult for the participants to see themselves and their community as worth saving. Instead, the participants take the brunt of racism and live with the burden of having addresses located in the less attractive neighborhoods in Ellsworth—areas that, as Collin stated, "no one cares about. That's just it. And since no one cares about 'em, people who live here don't even care."

The photography project was an opportunity for the participants to encourage each other, and other people in the school and community, to care about the way the community looks. The participants' message to the community, via the photographs, was simple, clear, and powerful: We do not like the way the community looks. We do not like the way people outside the community think about us because we live here. We want to do something about it. We want you to help us.

Exploring Strategies for Change

One of the first discussions in which the participants spoke about taking action to address specific community issues was during a review session in January 1998. We had just returned from winter break and were reviewing the activities we had participated in together thus far in the project: creating collages, visiting the local community center, storytelling, writing journals, large and small group discussions, and conducting the community resource inventories. In discussing these activities, the participants and the members of the research team identified some common themes that were emerging as the process evolved: violence, drugs, guns, education, and trash—the last being the one that elicited the strongest reaction from the participants.

> *Tee:* Trash. Man, it is the worst. And with trash, you get all the other junk, too. Drugs and drinkin' and stealin' and all that.
> *Bill:* It's like we said in those collages, this place looks like a junkyard. (January 18, 1999)

The individual and collective recital of the "trashy way the community looks" was a common one voiced by the participants multiple times during the months leading up to this meeting. Yet it was during this particular group session that they finally decided to address the issue in a concrete way.

In the midst of discussing how the community "looks like a junkyard," Tee stood up and said: "OK. So we all agree there is too much trash. So I think we need to clean up the neighborhood more and I think we can do that if we all pitch in." The participants agreed and decided that Tee's suggestion should be further explored. Thus, we brainstormed activities we thought might be effective in cleaning up the trash that litters the participants' community. After discussing a number of ideas, the participants decided that they wanted to organize a cleanup day which would target certain areas of the neighborhood. At the time, I was not enthusiastic about the idea or the subsequent proposal that the young people or participants later crafted. Many of them had already discussed with us the futility of organizing cleanup events. According to them they were "sick of cleaning up the school and the school garden across the street." They felt it was a waste of time to keep certain areas clean when, sometimes within hours, people "dirtied them up again."

Nonetheless, a core group of participants felt that cleaning up a part of community "just might work this time." Even though I had reservations about what I perceived to be a band-aid approach to the problem, I reminded myself that this was a PAR project and if the participants decided they wanted to organize an event, it was important for me to honor their decision and join with them in exploring their ideas for a subsequent action plan. I was also excited that they had initiated an idea for acting on the information gleaned thus far in the project and were willing to take action on an issue that concerned them.

So, on that particular day in late January we organized a cleanup event. The participants decided what we would need, who would participate, what preparatory things they would need to do, and who would take responsibility for various tasks: writing letters home to parents, speaking with Susan and requesting her support, creating fliers to be put up in the school and throughout the community, and getting in touch with city officials and requesting that they assist us by donating materials.

I wrote the participants' comments and suggestions on the blackboard, clarifying the dates and times and questioning them when I felt they were being too ambitious about their plans. I offered to write up the notes and return the following week with copies for everyone. In the meantime, the participants decided that they would choose a committee to oversee various aspects of the project and follow through on the ideas we had developed.

The next week I returned with the copies of the cleanup plan. The participants returned empty-handed. They hadn't taken any action about organizing their committee. Nor had they requested assistance from Mrs. Lawton, Susan, or any city officials. When I asked them why they weren't able to follow through on some of the ideas they had so enthusiastically embraced the previous week, they shrugged their shoulders, muttered under their breath, and basically agreed that "we forgot to do it."

We discussed various ways in which we could better prepare ourselves to undertake a cleanup project. The participants acknowledged that they needed to take responsibility for the things they had said they would do. They also mentioned that although they understood that this was a joint process and that they "liked being able to make decisions," it would help them a lot "if there was an adult around" who would remind them of what they had agreed to do and would share some of the responsibilities in developing a plan, such as taking care of transportation, making the necessary telephone calls, and gaining access to a computer and copy machine. I agreed with their assessment, although I explained to them that other than driving them to particular places, they were as capable as I or any of the other team members were of making phone calls, using a computer at school, and/or making copies of certain things on the school's copy machines. I also recognized that the school computers were not always available nor the school copy machines always functioning. Therefore we decided that when it was more efficient or effective for me and the team members to be responsible for certain items, we would do so. When the participants were able to and capable of taking responsibility for particular aspects of the project, they would do so.

Months went by, and although we continued to talk about "the trashy environment," the participants failed to initiate a discussion about how we might transform that reality. I was content to wait until they had more clarity about what and how they wanted to respond to the myriad issues that were emerging in the project, particularly as they related to the environment. That clarity came after we had implemented the community photography project.

It was only after the photography project that the participants seriously considered the possibility that they really *could* do something to improve the state of the community. Below, I present their second attempt to clean up the community, which occurred after we had completed our review and analysis of their photographs. I illustrate the ways in which dialogue, trust, creative activities, knowledge construction, shared decision making, collaboration, and a sense of purpose and intentionality converged with one another in a PAR process and ignited new ideas, new ways of thinking and doing, and contributed to the development of a youth-initiated action plan.

Tee: We could make a cleanup group. Because everybody says they gonna make up a cleanup group and they never do it.
Alice: Who is everybody?
All: The class, the class.
Collin: Could we make up a cleanup group to help and support our town to show that we care to clean it up? Could we do that?
Alice: Yeah, you could do that.
Collin: Let's do that now. Could you help us out with doing that?
Alice: Absolutely.
Collin: We will get the rakes and bags and everything. We will go around town and you know[

Blood: Yeah but [unint.] but we tried that and it didn't work.

Alex: It's not fair. It's not fair because every time we clean people throw it on the floor.

Tee: Here's something we can do. Like we can go out and put up signs in the school. We can talk to Ms. Lawton and we can make like "Don't Put Garbage on the Ground"[

Collin: Go around cleaning up and showing[

Tee: Right and we can go around town, around Ellsworth[

Blood: Go around The Courts and clean up stuff.

Tee: We can go to The Courts. I ain't saying The Courts is bad, but we can go just clean up stuff and we can get a little group. All we gotta do is get gloves, rakes, and stuff and make a rain date.

Alice: But what if you do that and you clean up everything on a Saturday. That is important but after everything you've told me, what do you think is going to happen next Saturday?

Tee: It's going to get dirty again.

Blood: We just don't do it.

Alice: Well, you could just not do it, or you could think of ways to do it but also to be doing something on a regular basis that will encourage the community to join you in this plan.

Collin: We pick up stuff and like make signs "Don't Dirty Our Town," "Help Our Town," "Every Time You Walk by a Piece of Paper Pick It Up" and all that. "Whenever You See a Piece of Paper Pick It Up." And have the city help us out a little bit. We need to be setting an example for kids, ya know? In the future it is going to be our world. We gonna be the presidents and all that and we have to start now. Start cleaning up and everything. They want to follow us.

Tee: Like the little brothers and little sisters are gonna say, "I want to be just like my big brother."

Collin: This is a trashy community. Nobody cares. . . . Kids all they want to do is litter and litter but if we show that we care and we start cleaning up maybe people will start helping us and coming in and putting more trees and stuff in our community. Helping us clean up and everything. Take off the spray paint and stuff. Maybe the city will help us out a little bit. If we start putting effort into it. . . . And stop all them kids thinking about getting guns and fighting and all that. . . . .

Tee: Yeah. They followin' us and we gotta do the right thing. So we can set an example for them. So we gotta do somethin'. We got to help out some-body. I will be[

Collin: Like once the bigger kids see us they try to help us a little bit every once in a while. We know how they are, "Forget that. They are stupid for getting dirty and all that." But at least we are trying to clean up. Our world is going to be our world pretty soon. We are going to have a filthy world if we don't start cleaning up and saving trees and doing all that and our world is going to come to an end because oxygen and all that is going lower and lower. We need to start cleaning up, planting more trees.

[ct]

Collin: We could start making up plans and we could start planning like when we are going to do this. Like plan and say we will do this one week. We will start saving up money to buy trees. We'll start saving money like havin' little buckets that say "Save Our Community" and all that and we'll go around and clean up an area that's all dirty and all that. Plant some grass for it to grow and all that.

[ct]

Blood: I got hope but if I were y'all I wouldn't do it because they're gonna keep on doin' it.

Alice: So what do you think the alternative is?

Tee: Keep on cleanin'.

Blood: I'm not gonna keep on cleanin' so they can keep on dirtyin' it up anyway.

Alex: They gonna take advantage of us.

Collin: [frustrated] So what? At least we tryin'.

Blood: We are going to do somethin' once and we see how it goes and people keep on dirtyin' then you just don't do it.

Collin: They'll stop trashin' and maybe they'll use the garbage can.

Blood: I be seein' $50 signs for litterin' in white houses.

Alice: In white people's houses?

Blood: Yeah, like in Beaconsville.

[ct]

Tee: We got to have meetings.

Collin: Like open houses. And talk to people and have people come into school like one time we use the gym and all that and have open house talks with everybody. (April 27, 1998)

A few weeks later, I engaged in a similar conversation with Mase, William, Chesterfield, and Bill.

Alice: Seems like what we want to do is address some of the issues that you brought up this year in terms of the community. If we have the opportunity next year to do something together, what is it that you would like to focus on?

[ct]

William: A cleanup crew wouldn't be that good because people just throw the garbage and we tell them not to throw the garbage and then nobody will listen to us because we are little kids.

Chesterfield: I would ask you to do, I would ask you to do a favor for us and if you can do it I'll tell you to take pictures of areas that are dirty and we could go around and[

Mase: Yeah, in the areas you took a picture of[

Chesterfield: We could make like a map and put all the photos on it and we could choose where to go here first and then there[

Mase: One group go here and the next group go there and then we could meet up at the same[

William: Or we can do that and take pictures of all the dirty spots and parts that are not nice and then we can put them in a big huge paper and hang it up so all the people can see how ugly it is.

Mase: And then one group go here and the next group go there. And from all the groups everybody meets up from the groups and we help clean up the biggest spot.

Alice: Let me just tell you one thing that we talked about in the other groups because the other groups said the same thing. I think cleaning up is very important to everybody. The question that the other kids had that you just mentioned is a really valid one which is what if we did that and we had small groups and we met after school and we devised this plan to take care of say six areas. Some of the kids said: "Yeah, but then a week is going to go by and it is going to happen again."

William: Exactly, it is going to be all dirty and the work isn't going to work. . . . And that adds to the drugs and the violence and the bad things that happen in our community.

Alice: That's what the other kids said. So what we talked about was maybe getting together and developing a program or a project that will do a cou-

ple of things: one, that will include the community, not just you, but trying to get the parents and other kids involved. The second thing is something that will be sustained, in other words something that will keep going
. . . something that you build up with the community over time.
Chesterfield: The goal is to clean it.
William: To keep it clean.
Chesterfield: Yeah, the thing is not to clean it but keep it clean. (May 4, 1998)

It was at this point in the project that the participants began to recognize that the violence in the community went beyond the more generally
accepted definition of violence as "rough or injurious physical force, action, or treatment" (*Webster's College Dictionary,* 1996). Through their visual stories, the participants demonstrated that there was also a preponderance of environmental violence characterized by trash, pollution, graffiti, abandoned houses, and drug paraphernalia in the streets.

Having understood that in a way that was different than their earlier
conceptualization of the relationship between violence and the environment, the participants decided that upon our return to school in September 1999, we were going to "get serious" about addressing the trash problem. And once back from summer vacation, that is exactly what happened.
We got serious. We also encountered a whole new set of challenges that
emerge when people move from talking about an issue to actually doing
the necessary work for effective change. Those challenges are described in
chapter 7.

Concluding Reflections

Photovoice (Lykes, Caba Mateo, Chávez Anay, Laynes Caba, Ruiz, and
Williams, 1999; Wang 1999)—the process by which people identify and
speak to community issues through photography—gave us an opportunity
to position the participants as recorders of their own lives and of their
school and community. The participants' photographs assisted them in prioritizing the aforementioned concerns and provoked stimulating discussions that generated ideas for change.

Similarly, the photography project was a point in the research project
that crystallized many of the activities and discussions we had engaged
in up to that point in the PAR project. The participants began to "see"

differently. Their visual images were reflected back at them and they began to understand the concreteness of some of their concerns. They were struck by their own representations, thinking it highly relevant that most of them had chosen photographs of pollution and trash as the most representative images of their community. Their photographs, their written descriptions of trash, pollution, and abandoned houses, and their feelings of disappointment, frustration, and resignation over the inability to clean up their neighborhood challenged all of us to broaden our conceptualization of violence to include violations of and to the environment, which, as their reflections reveal, have powerful implications for and in their community. Rethinking violence to include violations to the environment, which directly and indirectly violates the self and the collective, both complicates and enhances the ways in which educators and researchers address violence. Thus, we are invited to reexamine the social, economic, and political conditions that sustain the multiple forms of violence that exist in many low-income urban communities. Equally important, the participants' photographs, as well as their efforts to address what the photographs represent, invite educators to "revise and expand what we think we know about [urban youth]" (Way 1998:7) and the communities in which they live. By "listening" to what their visual stories say, researchers, educators, psychologists, and concerned adults can more effectively collaborate with young people in the construction of new knowledge that can ultimately be used to improve their individual and collective lives.

5

■   ■   ■   ■   ■   ■   ■   ■   ■

Becoming Somebody

IT HAS BEEN WIDELY DOCUMENTED that urban youth who attend inner-city public schools experience gross educational inequities due to lack of funding for urban schools (see, for example, Anyon 1997; Children's Defense Fund 1999; Council of the Great City Schools 1994; Darling-Hammond and Sclan 1996; *Education Week* 1998; Henig, Hula, Orr, and Pedescleaux 1999; National Commission on Teaching and America's Future 1996), discriminatory educational policies and practices (see, for example, Artiles and Trent 1994; Darling-Hammond 1995; Fordham 1996; Lipman 1998; Nieto 1996; Oakes 1990; Pessar 1997; Solis 1995; Townshend, Thomas, Witty, and Lee 1996), and a shortage of qualified teachers (see, for example, Grant and Zozakiewicz 1995; Haberman 1995; National Center for Educational Statistics 1999; Tellez, Hlebowitsh, Cohen, and Norwood 1995; Zeichner and Melnick 1997), to name a few of the problems.

In addition, many young people living in low-income communities contend with social issues that complicate their lives, and as an extension to that, their education: poverty, crime, toxic environments, poor housing, and other forms of violence. The challenges many urban youth face as they negotiate a system that promises them one thing—an equal education and an opportunity to achieve the American dream—and delivers another, are daunting. Although urban environments may produce heroism in some children as they negotiate difficult terrain, the majority of young people living in inner cities and attending urban public schools are too often "rendered invisible" (Tarpley 1995:3). The reality for many young people of Color, particularly those living in low-income communities, is that the American dream is, as Langston Hughes suggested, "a dream deferred" (1951:62). It is a dream that does not materialize for the majority of people of Color, economically deprived whites, and other socially marginalized groups.

In this chapter, I explore how the participants envision their dreams of "being somebody" within a system mediated by educational violence. In other words, the participants' education is embedded in a system that encourages young people to work hard and succeed in school, yet fails to provide the necessary resources for them to do so. I explore the participants' ideas about work, school, career, success, and "makin' it." In addition, I describe the experiences these young people live with and through that either sustain them in their desire to "be somebody" or contribute to their inability and resistance to learn, to hope, and to imagine their lives outside of their current situations.

For many of the young people I have met at the Blair School, staying in school is like treading water. They do just enough to stay afloat in an educational system mired in social, political, and economic institutions that simply do not provide equal and necessary opportunities for them, their peers, their families, or their communities to succeed and thrive. The participants' stories dispel the notion that public education provides equal opportunity for all. It doesn't. To really improve the chance for inner-city adolescents, particularly those of Color, to achieve the American dream, we must first rethink what that dream really means to and for these young people, and second, we need to increase young people's chances for living and learning.

"Being Somebody" within the Boundaries of Race, Class, and Gender

"I Wanna Be Somebody"

During the first few months of the project, the research team conducted community resource inventories (CRI) with the participants. In those one-on-one inventories, the participants talked a great deal about education and their desire to "be somebody" when they graduated from high school. When asked, "What are some skills or things you would like to learn?" the majority of the boys said, "a sport, like basketball." Other participants, both girls and boys, said "math and science." Still others wanted to learn more English, language arts, and/or social studies so that they could be successful, earn a lot of money, and "buy a nice house." Many of the participants expressed an interest in becoming some type of professional: teacher, lawyer, doctor, architect, astronaut, and one boy wanted to become an FBI agent.

During the "representing community" collage exercise referred to in chapter 2, one group of participants created a collage which focused on what they wanted to be when they grew up. When I asked the all-girl group (Veronica, Tina, Jeter, and Janine) to tell me about what they were designing on their collage and how it related to the community, they said: "This is what we do in our community. We think about the future." Veronica added, "I don't know what I want to be when I grow up 'cause it depends on what you do *now*, but I do think about it."

The girls in the group glued pictures of two babies—one girl and one boy—in the middle of the collage (see photo 11).

There were words coming from the babies' mouths that said: "What shall I be when I grow up?" and "What can I be when I grow up?" Some of the accompanying images were of Princess Diana, Toni Braxton, Jada Pinkett ("'cuz she's an actress"), a Black woman athlete ("'cause she's a runner, a gold medalist"), the picture of a *Cover Girl* model, Sally Richardson (an actress), a cover of *Jet* magazine, and a photograph of two businesswomen of Color.

The following conversation occurred when the girls presented their collage to the rest of the class for their interpretations and comments.

Janine: These are up here because the babies are thinking what we wanna be when we grow up. She could be an actress. The baby boy when he grows up, um, he could sing, he could play in a show[

Jeter: and she could be, like, a princess. Or she could be on a magazine or a cover girl. Or she could be a singer, or an actress.

Veronica: Or a model.

Photo 11. Collage designed by Janine, Jeter, Veronica, and Tina

Alice: Why did you choose to do that theme: what do you want to be when you grow up?

Jeter: 'Cause, we gotta, um, we gotta start thinking what we are gonna be in our future.

Janine: Instead of on a corner.

Alice: Do you think a lot about what you want to do when you grow up?

Girls: Yes.

Mikey: They still haven't told us what the runner lady is.

Group members: She's a runner.

Tee: But what does that have to do with the community?

Jeter: She's thinking she wants to be a runner, like a track runner.

Tee: But what does that have to do with community?

Tina: Well, like those are two businesswomen [pointing to another picture on the collage].

Janine: They can use their money to clean up the community and stuff. (November 10, 1997)

Some of the young people were confused about the girls' collage. This was indicated by Tee's question about the relationship between someone wanting to be a runner and the idea of community. At times the participants were quite literal in their meaning making, suggesting that the community was: "a place where you watch out for each other," "my neighborhood," "a group of people that help each other," "the environment," "family," "school," and "the part of the world you live in." Others said, "not being bad or in gangs," "people doing violence," "picking up trash and stuff," and "keeping the place clean." Other times, the participants moved beyond defining their community in terms of their material surroundings and began linking the notion of community to issues of education, work, and the way their community was perceived by those living outside it.

In response to Tee's question, the girls explained that one's future depends on what one is doing *now* and "right now, this community has a lot of problems that could get in my way of what I want to be when I grow up" (Veronica).

Thinking about the future had been a theme consistently at the forefront of the project. In a majority of the discussions we had about the future, the participants focused on education as the "way out" of the negative aspects of their community and a link to a successful life. Although the history and the educational experiences of the majority of African Americans and Latinos/as in this country suggest otherwise, many of these young people continue to believe that "getting a good education can get us off the corner" and can provide them with opportunities to fulfill their dreams, gain knowledge about the world, and find hope and pride in themselves.

A week after the participants had presented their collages representing the community to one another, I met with individual groups to further explore their creations. Below is an excerpt from a conversation I had with the four girls who designed the "What do you want to be when you grow up?" collage.

Alice: When you look at your collage, what do you think you need, as young girls, in order to be able to get to one of these places [pointing to the collage]?

Janine: A good education. No foolin' around in school. Payin' attention to the teachers. Don't go out on the corners tryin' to be stupid and do drugs.

Tina: Instead of gettin' in trouble, you shouldn't get in trouble. A lot of kids get in trouble when doin' things they ain't supposed to be doin'. I think you need to get like a good role model and stuff. Um, and don't steal. Don't get into trouble and get a good education and so you can be somebody.

Veronica: Like maybe your aunt or uncle. They probably did somethin' bad when they was young. But now they're like in the business or somethin' but they'll tell you if you're sittin' down talkin' with them, or your grand-father, if you're sittin' down talkin' with him, they'll be like, "Don't, do not try not to go down the path that I did. But see me now." But you be wantin' to say, "I wanna be like you" and they be like, "No you don't wanna be like me because I used to, see, you don't wanna get expelled from school or um, or sent away for doin' drugs 'cause they send you away to the penitentiary school and like you can't be around your friends." . . . You need, you just need to be yourself instead of tryin' to be like[

Janine: Everybody else.

Jeter: My uncle, right, not my uncle, my mother's uncle. No, my mother's cousin. He does drugs, right? And one day like two years ago, he shared the needle with somebody who had AIDS and he got AIDS. So, you have to get to, get an education, start workin' in school, um, don't pay atten-tion to drugs. Try to help other people to get off drugs so they can be somebody.

[ct]

Janine: You could try to convince them to stop this or um, instead of drop-pin' out of school, go back to school. Stop that and um, to not to go to the gutters and to be somebody. Not to be out here on the corner havin' babies. See, 'cause all the beautiful kids are in college learnin' stuff while you was out on the street. Or, um, you could have a program where peo-ple, you could make a little program, steps to teach about how to stop. Like the Nicoderm could help you to stop the smokin' and stuff.

Jeter: In school you learn a lot of new important things every step of the way and um, they teach you how not to go on the streets and stuff like that and you will be, when you grow up, you get to be somebody.

Tina: I like school because like it keeps kids out of trouble and you get a bet-ter education. . . . I think it's a good way to uh, say you should start thinkin' about what you gonna be so you won't end up on the street doin' bad things and get an education. (November 17, 1997)

Although the girls, as a group, tend to be more vocal than the boys about their views on education, and appear to be more determined to "do well in school," it would be misleading to suggest that the boys do not have similar perspectives about "being somebody." The following conversation took place with a mixed-sex group of participants who were revisiting their collage, which also included images related to education and "being somebody."

Alice: Why do you think education is important?

Monique: 'Cause like, if you wanna um, be somebody they look back on your records. [Starts singing a song she made up on the spot: "You gonna be somebody."]

Alice: What does it mean to "be somebody?" I hear lots of you say that.

Tee: Like, you wanna be somebody.

Monique: You wanna go somewhere.

Tee: You wanna go somewhere like, you wanna go to college. You wanna do somethin' with your life. Don't be a bum or somethin'.

Jason: Because um, you need to get an education to go to college. And you go to college you could be somebody. You could be whoever you want and um, you sometime you can . . . make a lot of money.

Risha: In order for me to stay in, in order for me to get a job, I'm gonna have to stay in school.

Tee: Yeah, I wanna go to college. I wanna make my mother proud. (November 17, 1997)

I have been an educator for over twenty years and although I want very much to believe that each and every one of these young people can "make it," and that they *will* overcome the barriers they face in their daily lives, I recognize that their education and the city in which they live "are subject to the strains and stresses of contradictory social, economic, and political pressures" (Shapiro and Purpel 1998:2), all of which mediate the teaching and learning processes that occur at the Blair School.

Ellsworth is located in one of the wealthiest counties in the United States. Yet the city has a disproportionate share of the problems that affect many urban communities throughout the country (such as high criminal activity, unemployment and low-wage jobs, poverty, and racial isolation). The contrast between the Ellsworth public schools and schools located in the surrounding suburbs is not an uncommon one in the United States. A number of scholars and researchers have documented the vast differences in material and cultural resources between those who have and those who do not, particularly when those differences mediate educational practices and policies (see, for example, Anyon 1997; Fordham 1996; Kozol 1991, 1995; MacLeod 1995; McQuillan 1998). Such differences all too often result in educational inequities that reflect the deep inequalities between races and classes in U.S. society and highlight the fact that "America now has some of the finest high-achieving schools in the world—and some of the most miserable, threatened, underfunded travesties" (Berliner and Biddle 1995:58).

The participants of this project are unfamiliar with educational inequities and the extent to which those inequities shape their schooling. Similarly, local dropout[1] rates, state requirements for graduation, national standards, and college entrance examinations are too remote from the worlds of these twelve- and thirteen-year-olds. What they *are* familiar with is their immediate surroundings and what they see around them, which is often fractured patterns of success and failure. They see some of their family members graduate from high school. They see fewer of their family members and peers pursuing higher education. That is not to say that their families or particular teachers and other people in their lives do not encourage them to follow their dreams of attending a university or pursuing a particular skill. They do. Yet the participants live in a society that refuses to implement programs and policies that support them in school, at home, or in the workplace. Instead, most people in the United States have low aspirations for urban youth and simply do not expect urban youth of Color to make it (MacLeod 1995).

Many urban schools cannot and/or do not provide young people of Color with the resources necessary to successfully transition from elementary school to middle school to high school and then on to higher education. Therefore, it is unrealistic to expect that all or even most of the differences in academic performance between urban and suburban schools will—or can—be eliminated. Coupled with underresourced schools, larger social systems also fail to provide urban youth of Color with access to educational and economic opportunities, thus increasing the likelihood that the participants will face significant barriers in attaining an education, in "becoming somebody," and/or being employed in the kinds of professions they spoke about in our group sessions.

"Ya Gotta Get a Degree"

Getting a high school and/or college degree is a gatekeeping experience in many people's lives. Yet, how one gains that degree and for what purpose is mediated by one's gender, race, social class, ability, familial history, geographical location, and a host of other variables. It is readily apparent from the participants' conversations that they have a different perspective about what it means to "get a degree" than their white suburban counterparts. In many white, suburban, middle- and upper-middle-class schools and communities, there is little need to explain, in detail, the trajectory from kindergarten to college. Most of the students attending these schools and living in these communities know where they are going and what they need to do to get there. That is not the case in many poor rural schools and communities, or in urban areas where the population of students is poor and poor working class, immigrants, and people of Color. Although all students in this country may hear a similar message—education is the key to success—how that message is heard, lived out, and experienced is mediated by a constellation of factors. Therefore, even though the young people in this project "know" they need to get a good education, watching them negotiate the educational terrain to achieve one is like watching players of a board game who may be familiar with the rules but don't have all the pieces.

Below is a brief excerpt from a discussion a group of us had one day about careers and the importance of "getting a degree."

Alice: Tonesha, what are some things you think you need to do to help you become a lawyer?

Tonesha: Well, first off, get good grades. Um, help my community. That's definite. And not to be a dropout. That's it.

Alice: Do you think school is an important place where you can do some things that would help you be successful?

> *Chesterfield:* Yes, because if you don't get a degree you won't be able to like, work or become something successful.
>
> *Bart:* You could work but you won't be able to make a lot of money, though. Like, you get money but like if you get a degree and stuff you gonna make like more money.
>
> *Bill:* With a degree um, you get a job, but you get a job like, picking up cars, like a tow truck. Or you can be a school bus driver.
>
> *Alice:* Is that what you want to do?
>
> *Bill:* No.
>
> *Alice:* Are you saying that if you get a degree you could do those things or if you *don't* get a degree?
>
> *Bill:* Yeah. If you get a degree. You don't get to do those things [if you don't have a degree.]
>
> *Bart:* You could but it's harder. (November 24, 1997)

This conversation is representative of many others we had during the first year of the project. As the excerpt shows, the participants have little knowledge about what it means to "get a degree," the value of a degree, and how a degree relates to specific jobs and careers.

The participants' access to knowledge is limited in part by societal and educational structures that were in place long before they were born. From birth through early childhood education on through elementary, middle, and high school, and continuing through college, Blacks and other people of Color, particularly if they live in low-income communities, suffer from a "pedagogy of the poor" (Polakow 1999:257) that culminates in an alarming record of educational failure and a limited number of opportunities for many young people of Color to "get a degree." As Connell argues, "In a country whose public traditions embrace the concepts of equality and meritocracy, the full weight of hereditary class and race distinctions begin at kindergarten and proceed ruthlessly and at an accelerated rate through high school" (1999:152), and, I would suggest, well beyond.

In order to inform the participants about the process of moving from kindergarten to college, and to clarify for them what is required to "get a degree," the research team made a conscious effort to share our educational experiences with them. Thus far, fourteen graduate students have participated as team members in the project. Some of the team members were in their early twenties, which did not go unnoticed by the participants. (I recently had lunch in the cafeteria with some of the girls and mentioned to them that Jen and Nicole were coming by on Monday to see them. Rebecca smiled and said, "Thank God!" I looked at her askance and said, "Oh, yeah? Am I boring you too much on Monday mornings?" She quickly replied, "No. Not at all. It's just that you're old. We need the youngness around here.")

The team members related very well to the participants, spending a good deal of time "hanging out" with them and answering many of their questions about the team's families, their boyfriends and girlfriends and husbands and wives, what they did over the weekend, and other subjects that are of interest to twelve and thirteen-year-olds. The multiple conversations the team members had with the participants assisted the young people in better understanding the trajectory from kindergarten to college. They learned the differences between being an undergraduate, graduate, and doctoral student. They understood that Ph.D. meant Doctor of Philosophy, not "player hater degree"—slang for someone who cheats on her or his boyfriend or girlfriend. They also gained important information about what was expected of university students and the importance of developing learning strategies *now* which would assist them as they progressed through school.

I am not suggesting that adolescents elsewhere in the country do not or would not benefit from similar information. Nor am I suggesting that by providing factual information about how students move through the educational process we made a dent in the structures that keep these young people from entering "elite" educational spaces. Yet gaining knowledge, limited though it may be, about how educational systems are structured—knowledge almost entirely out of reach for many urban youth—is one more step toward defining one's reality. That, in turn, could lead to the participants developing a greater understanding of what it will take for them to achieve their personal and academic goals. In addition, the participants can begin to see themselves as being capable of using knowledge as a "resource for challenging the hegemony of the dominant ideas" (Gaventa 1988:24–25) which, in this country, are framed within an anti–youth of Color discourse that blames them for educational failure.

In a related discussion that was generated during the collage exercise, the participants discussed what it meant to be a "businesswoman"—a topic that came up a number of times throughout the project. One of the mixed-sex groups, and the all-female group already referred to earlier, used businesswomen to represent their community when they designed their collages. During a class discussion about the collages, I asked the participants if they knew any businesswomen in their community.

> *Mase:* Yeah, my mom.
> *Alice:* Your Mom? And what does she do?
> *Mase:* Works at the bank.
> *Janine:* My aunt, she work at McDonald's.
> *Bart:* My aunt works at a company that repairs cars. She's an executive or something. She uh, she works in the office and does the bills and stuff.
> *Mikey:* My mother works at the sneaker factory.
> *Puffy:* My mother, my mother she works at [a department store].
> *Veronica:* My cousin works in an office.
> *Monique:* My mother's friend works at the bank.
> *Tee:* My cousin works at the [neighborhood grocery store].
> *Janine:* My other aunt, she works at the bus company and my mother works there.
> *Jeter:* Um, my aunt is a teacher.
> *Veronica:* My aunt, she works at the limousine company. (November 10, 1997)

The participants are proud of the work their mothers, fathers, relatives, and friends engage in and feel that, as Mikey said, "It's good to have a job. You feel pride in yourself when you go to work." Unfortunately, that sense of pride in one's work diminishes if it is carved with the knife of racism, sexism, and discrimination. There is a pervasive view among many people in the United States that the majority of urban residents simply do not work, but spend their time playing basketball, drinking on the corner, and collecting welfare checks (see, for example, Gilens 1999; Kelley 1997; Polakow 1999; Pope 1999). This view has powerful implications for the way the participants conceptualize the notion of welfare, a subject that first came up during a discussion I was having with Jason, Monique, Tee, and Risha about the cost of higher education.

> *Tee:* You know somethin'? I wanna know why people pay for college. 'Cause um, when you really want to go to college, and then you gotta pay and

you don't got the money and so you gotta work and pay all of this money[

Monique: But I'm goin' to college anyway.

Tee: And it's the twentieth century and you'd think you could go to college for free. They should let people get an education for free.

Alice: It is the twentieth century but not for long.

Tee: [unint.] It gonna be a boring next century 'cause I don't think there's gonna be any jobs 'cause they cuttin' all the state money for jobs and people gonna be bored.

Jason: Cuttin' welfare, too. They said they was gonna cut people off.

Monique: Like, if I started on welfare now, I can only be on it for twenty one months. In this state, I would have to stop in twenty one months.

Alice: What do you think about that policy?

Tee: That's a shame.

Monique: No, that ain't because people is gettin' too lazy.

Tee: Oh, yeah. That's true sometimes, too, but[

[ct]

Monique: And look, people have more babies and they get more money. But now, now they [the government] is stoppin' it.

Tee: And now, the kids, when they be havin' babies and hey, wait, excuse me. Don't interrupt[

Monique: Wait, wait. Look, now, these grown-ups and some kids have a lot of babies and they tryin' to get extra money from the state. Now they [the government] stoppin' it. Now they stoppin' it, the limit of babies you can have.

Risha: And they only givin' you fifty dollars more each time you have a baby.

Jason: Excuse me. Now if you have over two children or is it three, you have to work and you have to stop welfare because they[

Tee: You gotta work. That's it.

Jason: Yeah. You have to work 'cause they not gonna give you welfare 'cause you have too many kids. You have too many kids for them to be payin'. And they noticin' now that people just havin' a lot of kids to get the money. So they said if you have over three kids or two, then they ain't gonna give you welfare 'cause we, we payin' you too much money and you just gonna go out there and waste it on drugs or somethin'.

Tee: People think welfare is bad.

Alice: What do you think?

Tee: I think it's good because people tryin', they tryin' but in a way I think it's right and in a way I think it's not.

Alice: Uh-huh.

Tee: People think it's bad because, they like, "your mother is on welfare" whatever, but they think um, 'cause it's bad because people, like they lazy or somethin'. They don't wanna have a job. But if people can't get a job, they can't get a job. (November 17, 1997)

Later that day the issue of welfare came up again in another discussion I was having with Janine, Tina, Veronica, and Jeter. The girls were discussing the kind of jobs they wanted to have when they were older.

Janine: I want to have a job so I can take care of my children and support them. Not have to be[

Jeter: On welfare.

Veronica: Yeah, you have to be on welfare sometimes 'cause ya can't afford to take care of ya kids. And I just wanna get a job and work and be all I can be. I don't wanna go out and be a prostitute, sell drugs, or nothin' like that.

Jeter: Yeah, instead of bein' too young and havin' babies.

Alice: Do you know a lot of girls or are there a lot of girls in the neighborhood who are young and having babies?

Veronica: There's a lot of girls who have babies and they're just young teenagers. I know there's some high school dropouts[

Janine: This girl I know, she had her baby when she was fourteen.

Veronica: Yeah, and I know this girl, she had her baby when she was twelve and she ran away[

Jeter: My cousin, she had her baby when she was twelve and she had to move to Puerto Rico.

[ct]

Tina: Um, a lot of teenagers get pregnant at young ages around my neighborhood.

Alice: Yeah, and what do they end up doing?

Veronica: They just end up droppin' out of school[

Tina: Some of their parents get upset and they kick them out and they have nowhere to go 'cause their parents can't take care of them and their baby. And so like a lot of babies could end up dying because of that and the girls drop out of school 'cause they have to try to take care of the babies. And then they have to get welfare.

Veronica: Remember that movie that had that um, that lady, that white lady and that Black lady that dropped her baby in the dumpster?

Janine: Sad. 'Cause she was on crack and she didn't know what to do. He kept cryin' and cryin' and cryin' and she wanted to go to the store. . . . So she put him in the garbage can and tried still to go to the store. But she got caught. Um, and she had to go to jail. Then, [unint.] then the baby started to cry and they took him out and they put him in the hospital[

Veronica: and in the hospital this white[

Janine: and they treated him and this white lady and she felt so sad 'cause of the baby and so she took him. Then he grew up and he was so good and then the lady, she stopped doin' crack. She got a good job and she fixed herself up. Then she found out who had the baby and she wanted to take him back and they had to go to court and she won. But the little boy didn't like her. He liked the white lady 'cause he was so used to her and he wouldn't go.

Veronica: And he started cryin' when she took him away from the white lady so at the end, she was like, she was like, um, "You gotta take," the Black lady said, "You gotta take care of him 'cause I wasn't the one there when he was growin' up." 'Cause he wasn't even one yet when she dumped him in the garbage can.

Janine: He was a couple of months. He was just been born.

Tina: Yeah, so ya have to stay away from drugs and not have babies so young and everything 'cause you can't take care of the baby and then you could go to jail or go on welfare.

Veronica: But you should get help, too. You shouldn't be left out on the streets. That's not good either and not fair to people.

Tina: Yeah, that's why they need to have welfare and stuff so that people don't end up homeless and then they feel bad and then they do bad things. (November 17, 1997)

The girls continued to discuss the hazards of teen pregnancy and the losses young girls incur when they "play around" and get involved with boys and drugs. They clearly recognized the dangers of both and were confident that if they "stay in school and get good grades" they would sidestep the problems they see other girls their age encounter as they negotiated teen pregnancy, welfare, parents, drugs, school, and the host of other issues that arise for young people living in their community.

Two weeks after this discussion with Janine, Jeter, Veronica, and Tina, I heard similar sentiments about teen pregnancy from Tonesha, Bart, Bill, and Troy.

> *Tonesha:* It is a disgrace how teenagers go out and they have all these babies and that's[
>
> *Bart:* I know.
>
> *Tonesha:* They should have them when they be older.
>
> *Alice:* Why do you think so many teenagers have babies?
>
> *Bart:* 'Cause they be thinkin' like, they all big, like girls, like think they're old enough to do stuff like that.
>
> *Alice:* Are there a lot of teenagers in this neighborhood who have babies?
>
> *Everyone:* Yes.
>
> *Alice:* Why do you think that is? Bart says it's because the girls think that they're old enough and they can do that. But what about boys?
>
> *Chesterfield:* 'Cause I think they're curious and they um, and they just feel good about it if they, well, you know what I mean.
>
> *Bart:* They want to experiment.
>
> *Alice:* Chesterfield, you can say that word. It's not a bad word.
>
> *Chesterfield:* Yeah, but I don't like saying it.
>
> *Alice:* You don't? OK. Can I say it then?
>
> *Chesterfield:* Yup.
>
> *Alice:* So you think they are curious about having sex but they don't really think about having a baby?
>
> *Chesterfield:* Yup, it just sorta happens and they don't think about it. . . . .
>
> *Tonesha:* I just think that teenagers, thirteen to sixteen, they can't hold their hormones. I think it's because, it's because the boys is involved too, because the boys, the boys are like eighteen to nineteen years old. Why these girls are thirteen to fourteen years old! And that's a shame right there. 'Cause that's like, that's like, if a person was twenty and a girl was like nine or ten years old, that's like sexual harassment right there. All that stuff. That's a disgrace. That needs to stop. But I don't think I could stop the hormones 'cause that's in their body.
>
> *Alice:* You think that happens with girls and boys?

Tonesha: Yeah.

Alice: And so do you think like Chesterfield that they don't really think about the consequences of it?

Tonesha: Yeah, 'cause like, you can, you can die bein' young and givin' birth. And havin' a baby is like nine months with a little thing in your stomach. That's, I just can't deal with it. . . . And, oh, teenagers. Shorts up to here that show your butt. That's nasty. In the summer, they're a disgrace. Poom-poom shorts come up to your butt and I didn't want to say the other word. . . . It's, I can't say it. OK. I'll say it. Coochie-cutters.

Bart: I saw this girl, she had a skirt on, it was all the way up to here. Like all the way up to here. The end of it.

Chesterfield: I saw this man yo', his shirt was like this. You could see all his hairs and his stomach.

Alice: So men dress like that too, huh? It's not just girls.

Tonesha: I know this is not true to be scared by this, but it scared my mind because I was um, watchin' the TV, and on this channel they were showin' these people naked, but I just kept on clickin'. That's nasty. . . . That's just not good. These girls havin' babies. Soon as they have the babies, that's the end of their life, goin' to school and everything. They can't go to parties, nothin'. Welfare and nothin'. (November 30, 1997)

The participants' perceptions about welfare and teen pregnancy emanate from their experiences as young people living in an inner-city environment. Equally important, their views about social issues are informed to a large extent by the media and the dominant discourse in the United States that portrays them, and people like them, as undeserving recipients of public assistance. Due, in part, to their age, but more importantly to the power of the national condemnation of "welfare mothers" in shaping people's perceptions, the participants blame individual teenagers for making poor decisions and "endin' up on welfare." Their judgments of their friends, relatives, and neighbors are skewed by their lack of knowledge about how the welfare system functions in this country, the accusatory tone of the American people regarding people "on welfare," and the depiction in the media of welfare recipients as being predominantly poor and Black. As Gilens suggests, 65 percent of poor Americans shown on television news are Black, while 62 percent of poor Americans portrayed in news magazines are Black. This "despite the fact that African Americans constitute only 30 percent of welfare recipients and only 27 percent of all poor Americans" (Gilens 1999:3).

The participants live in a sociopolitical climate that dehumanizes their mothers, aunts, cousins, and sisters, by promoting the myth that welfare only wears a Black face. As Dill, Zinn, and Patton argue, "This occurs in part because racial animosity and suspicion remain a fundamental (and largely unaddressed) aspect of U.S. culture" (1999:282). The attack on "welfare mothers" also occurs because we live in a culture that "confers honor on those who hold jobs over those who are outside the labor force. Independence and self-sufficiency—these are virtues that have no equal in this society" (Newman and Ellis 1999:178).

Within the PAR process, we opened up spaces to address the meanings of independence and self-sufficiency, of animosity and suspicion. The participants and the research team engaged in multiple conversations over the course of the project about teen pregnancy, how boys and girls dress, who should be on welfare and who should not, and what constitutes work. We did not resolve these issues. Yet by speaking about complicated and complex issues that are not usually addressed in the public spaces inhabited by urban youth, and by posing questions that generated new knowledge about the complex nature of people's lives, we afforded the participants the opportunity to more fully explore the various dimensions of welfare, race, and what it means to "be somebody" within the context of United States society.

"We Look Up to People"

How the participants define what it means to "be somebody" and how they envision the process of "getting a degree," are closely related to the role models that they admire, look up to, and want to emulate.

> *Monique:* Oh, we got the singers [on the collages] because like, everywhere you go you hear different music like, Busta Rhymes, Usher.
> *Tee:* Lil' Kim.
> *Monique:* We have Missy up there. She's a singer. And Brandy.
> *Tee:* And we got the basketball players because basketball players in the community, in some communities, we look up to the basketball players.
> *Jason:* We look up to sports.

Alice: Why do you look up to people in sports?

Tee: 'Cause we like how they play and what they do and they make a lot of money.

Monique: They make a lot of money.

Alice: Is that something that you want to do?

Tee: Yup.

Jason: Or they could grow up to be a movie star.

Monique: Yeah, they could look up to a star. They could look up to them or a singer, anybody. You know, some um, big boys look up to other big boys.

Tee: Like, suppose like, she looks up to you, and then she wanna do what you do. But like, they do bad things like, suppose my father he be doin' drugs and stuff that makes me wanna do drugs.

Alice: So what's going to keep you from doing that from looking up to people that[

Tee: Do bad stuff?

Alice: Yeah.

Tee: Try to get a good education and do our own stuff. Make your mother proud and stuff. (November 17, 1997)

A similar conversation took place the following week with another group of participants.

Bill: The people that um, you look up to play basketball. Like um, kids playing basketball.

Alice: Are there a lot of kids playing basketball around here?

Mase: Yeah, it gives them something to look up to.

Tonesha: I look up to successful people.

Troy: They [athletes] get paid good money.

Chesterfield: They're really good at something.

Mase: Yeah, they be like usin' their talents to amuse everybody. To like um, to like make everyone like them and make them happy and like, amuse them and stuff.

Tonesha: I don't [look up to them]. I look up to successful people.

Alice: So why do you think sports people are not successful?

Tonesha: 'Cause there's other things you can do with your life.

Mase: But, basketball, like, you get paid a whole mess of money for playin' that.

> *Tonesha:* Yeah, and lawyers do, too.
>
> *Alice:* Do you think about success as making money?
>
> *Mase:* Yup.
>
> *Tonesha:* Well, I would like to grow up to go to college and get a degree or somethin'. And I will like to be a lawyer because I would like for all the violence and stuff out here, I would like help innocent people and stuff like that. Not go against them, but help them. So, I don't think y'all should look up to them people [athletes]. Well, you could look up to them if you want because they make a lot of money. But still, you could still be um, another successful whatever. But you could still go on with your life, like as being a doctor, a lawyer, a secretary, and all that other stuff. Mechanic and stuff. Sports you can play everyday. That's what I think. I think everybody here at this table, the boys, look up to like, basketball, sports, sports, sports.
>
> *Bill:* I look up to wrestling.
>
> *Mase:* Wrestling? That's all fake.
>
> *Bill:* Doesn't matter if it's fake. They still get paid for it. (November 24, 1997)

A handful of girls aspire to and are determined to be professionals (such as teachers, lawyers, businesswomen, and doctors). Another group of girls want to be singers, models, and actresses, make lots of money, and travel. While conducting the community resource inventories with fifteen girls during the first year of the project, we asked them: "What are some skills or things that you would like to learn?" The majority of the girls' answers demonstrated their desire to work with people. Rebecca wanted to "learn how to work on the human heart because I want to become a doctor"; Flanango wanted to "counsel kids"; Monique wanted to "learn about another person and what they do"; and two of the girls wanted to be lawyers. A few of the girls were interested in learning particular sports (such as figure skating, karate, and swimming). Many of the girls also wanted to learn more about math, science, and social studies.

We asked the same question—"What are some skills or things that you would like to learn?"—to sixteen boys during the first year of the project. As Tonesha noted in the preceding discussion, the boys "look up to sports, sports, sports." Fifteen of the sixteen boys said they wanted to learn some type of sport (such as basketball, karate, baseball, or boxing). Some of them also wanted to learn how to work on machines, computers, and bikes. (Mase is an avid bike rider and spends much of his time riding through various neighborhoods on his bike—a bike that has no brakes. The boys purposely disengage the brakes so they can have "more fun.") Although the boys also mentioned things like wanting to "write cursive better" (Chesterfield), wanting to "study astronomy" (Tee), and wanting to be an "actor because I always wanted to be on TV" (Mikey), their main focus was learning how to play a sport.

The emphasis on sports and looking up to sports figures is not surprising. The boys' belief that playing basketball would provide them with money, fame, and success, and the fact that admiring basketball players "gives them something to look up to" is based in part on what they see around them and the portrayals of advertising and other media outlets. As Kelley points out,

> Nike, Reebok, L. A. Gear, and other athletic shoe conglomerates have profited enormously from postindustrial decline. TV commercials and print ads romanticize the crumbling urban spaces in which African American youth must play, and in so doing they have created a vast market of overpriced sneakers. These televised representations of "street ball" are quite remarkable; marked by chainlink fences, concrete playgrounds, bent and rusted netless hoops, graffiti-scrawled walls, and empty buildings, they have created a world where young black males do nothing *but* play. (1997:44)

Kelley's description of the public play areas in which inner-city youth play basketball closely resembles the places where the young people I work with play basketball, hang out with friends, and dream of being the next Michael Jordan. What the television ads and the commercials do not show, and what athletic companies fail to make known to the thousands of inner-city youth who buy their sneakers, is the fact that the vast majority of urban youth will never play college or professional basketball. Nonetheless, the male participants retain a sense of hope and idealism about their "careers" in sports. Their idealism may help them cope with their daily lives. Yet it also keeps them from imagining themselves as being capable of succeeding in other careers or work-related areas—an issue we addressed in a more intentional way during the second year of the project (see chapter 6).

Although the participants' career interests appeared to fit traditional patterns of occupations that are usually associated with females and males (the girls wanting to work in the helping professions and the boys wanting to play sports), such an analysis obfuscates the more nuanced dimensions of the participants' curiosity about various careers and their desire to learn more about different occupations. By analyzing the information gathered throughout the first year of the project with regard to education and the world of work, the participants entertained new ideas about the kinds of careers they wanted to investigate, which led to the development of a career exploration program and the creation of a shadowing program. Both of these assisted the participants in exploring their ideas about "what they want to be when they grow up" and are further explored in the following chapter.

Concluding Reflections

As the data reveal, the participants were hopeful, eager to learn, and were openly exploring a host of ideas and dreams about their futures. They maintain a firm belief in the American dream even when they do not see it manifesting itself within their own families and communities. In their daily lives, the participants see many of their neighbors and relatives working full- and part-time jobs in order to pay the rent, purchase food and clothing for their families, and ensure that their children are cared for. What they do not see in their daily lives are their friends and relatives becoming doctors, nurses, lawyers, policewomen and policemen, sports megastars, successful rap singers, and professional models—the professions that they are interested in pursuing and the ones that they associated with the American dream.

In some respects, the participants know too much. In other respects, they don't know enough. They are at an age in which they still retain a sense of naiveté about what lay ahead of them in terms of high school and pursuing a higher education. Even though they do not see many versions of the American dream manifested in their lives, they continue to believe that if they "don't act stupid" and as, Tee said, "put our heads to good use," they will succeed. In the meantime, educators, psychologists, researchers, politicians, and a majority of the American public continue to tell them that if they work hard, get good grades, stay in school, and don't do drugs they will succeed.

We hold education up as the beacon of hope, fueling the belief that if students succeed academically, they can be anyone or anything they desire. We do all this while simultaneously cutting budgets for public schools, increasing funding for vouchers and the privatization of schools, designing charter schools, eliminating affirmative action policies, refusing to repair unsafe schools, failing to fill teaching positions in urban areas with qualified teachers, holding on to low expectations for poor children and children of Color, and overall, ignoring large segments of the population.

Given those realities, it remains to be seen if Tee, Tonesha, Mase, Melinda, Janine, and the other participants will actually graduate from high school and go on to further their education. They are at an age where they still retain a degree of idealism that I hope will sustain them as they continue throughout their adolescence. Yet idealism, though valuable, is not enough to change the educational landscape and make it possible for them to succeed in achieving their dreams. As the participants told me many times during the project, "We need adults around once in a while to help out with the things we don't know yet or that we can't yet do" (Mase). I, too, hope that we are "around once in a while" so that we can learn from and with urban youth about "things we don't know yet or that we can't yet do." I hope those of us who have contact with voting machines, telephones, pens, computers, faxes, and keys to offices that hold a wealth of information about how we can transform education, take their request seriously and move a little faster to create opportunities for these young people to fulfill their dreams, realize their hopes, and discover for themselves what it means to "be somebody."

6

■   ■   ■   ■   ■   ■   ■   ■   ■

Exploring Racism, Whiteness, and Careers with Urban Youth

IN LATE SPRING 1998, Jen and Nicole came to me with an idea for a career exploration program (CEP) they hoped to develop with the participants over the course of a semester. Jen and Nicole were two graduate students in the school psychology program who wanted to fulfill the requirement for their master's theses by engaging in the PAR project. Jen was a graduate assistant in the department I belong to and had worked closely with me on a number of projects over the years. She had also been involved in a host of activities with the participants during the PAR project.

Jen and Nicole were excited about the idea of collaborating with the participants in developing a program designed to assist urban youth in thinking about future career opportunities. After listening to Jen and Nicole's ideas, I suggested that they visit the participants, describe some of the activities they wanted to engage in with them in terms of exploring educational and career issues, and invite the participants to frame the project in ways that would be most useful to them as middle school students.

As Jen and Nicole reflected on how to frame a participatory CEP, I reminded them that an important aspect of PAR is the attention to the daily lives and the subjective realities of the participants. Creating predetermined exercises and imposing a preset recipe for exploring particular issues runs the risk of constraining the emergence of the participants' experiences. Although I understood the need to define certain goals for the group sessions and to develop a framework from which to proceed in their investigation, particularly due to the fact that they had to write an institutionally required proposal for their theses, I cautioned Jen and Nicole against perceiving their proposal as fixed. Rather, we talked at length about the underlying principles of PAR and agreed that the *process* of engaging in the CEP was as important, if not more so, than the product. Jen and Nicole agreed and assured me that they were flexible about the schedule, anticipated the need for modifications to the program, and fully supported the idea that the participants be the primary designers of the career exploration program.

As the CEP evolved, it became apparent that Jen and Nicole were not as flexible as they had originally stated. Like me when I first attempted a PAR project as a doctoral student, they failed to see that reading about PAR and discussing the various dimensions of PAR are drastically different from the actual process of engaging in a PAR project. Jen and Nicole were immediately afflicted with the urge to move quickly (they needed to complete their theses), and to control every facet of the project.

I discussed my concerns about how I saw the CEP evolving with Jen and Nicole many times during highly charged team meetings—meetings usually characterized by one or two emotions: joy or despair. The research team for the CEP (which also included Amy, a student in the elementary education program who chose to participate in the PAR project as part of her coursework) either came into the meeting smiling and telling me that the group session had been "great," or they came in telling me that the session had been a "disaster" and they felt like they were baby-sitting. As they described their sessions, it became clear that their feelings about the group sessions were directly linked to the participants' behavior. If the participants did what Jen, Nicole, and Amy wanted them to do, the team members felt that they had done a good job and could assure themselves that what they were doing was important, well-received, and making a difference in the lives of the participants. But if the participants didn't do what Jen, Nicole, and Amy expected them to do, they felt like failures. When the participants did not live up to their expectations, the team became angry, discouraged, confused, and began to doubt whether they were "doing the right thing."

In our team meetings, Jen and Nicole discussed their concerns about what was happening in the CEP sessions as well as their reluctance to give up control over what they deemed "a chaotic process." At that point in the CEP program, Jen and Nicole realized that some of the participants were uninterested in the activities they had planned. When a few of the participants mentioned that they were thinking of quitting the program altogether, Jen and Nicole realized that if they were going to engage in a PAR process, they had to stop insisting that the participants do it *their* way on *their* timetable.

For Jen and Nicole, the letting go process was a slow one. Over the course of the next few months, they continued to experience moments of panic, "giving up control, going along for the ride, and not always having hold of the steering wheel" (Marecek, Fine, and Kidder 1997:634). Yet, in surrendering their need to control *for product*, Jen and Nicole were better able to engage *the process*. Equally important, they learned that, given the opportunity, young people can and will create spaces for themselves in which they can effectively speak to issues that concern them.

Two examples of the participants speaking to issues related to careers and the world of work, which were not defined in Jen and Nicole's original outline for the CEP but figured prominently in the program and in the overall PAR project, are described below. Both issues—racism and future career goals—were constant themes in the PAR project and, as the data reveal, are salient issues in the participants' lives.

"A Lot of People Think We Can't Do Anything"

Jason, who has a Puerto Rican father and a European American mother, made an insightful observation about the relationship between race, racism, and work during one of the career exploration sessions.

> *Jason:* Other people can have like careers and jobs, too. Not only people like us [light skinned], our color, like African Americans can have jobs, too. Um, 'cause some people think that like other people can't make it. Like, um[
>
> *Tee:* That Black people can't get jobs.

Jason: Yeah, think that Black people can't get good jobs.

Nicole: Who thinks that?

Group: The racist people.

Nicole: Why do you think people think that?

Mase: Because they think they are better than them. They think 'cause they are better than us[

Tee: They racist. This is what they are trying to say. Some people think that Black people, they're like bums, or whatever, they don't[

Tonesha: We don't think that it's, like just white people. It's all kinds of people. It could be Black against Black, white against white, Chinese against Chinese.

Tee: Some racist people don't like Blacks because they think that Blacks can't do nothin'. So we can't get to have careers or whatever. We can't get to that place that they're at. So they're tryin' to say that they're better than Blacks.

Mase: That's right, man.

Tee: We can get, we are just like equal like any other people.

Tonesha: Just because people live in the projects don't mean that they can't get a job.

Tee: We can get the same job they can get.

Mase: That's right, brother.

Tee: You can live in the projects or the rich houses, the apartments or whatever we can still get the same job.

Mase: That's right, we have pride.

[Group starts clapping]. (November 2, 1998)

After this conversation took place, Jen, Nicole, and Amy arrived at the team meeting excited about experiencing what they had read about in the PAR literature. By developing relationships of trust with the participants, and by cocreating space for the expression of their concerns, the team members felt they were engaged in a cyclical process of knowledge construction and reflection. In this instance, the participants brought the raw, often unexpressed knowledge about themselves as young people of Color, vis-à-vis the eyes of "the other," into the open. They did so with three white females who, unbeknownst to them, were eager to incorporate the young peoples' experiences with racism into their goals for the project but were not sure how to tackle a topic that "felt" unapproachable to them.

The team members and I discussed strategies for linking the participants' discussion about racism to the career exploration program. The participants made it clear that they were aware of how racism intersects with job opportunities. The question for the research team was what to do with that information. Although I am the primary researcher and supervise the research team, I was not present at the CEP sessions. Nor was I responsible for implementing the activities, facilitating the group discussions, or making the on-the-spot decisions that need to be made when engaging in a PAR process. Although I felt that it was important for the members of the research team to follow up on the subject of racism with the participants, I was concerned about how Jen, Nicole, and Amy would approach it. I felt strongly that Jen, Nicole, and Amy needed to be self-conscious about their engagement in the research process and attend to their assumptions and beliefs about racism and how those categories of meanings informed their roles in the project. Yet, from my own experience, I understood that reflecting on personal issues about whiteness, privilege, racial identity, and how being white informs participation in a PAR project can be a challenging and difficult experience (McIntyre 1997; McIntyre and Lykes 1998).

At times, I wanted to "take over" their project, afraid that the team members were not ready to address racism in a critical way and that somehow, albeit inadvertently, they would be unable to clarify the complexities of racism with a group of twelve- and thirteen-year-old adolescents of Color. I was also concerned that the team would not adequately address Tonesha's comments about racism, that "it isn't just about white people." I felt that the team was ill-equipped to address the fact that intergroup and interethnic conflicts are created and maintained within a larger system of whiteness which sets the stage for hatred, mistrust, and discrimination between and among ethnic and racial groups.

I discussed my concerns with Jen, Nicole, and Amy. In turn, they discussed theirs with me. We each took time to write about our feelings and reflect on how we could most effectively address the issue of racism within the career exploration program. Through our discussions and self- and collective reflections, it became clear that the research team was afraid "to say anything in case what we say is wrong" (Nicole). What resonated in our team meetings was a feeling of shared reluctance by the team members to engage in a critical conversation with the participants about racism. Even though Jen, Nicole, and Amy were initially excited about the fact that the participants had initiated the discussion (it made them feel that the participants trusted them), they dreaded the idea of facilitating any further discussions on the topic.

Through reading, writing, reflecting, and engaging in critical dialogue among group members, we worked through some, though not all, of the team members' anxieties. Over time, Jen, Nicole, and Amy recognized that addressing racism within the PAR experience was a teaching-learning process in which they could learn, and unlearn, racism from privileged social locations that heretofore had prevented them from effectively addressing the issue of racism both in their personal and professional lives.

After further discussions, Jen, Nicole, and Amy decided to meet together and formulate a new set of ideas and questions that would facilitate a conversation with the participants about the relationship between racism, education, and the world of work. For example, they invited the participants to view the ABC film *Eye of the Storm*, about a white teacher examining racism and prejudice in an all-white third-grade classroom. Following the film, Jen, Nicole, and Amy discussed the effects of racism and discrimination on one's learning and one's interpersonal relationships with the participants. Equally important, Jen, Nicole, and Amy made room for the participants to discuss and name the racism and discrimination they experienced in their daily lives without trying to interrupt, control, or abort the conversation.

Below, I present a lengthy excerpt from one of the CEP group sessions which again reveals how PAR provided an opportunity for both the members of the research team and the participants to explore the meanings they attached to racism and whiteness and how both systems shape and inform their daily lives.

Jen: Jason, do you remember there was a picture of two people graduating from high school or college on your collage?

Tee: Yeah, and that we talked about how Black people can't get jobs.

Mase: I don't know 'cause we're not different than anybody else.

[ct]

Rebecca: [who is Puerto Rican and European American] I think that everyone thinks that Black people are bad and you have to stay away from them.

They are bad. They are no good. And they don't realize that they are just the same as everybody else just a different color and it really doesn't make no difference.

Tee: That's what some people think.

Jen: Why do you think people think that?

Rebecca: They just think that and they just don't care.

Tonesha: They think they better than everybody else.

Monique: Oh, slavery and history, yup.

[ct]

Tee: Some people think they are better than others.

Jason: Since, like in history way back Black people used to be in slavery. White people used to overpower them.

Tee: Some white people, not all.

Jason: Some white people used to think they could overpower Blacks and they still think they can do it.

Monique: They scared of Martin Luther King.

[laughing]

Rebecca: Whites think, "We're white. We are better than them. They were nothing but slaves. They will never accomplish anything" and a lot of Black people accomplish a lot of things that white people don't. A lot of people think that they are stupid. They can't do anything. They are ignorant, push 'em away, and they don't realize they are bringing more hatred and they are [unint].

Monique: You always do give a long speech.

Tee: Anyway, we all equal. Some people, when they keep on tellin' them that they start gettin' it in their head and start believin' that and there are gonna be wars.

Jason: Some Hispanic people hate white people, too. Some, because of the same thing. Some people just think they are better than a lot of people but it ain't true.

Blood: I ain't white. I am Puerto Rican, brother.

Tonesha: It is Blacks against whites though, too. A lot of Black girls do not like no white girls.

Tee: Blacks don't like whites because of the slavery days and our ancestors and all of that. There are even stories about[

[ct]

Tee: They just cut me off.

Tonesha: Be quiet and let me talk. My friend; her name is Sandy. So we went to the movies like two weeks ago, and these white girls came and to be specific, they are another species. They came in the movies and my friend was like, "Look at those girls. They think they can dress and all that." That could be another reason why there is all this[

Tee: hatred[

Monique: [who is Puerto Rican] But Black people think they the bomb, too.

Tee: Not all whites, some, some.

Monique: All whites.

Tee: SOME, SOME!!!

Monique: Yeah, OK., just like when I went to the arcade the other day. The girl rolled her eyes at me. I almost hit her but I didn't and I calmed my nerves down.

Tonesha: And she was white?

Monique: Yes, she was white and I was about to knock her out.

[ct]

Tee: There is a story about Martin Luther King or Malcolm X. One of them had a friend. They had a white friend and their father told them not to play with the Blacks. Some of them kids have their fathers telling them the same thing that was happening to Martin Luther King and Malcolm X. Same thing. Their parents are telling them that whites are better than them and everything. So that is how it is comin' up now. They are followin' the old days.

Jason: The other day I was at [the mall] and there was this white kid behind me and I was buying magic things, and um there was this white kid behind me in line and he said, "Excuse me." The cashier said it to me too, "Excuse me." He was like "Excuse me" and I just put down the stuff and left. 'Cause he just kept on bothering me and saying, "Excuse me."

Mase: Well, I would have stood there and said[

Tonesha: I would have been like "Excuse me. Excuse me" right back.

Mase: I'll excuse you with my fist.

Monique: Um, I was in downtown in a hair store. And this white man came in the store and bumped me.

Jen: He bumped you?

Monique: Yeah, he bumped me and he did not say excuse me, I said "Excuse me" and he kinda walked by. I almost hit him.

[laughing]

Nicole: Do you think that he intentionally did it because you were of a different race?

Monique: Yeah, yeah. And he didn't say "excuse me." He just bumped me.

Mase: He was white?

Monique: Yeah, he was white.

Tee: I was in [a grocery store] and I had my little brother and I had the buggy. I put him in the buggy and I am walkin' and I am rollin' by with the buggy cruisin', mindin' my own business whatever, just shoppin' with my grandmother and this lady, she started cussin' at me and my little brother so I went to get my aunt. We just rolled back over there. And the lady was like "I didn't do nothing to your son" and whatever.

Blood: She was white?

Tee: Yeah, she was white.

Rebecca: There was this old lady in the store and she is so racist and she says, like my brother was pushing me around in a cart, 'cause we kind of took it. We were playing with it 'cause it was fun and she was like, "Oh you damn spics. . . . I see you been hanging around with those f——ing niggers?" (November 16, 1998)

I listened to the participants' taped discussion and can attest to the level of energy and exuberance with which they engaged this topic. Like some of the discussions of violence presented in chapter 3, there were striking similarities across the participants' narratives and interpretations about their experiences with racism and discrimination. Their discussions were also infused with anticipation and high energy. Just as one participant finished a story about an experience with racism and discrimination, another would follow. The participants also affirmed each other's experiences by instantly and openly identifying with one another, thus refusing to dismiss each other's experiences as singular events unmediated by white racism.

As the data reveal, the participants are at an age in which they were more apt to *describe* how they are discriminated against by whites than to express how they *felt* about it (at least in my presence and in the presence of other members of the research team). Rather than explore their feelings of anger, rage, fear, and mistrust in the group sessions, they tended to respond to their experiences with whites much as they did when they responded to their experiences with violence. They became angry and frustrated and responded to those feelings with humor, offhand remarks, or by wanting to "knock her out." Their reactions are understandable given what has already been suggested in earlier chapters. By "acting phat" they often countered some of the damaging effects that come from living on the outskirts of mainstream society. Such a stance may be a protective strategy that helps them feel confident and in control in the face of racism and discrimination—at least when they are among white people. Yet it can also be self-limiting, by making it difficult for them to express deeper feelings about particularly painful life experiences.

"Not All White People Are Bad"

Although I consciously attended to the way my whiteness intersected with the PAR project, as well as with the way it mediated my relationships with the participants, it was (and is) rarely the focus of our group sessions. Yet in the early stages of the PAR project, I often wondered how they felt about participating in a long-term PAR project with a white person. So, one day, after "hanging out" with them for about a year and a half, I invited them to tell me how they felt about collaborating in a project with a white woman. They rolled their eyes at me (a normal reaction when they perceive my questions and comments as "dumb") and said,

Tonesha: Now what is this all about? What's she talkin' about?

Blood: How is, how do you feel whatever, hangin' out with a white dude? . . . . Ms. McIntyre, why was they givin' a lot of Black people and white people awards on TV yesterday?

Alice: What?

Blood: They was givin' *Malcolm X, Amistad,* they was givin' awards for those movies.

Monique: Yeah, they was talkin' about movies and slavery and stuff[

Janine: Yeah, *Amistad.*

Mase: And *Malcolm X.* They was givin' the whole movie awards.

Rebecca: They gave one to um, I think it was *Glory* with Denzel Washington.

Mase: I saw *Amistad.*

Alice: What did you think?

[ct]

Mase: I feel bad y'all.

Janine: But at least they got to go back to Africa.

Mase: The family was dead though.

Janine: No, they were sold to some people.

After a discussion about the award show and how Black filmmakers and entertainers address racism and slavery in film, I once again invited the participants to respond to my earlier question.

Alice: OK, so you didn't answer my question.

Mase: What question?

[laughter]

Rebecca: Do we have to answer?

Alice: Well, considering we have had many conversations about race and racism and since many of you have experienced racism, I was just wondering how you felt about me, as a white person, participating with you in a project that we may not even be doing if it wasn't for the consequences of racism and other things that make it difficult for you as young people.

Monique: It's fun. It's OK.

Tonesha: It's just some whites. It's just some of them who be thinkin' they're it.

[laughter]

Melinda: Not all white people though.

Blood: Yeah, you're cool, Ms. Mac. (February 22, 1999)

When we discussed issues of race and racism, the participants were usually quick to point out that "not all white people are bad." Recently, I reviewed the chapters of this book with them for their feedback and contributions. They each took turns reading brief summaries of each chapter and then we discussed issues relevant to the particular book section that was read. Mase read a summary of chapter 5.

Mase: One aspect of this chapter focuses on education and the difference in education between the poor and the rich, between the whities and[

[laughter]

Mase: I mean whites.

[laughter]

Mase: Whities or whites, whatever. I don't mean you. OK. Let's start again.

Tee: (whispers) Whities.

[laughter]

Mase was embarrassed by his use of the term "whities." He lowered his head and ignored the collective laughter directed at his word slippage. The rest of the participants laughed hysterically over what they considered a major faux pas on Mase's part. I smiled at Mase and reassured him that I was not offended by his terminology. He smiled back and continued reading the text.

A little over two months later, we christened the third year of the project by holding our first group meeting at the local McDonald's. The participants had been in school for one week by then. I invited them to join me and the members of the research team for a "working lunch" where we could talk about their summers, their new classes, and review the current status of the project.

As the participants ate cheeseburgers and french fries, I brought them up to date on the status of the cleanup project we had developed the previous year (see chapter 7). I informed them that we had still not heard from any city officials about our proposal to work with them to clean up particular neighborhoods in Ellsworth. Instead, I had been told by a City Council member that there was no room in the budget for trash receptacles and that some people in the city government "spoke too soon" when they told us that they would assist us in our undertaking.

I then explained to the participants how during the summer months the city beautified the area of Ellsworth that I live in—an area that did not need beautifying and that I describe in more detail in the next chapter. After further discussion, I asked them why they thought their neighborhoods were not being given the kind of attention that my neighborhood was. Monique immediately said, "'Cause y'all white." Immediately, a shocked expression came over her face. She covered her mouth with her hand while the rest of the participants engaged in collective hilarity over what she had blurted out. I walked over to her to put my arm around her— a gesture she interpreted as meaning I wanted to "high five" her—which I ultimately did. I reassured her that I agreed with her—that being white was one of a host of reasons why one area of Ellsworth was well-kept and other areas suffered severe neglect. Monique breathed a sigh of relief when she realized that I wasn't "mad" and said, "Whew! I thought I said somethin' wrong there."

Whenever the participants spoke about white people in our group sessions, they did so within the context of a good-bad dichotomy that, for them, was straightforward and made a great deal of sense. Some whites were good and some whites were bad. The white people who never said anything derogatory, who "liked Black kids," and who didn't "talk funny," were "good whites." The white people who stared at them when they entered a store, "talked nonsense," used racist comments, and thought "they're it" were "bad whites." The participants willingly described their experiences with white people to me and other members of the research team within the group context. Yet they did so only when they felt we would not be offended by their stories. In other words, their categorizations of whites let me, as a "good white," off the hook.

I am deeply aware of how easy it is for white people, particularly white educators, to perpetuate the good white–bad white dichotomy. Embracing such a belief dilutes a critique of the multiple ways in which white people—both "good" and "bad"—perpetuate, and benefit from, white racism. Similarly, it relieves "good whites" from taking responsibility for racism (McIntyre 1997). I am also deeply moved by and concerned about how the participants negotiate race talk with me and the other members of the research team. Although I appreciate their concern that I will be offended by stories of "bad whites 'cause we don't want you thinkin' you're one of them," it is disconcerting to watch a group of young people of Color having to construct narratives of racism and discrimination while simultaneously having to remain conscious of how they might offend a white person while doing so.

I experienced, and continue to experience, a reconstruction of my own whiteness as a result of my participation in this project with this group of young people. Their trust in me and their continued efforts to collaborate with me in the goals of this project have affirmed for me PAR's ability to create spaces for rich and critical dialogue between urban youth of Color and "old" white educators. In a very real sense, these spaces have generated a process of transformation for all of us, "a process that we are living through, creating as we go" (Maguire 1993:176).

"We Want to Go to the University"

In thinking about work, careers, and schooling, the participants expressed an interest in returning to the university, both to partake of the student cafeteria (a place they have grown very fond of) and to meet some of the people who work at the university and listen to them discuss their various career choices. In particular, the participants wanted to speak to a lawyer, an athlete, someone who was in charge (they invited a Dean), and a person from the admissions office (they wanted to know how you get into college). Although the idea of visiting the university was not in the initial proposal crafted by Jen and Nicole, they both realized that it was important to incorporate the participants' ideas in a concrete way into the overall PAR project. Thus, they and the young people mapped out a trip to the university which included a tour of the new athletic center, a discussion session with the panel of speakers mentioned above, and lunch at the cafeteria. The participants designed cards inviting the selected panelists to a group session and also generated a list of questions which were then used to initiate a group discussion with the panelists.

The participants enjoyed the tour of the athletic center, relished the choice of food at the cafeteria, and engaged the panelists in a lively discussion, asking them about what they had wanted to be when they were young; what had brought them to the university; whether they were ever on the honor roll; what their best strengths were; whether they got nervous talking in front of people; what kind of work they did in college; what their expectations of life were; what they had to do to get where they were today; and whether they liked their jobs.

The participants left the university wanting to know even more about various professions. They also wanted to further explore how to prepare themselves for higher education. When they met with Jen, Nicole, and Amy the following week, they discussed some of the things they had learned during the trip and throughout the CEP program: "You gotta work really hard to get where you want to go" (Melinda); "It ain't easy to be what you want to be" (Jason); "I learned that it takes time to get where you are, where you want to go" (Mase). The participants also generated a list of qualities they felt they needed to possess if they were to succeed in a chosen career.

Monique: You can't be lyin'. You can't lie 'cause you ain't gonna get nowhere lyin'.

Risha: Be on the honor roll. Get a good education. Try and stay out of jail. Have to be healthy and you can't be shy.

Monique: You have to dress appropriately.

Jason: Get a scholarship. Get good grades.

Janine: Hard work. Finish high school. Be involved. Go to college. Go to graduate school. Be a leader. Respect what you do. Build bridges to the highest point. Follow your expectations. Do what you think is interesting. Respect yourself and others.

As the data reveal, the participants stressed education, self-respect, leadership, and honesty as the salient aspects of what they had learned in the CEP program. The qualities they chose as being significant contributors to their success in later life were some of the basic tenets for "makin' it" in this country—qualities that the participants had little doubt believing in. They were certain that if they possessed those characteristics, they would succeed in life and achieve their stated goals.

As revealed in chapter 5, the participants have an optimistic attitude about themselves and their ability to "be somebody" in the world—an optimism that I find both heartening to witness and unsettling to ponder as they mature and graduate from middle school. On the one hand, the participants *have* to believe that they have a future beyond much of what they see around them. As Way argues, what would it mean for young adolescents like Tee, Tonesha, Janine, and Mase "to believe that their futures would reiterate the ones they see around them" (1998:171)? On the other hand, as young adolescents, the participants have yet to fully recognize and experience the full implications of racism, classism, and other structural constraints on their ability to gain access to the professions of their choice.

Many researchers and scholars (see, for example, Fine 1991; Fordham 1996; MacLeod 1995; Pastor, McCormick, and Fine 1996; and Way 1998) who have "studied" urban youth suggest that, although resilient and sophisticated in their forms of resistance, most urban youth experience debilitating moments of disillusionment and despair when they have to face "the real obstacles that impede their investments in the future" (Leadbeater and Way 1996:9). Yet it is important to note that the populations the above researchers studied were young people between the ages of fourteen and twenty one. It is my experience that the group of twelve- and thirteen-year-old middle schoolers participating in this PAR project are more optimistic than their high school counterparts presented in the above accounts. This is due, in part, to the fact that the participants have not yet fully grasped how obstacles like sexism, racism, classism, SATs, high school tracking, overworked guidance counselors, lack of advanced placements courses, limited access to computers, and a host of other issues that are pertinent in one's journey from high school to the world of work will and do mediate their personal and academic lives. Nor have they reached a stage in their lives where they can analyze the "*discrepancies between what they are told they can achieve and what they witness as possible in their social contexts*" (Pastor, McCormick, and Fine 1996:28, italics in the original).

As the participants graduate from middle school, enter high school, and begin to recognize that it takes more than a consistently solid performance in school to "make it," they may lose some of their optimism. With an increased awareness of racism, privilege, and how one gains access to educational and societal resources, they may begin to understand that personal effort alone cannot guarantee success. As they progress through high school, they are also more apt to stop *describing* how they are denied academic and career opportunities because they are Brown and Black and living in low-income areas, and begin to actually understand that the price they pay for being who they are is much greater than they had once imagined. Internalizing that knowledge has powerful implications, not just for the way they envision their futures, but also for the way they live out their present day-to-day lives.

This is where PAR contributes significantly to the question of what we do *after* we have unearthed and named some of the obstacles that interfere, interrupt, and deny urban youth their rightful place in U.S. society. As Pastor, McCormick, and Fine argue, "Simply learning about social oppression can be problematic for young women (and men) of poverty or color, if they cannot imagine that their oppressive conditions can be interrupted and transformed. If young people see pervasive social inequity and its adverse consequences, but they cannot imagine transformation, such information may simply fold into a heap of hopelessness, cynicism, or alienation" (1996:29). As is clearly revealed in this book, PAR provided the participants with opportunities to see some of the adverse consequences of living in a low-income, inner-city environment and, once seen, to take action to improve community life. Linking the awareness of injustices to formulating actions to address those injustices may not eliminate the horrors that characterize many urban schools and communities, but it did increase the participants' knowledge about how to deal more effectively with their realities. It also helped these young people to "keep hope alive," as Jesse Jackson often puts it, which is just as essential to them as "good grades, hard work, and gettin' through school."

"I'd Like to Spend the Day with . . ."

As the third year of the project began, Kay, a university staff member who had worked closely with the participants and me in securing funding for the PAR project, felt that we could expand the CEP program by inviting the participants to spend a day shadowing someone who worked in a profession or at a job that was of interest to them. The participants liked Kay's idea. In preparation for the way that program might take shape, they and the members of the research team discussed a wide range of jobs and professions that might "fit" their interests, taking into consideration our geographical location, the age of the participants, access to the kinds of people they wanted to spend the day with, the availability of research team members to assist in coordinating the program, teacher support, school scheduling, parental consent, and other pragmatic concerns that needed to be worked out in order to make connections between and among diverse groups of people.

Each of the participants chose three types of people they wanted to shadow. Tonesha said, "My number one goal is to become a lawyer because they help people. I'll go with a lawyer. Then a model because they make great money, and then a superstar because that is a great position for me because I'm very athletic."

Bill read his list of people he wanted to shadow and told us that first he wanted to follow a male basketball player "to learn some moves." His second choice was to shadow a "One Time." Bill's third choice was to shadow a rap singer. After Bill had shared his list with us, I asked him for clarification about his reference to "One Time." The rest of the group immediately informed me that it meant the police. "One time. The police. Ya know, when there is one cop car, it is called one time. If there are two cop cars, two times, three cop cars is three times" (Blood). Monique continued with, "Yeah and five times means five cop cars which means narcs." I replied, "You forgot four times. What does four times mean?" "Four cop cars. That's all," she replied. I then asked them if it mattered how many police were in each car. Did it change the terminology? They rolled their eyes (a normal response to questions that indicated my ignorance of the commonplace in their neighborhood) and informed me that it had nothing to do with the number of police in the car. It was the number of cars that mattered. "For your information, Ms. Mac, if you do see a person in the back seat, that's not the police. That's the FBI." (Monique).

> Like we had a car outside our house 'cause the lady upstairs, her boyfriend killed someone, so I looked out my window and I knew they were detectives 'cause you can tell. So I slipped out of the house the back way and then went around another way and they were still there. And they stayed there all day just watchin' and we knew what they were. (Tonesha, June 7, 1999)

Blood wanted to spend the day with a basketball player. If that didn't materialize, he wanted to shadow a lawyer to "see how they work" or a doctor "because I want to see what they do in the hospital." Risha's first choice was to spend the day with a "nurse that takes care of babies because I like little babies. Then a police officer because they help people when people least expect it sometimes." If she couldn't be placed with a nurse or a police person, Risha wanted to spend time with a model "because I would like to learn how to model."

Mase preferred to spend his time with a basketball player, because "I like to play basketball, but I like flipping, too, so I could spend the day with a gymnastics person, too. Or, I could be with a doctor because I want to know how they work in the emergency room." Monique also wanted to shadow a model because "they make good money. But I would also like to be with a basketball player because I love playing basketball, or a graphic designer because that is what I am going to take up in high school." Jo-Anne also wanted to shadow a police person. If not a police person, she wanted to spend the day with a lawyer because "I want to know what kind of work they do or with a singer because I want to be a singer, too." Melinda wanted to help people by being a nurse or a psychiatrist and wanted to spend a day doing one of those things or shadowing a "CEO of a company because they build companies and I'd like to build a company." Janine only wanted "to be two things in life: a lawyer 'cause people shouldn't be doing wrong and lawyers can help them or a doctor 'cause they make people feel better. They risk their lives for someone else."

Rebecca told me that she would not participate in the shadowing program because "I'm not spending the day with anyone I don't know. I don't trust anyone. So, no thanks." I told Rebecca that I understood her hesitancy about spending the day with someone she didn't know and asked her if it would help for one of the other participants to join her. Or, if that did not work out, would she like to have a member of the research team, or myself, to spend the day with her? She declined the offers, saying, "No way. I'm not doin' it. I don't trust anyone I told you. You, yeah, but still. I don't want to be with a stranger all day." She did agree to tell me what she wanted to be when she graduated from college. Rebecca wanted to be a psychologist so she could "help the mentally ill who have so many problems and need the most attention." If she didn't become a psychologist, she wanted to be a high school biology teacher "because that is about science and the human body and studying the human body is so interesting." If those professions didn't work out, Rebecca would return to "what I wanted to be before I changed my mind to psychologist—and that is being a lawyer so I can help people in trouble who have no one else to fight for them." Rebecca also told me that she thought we should "talk about gender stuff next year when we do the shadowing program because so many men discriminate against women because we are female and because they still think that we should not have a state of mind and we should not be intelligent. They also think we should stay in the house and not work."

Acquiring knowledge about "gender stuff" and about how gender, race, and social class mediate education and the world of work are important areas of consideration in terms of how the participants negotiate the journey from school to work. Similarly, understanding how one's race, sex, and social class positions relate to one's access to certain careers is a significant contribution in the participants' efforts to "become somebody." As suggested earlier, the participants are still young adolescents and therefore do not spend their time dissecting the underlying nature of sexism, racism, and discrimination and how systems of privilege and oppression organize people's lives or mediate their career opportunities. Yet that is not to say that the information gleaned from the multiple discussions we engaged in has been wasted. An important contribution of PAR is that participants can develop a text that "can act as a template in later stages of development, when increased sophistication will allow the material to be recast fruitfully" (Garrod, Ward, Robinson, and Kilkenny 1999:xiv–xv). In the meantime, the participants and the members of the research team continue to engage in interactive processes that provide the basis for a more comprehensive understanding of the conditions that facilitate and constrain urban youth in their efforts to "be somebody" in U.S. society.

Concluding Reflections

McTaggart highlights the distinction between "involvement" and "authentic participation" in participatory action research. Authentic participation in research means that the participants share "in the way research is conceptualized, practiced, and brought to bear on the life-world" (1997:28). This is in contrast to participants who are merely "involved" in PAR and do not have ownership over the project, or do not actively contribute to all aspects of the research process.

As the data reveal, the participants didn't simply want to be "involved" in the career exploration program. They wanted to participate in its development and implementation. They had already been participating in the overall PAR process for a year prior to entering into a collaborative process with Jen and Nicole. Thus, they had a taste of what it was like to have some sense of ownership over their own learning. They had engaged in multiple discussions that increased their critical awareness about issues that were important to them. With that awareness, they had begun to understand how they could mobilize the resources available to them to address particular issues.

The data in this chapter (and throughout the book) also reveal the extent to which race is a principal variable in the participants' lives. Throughout the PAR project, the participants have described how racism is a factor in gaining employment, attending particular schools, getting into college, owning a "nice house, not like the ones around here," and living in a clean and safe environment. They have also discussed the role of white people in their lives. There are the white people who are "cool. Like this white boy who goes to the club. He don't act like those other white people who always got somethin' to say" (Monique). Then there are the "other white people"—the ones who "think they got it goin' on. Like they just make me sick. Thinkin' they all that" (Rebecca).

As we developed levels of trust with one another, the participants became more willing to speak with and to me and the other members of the research team about racism and whiteness, topics not usually discussed between youth of Color and white people. We, the members of the research team, became more willing to be self-reflective about our positionalities within the project. In addition, we became more willing to listen to what the participants had to say about racism and other subjects, and to link those conversations to the actions they wanted to take in order to address issues of concern to them.

In chapter 7, I describe the process we engaged in to address one of the gravest concerns the participants had and have about their community—"the trashy way it looks." Through joint knowledge construction and joint analysis about the participants' realities, we took steps to "make things better around here."

7

■　　■　　■　　■　　■　　■　　■　　■　　■

From Dialogue to Action

TO MOVE FROM CONSTRUCTING KNOWLEDGE about our lives and the issues that concern us to mobilizing ourselves to tackle those issues is one of the principal aims of a PAR project. Yet there is no blueprint in PAR for how groups formulate plans for concrete action. Each project is unique, embodying the characteristics, personalities, questions, concerns, and contexts of a particular group. Therefore, how action manifests itself within a PAR process is dependent on, and mediated by, a set of variables that are malleable, often unpredictable, and directly linked to the multifaceted nature of human beings. In this case, such action was also limited and constrained by educational institutions, government bureaucracies, funding organizations, and other social structures. Equally important, the human beings in this PAR project were twelve and thirteen years old, which put a particular spin on the decision-making processes that led to the collective action generated in this project.

The participants made decisions about what to do, how to do it, when to do it, and if doing it was going to have any effect on their lives by defining their concerns, developing the research tools to investigate those concerns, interpreting the data, and deciding whether to take new action or to move into further research. In this chapter, I discuss the gradual, cyclical movement that occurred when we switched from gathering information about the participants' experiences living in their community (phase 1), to reflecting upon the information they had discovered in that process (phase 2), to the formulation of action and intervention plans aimed at addressing their concerns (phase 3). I present some of the tug-of-war we experienced between *knowing* that there were actions we could take, however limited they may be, and actually *taking* those actions. In so doing, I illustrate how PAR enabled us to implement new learning, further our research, and cultivate a sense of agency and activism among a group of young people committed to "makin' it nice to live around here."

From Dialogue to Action: Resistance and Responsibility in Participatory Action Research

We began the second year of the project with a new set of challenges. First, the research team was reconfigured. Due to other commitments, the majority of the team members who had participated during the first year of the project had to leave it and were replaced by three new team members. Second, during the summer of 1998 eight of the participants moved out of the area or were transferred to other schools in Ellsworth. The remaining participants were placed in three separate seventh-grade classrooms, all of which had different class schedules. Different schedules meant there were different teachers at different times of the day.[1] Separate classrooms and new schedules also meant we had to find a new meeting place. No longer could we meet in Susan's classroom. The only remaining space was the school cafeteria—not the most intimate setting for the project, but a space nonetheless. We managed to hold onto this space even when other school events were held in the cafeteria during our scheduled sessions. Notwithstanding our surroundings, on most Tuesdays we could be found huddled in one corner of the cafeteria constructing knowledge together.

The levels and types of participation also changed during the second year of the project. We were no longer simply "talking about" the participants' concerns about the community. We were actually formulating ideas and learning how to take responsibility for what we wanted to see happen regarding some of the issues we had discussed the previous year. In addition, the participants were no longer under the guidance of Susan who had been a firm and powerful influence in their lives and who had been a part of many of the activities we engaged in during the first year of the project. Now the participants were "on their own" in many respects. They didn't have a teacher present prodding, pulling, and challenging them, as Susan often did, "to honor their commitment to this project and do what they said they were going to do." Although I certainly prodded, pushed, and challenged the participants at various points throughout the project, they knew that I was leaving at the end of the session. I may be back the next day, but I wasn't an ever-present figure in their day-to-day lives at school. Nor was I going to make sure that they completed this or worked on that for the next session. They were responsible for doing certain things from one session to the next and it was up to them, for the most part, to remind each other of what needed to be done and cooperate with one another in completing certain activities.

Numerous times throughout the project I reminded the participants that this was *their* project, these were *their* ideas—not mine—and that any notion they carried in their minds that I was the one who was "making" them do *anything* was a gross distortion. They didn't always like hearing that—nor did I always like to practice it. They were accustomed to being educated by being told what to do and how to do it. Although they often rebelled at being told what to do while in school, in many respects they had come to expect a hierarchical, authoritarian relationship with teachers and other staff members. Thus they were unfamiliar with how to question preexisting knowledge and had little experience taking responsibility for their own learning. They had been subjected to the traditional "banking" system of education (see Freire 1970, for a fuller discussion) that continues to dominate the way teachers teach and students learn in this country and results in many young people being unfamiliar with dialectical processes of learning.

In this PAR experience, the participants were confronted with a different way of learning and constructing knowledge. Here, they were invited to engage in a participatory, democratic process which required that they remain open to uncertainties, confusions, disagreements, mistakes, and the challenges that result from taking responsibility for the direction of a consciousness-raising process that leads to action. They needed to relinquish their need to be *spoken to* about their concerns and life experiences, and instead to *speak about* issues that were salient to them. Then, once spoken about, explored, and critiqued, they needed to address those issues in ways that felt right for them and that exemplified their desires, goals, and commitments.

As a classroom teacher for many years, I too had become accustomed to engaging in the teaching-learning process in particular ways. For example, when I became frustrated with Freirian pedagogy and the democratic process of learning, both of which I value in my classrooms, I "took charge" of the situation, the classroom, and the students. Therefore, just as the participants struggled with believing that they were responsible for the progress—or lack thereof—that occurred in the project, I struggled with believing that I didn't need to "take over" when I felt they were being irresponsible or inattentive to the project. As the data in this book reveal, I often resisted the urge to make unilateral decisions about project-related concerns, particularly when the participants forgot to do something or dismissed something as unimportant. It was at those junctures that I most needed to remember that the participants were twelve and thirteen years old. They were at a transitional age, addressing serious issues while also, negotiating adolescence. Therefore, one minute they were excited and eager to work on a certain aspect of the project. The next minute, they would be distracted by adolescent life, lose their enthusiasm for the activity we were working on, and tell me that they "just didn't care right now" about the problems at hand.

These shifts in attitudes and behaviors were not only evident in the participants. The team members experienced similar feelings at different points in the research process, fluctuating from being highly engaged in the day-to-day research process to being discouraged, frustrated, and convinced that they had made a mistake in choosing to engage in a PAR experience. Yet, even in the midst of these shifting and humanizing emotions—many of which mediated people's participation in a host of different ways—we managed to maintain, sustain, and collectively move in and out of creative processes of change. I describe one of those processes below, foregrounding how we developed and implemented a long-term, ongoing community cleanup project aimed at eliminating the "trashy way the community looks."

"We Can't Wait for Adults to Do It"

I don't want to live in a dirty community. I was at the library. One piece of paper takes three weeks to disintegrate. And like, more paper that's thrown out, just keeps on piling up and piling up and that stuff eventually disintegrates and goes to the dirt. Makes the dirt not very good. The air starts getting bad, then the dirt when it rains, the evaporation starts and the air comes up again. That dirty air comes into the sky and causes acid rain. So that one piece of paper that you threw down does all that stuff. (Monique, September 24, 1998)

One STEP (Save the Earth Program)

As noted in chapter 4, the participants encountered a whole new set of challenges when they decided to "do something" about the trash in their community. The action program that was created out of those challenges is described below.

When we returned to school in September, the participants requested that we schedule meetings for the as-yet-to-be-developed cleanup project *after* school (as opposed to during the school day) so that we could accommodate the career exploration program described in the previous chapter. We took a vote—as we do on *all* decisions that affect the group—and the unanimous decision was to meet every Thursday after school for two hours. I spoke to the seventh-grade teachers, rearranged schedules (no easy feat), and even discovered an empty classroom where we could hold our meetings. The participants were excited about the possibility of moving from dialogue to action and told me that if I supplied the snacks, they'd supply the ideas.

I supplied the snacks. Only a few of them supplied the ideas. Our first after-school meeting was attended by only three participants. The following week, five participants came to the meeting. The week after that, seven. I was somewhat discouraged by the turnout. Even though eight of the participants had moved or been transferred to other schools during the summer, the majority still attended the Blair School and repeatedly made references to wanting to come to the after-school meetings but for a variety of reasons were unable to attend. Sometimes, they simply forgot to come to a meeting; others waited outside until they were coaxed in and if that didn't happen, they turned and walked away. Some of the participants came to the meetings and simply sat and watched. Others came and immediately ran the meetings, engaging their peers in a variety of project-related activities. Some days the participants were ill. Some days they had to baby-sit their younger siblings or had other familial commitments. Some days they had a school event that took precedence over the project. Other days, the lack of attendance at meetings was the result of detentions, suspensions, or needing to stay after school and complete homework assignments. On two occasions, I arrived at the school prepared to meet with the participants and the building was empty. The school had early release days that I was unaware of.

After eight weeks of inconsistent attendance and participation, I offered to explore other possibilities for meeting times that would be more accommodating to the group. But those who were attending the meetings on a regular basis disagreed with the option of changing the time of the meeting, stating that "If they want to come they can come. If they don't, they don't. Sometimes, you can get more done with a few people anyway" (Mase). Mase's friends agreed and therefore the meeting time was not changed. As it turned out, the attendance fluctuated during the first few months of the project. Nonetheless, a core group of six participants continued to attend the after-school meetings and initiated what later became known as One STEP (Save the Earth Program). They created a logo for the One STEP group, decided to organize a schoolwide assembly in the spring of that year, and developed a list of people to write letters to, inviting them to participate and contribute to the program.

The participants had two goals. One was to inform the students and staff at the Blair School about the PAR project, paying particular attention to the One STEP program. Second, the participants wanted to invite the Blair School community and the officials from the city of Ellsworth to participate with them in cleaning up the community.

By the end of December 1998, the participants were excited about their progress, even though they felt it was taking "way too long." As Tee remarked, "I can't believe it took us a month to decide what a logo should look like." It was also during this time that I was invited to present aspects of the PAR project to faculty members and graduate students at a university research symposium. I asked the participants if they were interested in joining me at that event. I explained to them that if they chose to do so, we would need to decide together what we wanted to present, how we wanted to present it, and what questions, if any, we had for the audience. The participants agreed that "it would be a great opportunity to speak to people about our community." Yet not all of them were eager to "stand in front of a bunch of people we don't know." After two weeks of discussing the event, Blood, Tee, Mase, Melinda, and Janine decided that they wanted to "give it a try." Therefore, the six of us spent a number of sessions reviewing the data we had gathered and crafting a presentation that later became the framework for the schoolwide assemblies the participants organized the following year.

Janine, Melinda, Mase, Tee, and Blood presented their work at the university with a clear sense of purpose. Watching them stand before a group of graduate students and university faculty members and present stories about their lives was a deeply moving experience for me, and for them. They were articulate, poised, "dressed in their church clothes," and answered questions from faculty members and students with ease, confidence, and a clarity about themselves and the work they had done that was commendable. Their presentation exemplified the best of what can happen in a PAR project when we provide opportunities for young people to speak for themselves about their lives, their concerns, and the ways in which adults can assist them in realizing their hopes, dreams, and ambitions.

The process of developing a presentation for the university community also provided the participants with an opportunity to reflect on, analyze, synthesize, and make sense of the information we had gathered thus far in the project. The interpretive process assisted them in formulating their ideas, prioritizing the themes most salient to them, and organizing the data in ways that were congruent and supportive of their goals. In addition, by crafting a presentation for the university symposium, they were better able to shape the upcoming assemblies that are described below.

The One STEP Assemblies

When we returned to school after winter break, we faced yet another schedule change. The participants requested that we cancel our after-school meetings and meet during the regular school day. They had discussed the level of participation among themselves and as Tee said, "We thought that meeting after school would be a good idea. And it was. But now we've changed our minds because we want everyone to come. We should have told you earlier but we didn't want to let you down." I assured Tee and the others that they had not "let me down" and reiterated that this was a participatory project and that *every* decision was up for discussion. I also reminded them that *they* had chosen to meet after school and therefore, they could choose *not* to meet after school as long as we could work out a schedule with the teachers.

Once the new schedule was developed with the teachers and other staff members (again, no easy feat), we focused more intently on the ideas that had been formulated during the after-school sessions. The core group of participants took the lead and presented what they had developed over the prior months to the remainder of the group. Once presented, we began the process of deciding how the assembly would be organized, what its goal would be, and what we needed to do to prepare ourselves for the event. We returned to the data and discussed Chesterfield's idea of taking photographs of specific areas of the community that needed attention. We decided that once we had developed those photographs we would present them to the mayor and other city officials along with a request that trash receptacles be placed in those targeted areas. Within a few weeks, we took that walk and discovered that over a three-mile area there was "tons of trash" and only one trash receptacle. We developed our photographs and created a collage that was displayed at the two schoolwide assemblies—an idea originally brought to the group a year earlier when Collin had suggested we hold open houses with people so we could talk about the trash problem.

The participants also decided to hold two contests at the Blair School, the winners to be announced at the assemblies. The first contest was "The Trash Can Decorating Contest." Each class was invited to decorate a trash can. They could do so in any way they chose as long as it related to the environment. The three winning classes received framed certificates. Initially, the participants wrote to the mayor of Ellsworth and requested twenty seven trash bins which they wanted to give to the twenty seven homeroom teachers in the Blair School. The mayor's secretary telephoned me explaining that "Trash cans are expensive so we can't provide them to the school. But we can give you twenty seven recycle bins if you want those." When I informed the participants that we would not be receiving trash receptacles from the mayor but that we could have twenty seven recycle bins, they laughed. Mase said, "What are we supposed to do with blue bins that have writing all over them?" After a lengthy discussion about how to address the problem, we decided to purchase white kitchen wastebaskets (which we referred to as trash bins) for the contest. We also decided to accept the city's offer and gave the donated recycle bins to the teachers for classroom use.

The second contest was "The Cleanest Classroom Contest." The various classes had to keep their classrooms clean and be prepared for a surprise visit from an inspection team made up of members of the One STEP program. The winning classes were rewarded with a pizza party. In addition, the participants wrote and performed a skit and a dance highlighting the above issues.

As I write about this sequence of events, the process of developing and implementing the One STEP program and the One STEP assembly seems to have been orderly and well organized, and to have been completed without a great deal of resistance and confusion. Quite the contrary. For the most part, the participants and I, and the members of the research team, have always agreed on the main points of what we have tried to accomplish. It's the finer details that require patience, a willingness to compromise, flexibility, and a determination to persevere in the face of frustration, apathy, disagreements, and stubbornness. Both the team members and the participants engaged in their own forms of resistance throughout the decision-making processes that characterized this PAR project—resistance that often required a great deal of energy to overcome.

For example, during the initial stages of the One STEP program, the participants were convinced that the skit, as well as the dance they were creating, were going to be written, rehearsed, and "ready to go" by December. However, by December they had not written a word of the skit nor decided what kind of dance they would do or what type of music they would use. By February, the people who had decided to participate in the skit disagreed about who was responsible for doing what. They also convinced themselves that they were never going to be ready and were going to embarrass themselves if they went ahead with their plan. By early April, there was a written draft of the skit and eight people had volunteered to participate in it. Two weeks later, the draft was rewritten and only four participants wanted to be included in the skit. Three days prior to the assemblies, most of the participants wanted to opt out of the skit altogether because they were nervous, anxious, and did not want to embarrass themselves in front of their peers. Some said they would do the skit but not the dance. At one point, Tonesha said, "Fine. Forget y'all. I'm doin' a solo." Two days later at the dress rehearsal for the assemblies, seven of the participants were back in the skit and four were determined to do the dance.

Although I fully supported the participants' desire to perform a skit as a way to both inform the students and the staff at the Blair School about the project, as well as entertain the audience (and themselves), I let them know early on in the process that the skit was 100 percent their responsibility. I told them that I, and the members of the research team, would assist them in various ways to facilitate the implementation of the act, but they were responsible for writing the script, arranging rehearsal times, making sure the sound system was available, gathering props, and working with the other participants in integrating the skit into the overall presentation. There were times when I reconsidered my role in the creation of the skit, thinking that if I didn't intervene it would never materialize. But I also knew that if the participants wanted the skit to be a part of the presentation, they would work through their differences, take responsibility for developing the message inherent in the skit, and make sure that when the day arrived they were prepared to, as Tonesha stated, "show the people how talented we are." Ultimately, six participants performed the dance and the skit and they most definitely showed the audience how talented they were.

As a collective group, we also disagreed about which class had decorated the most creative trash bin. During one particularly long day, we struggled with a decision-making process that left me frustrated and the participants arguing about how many points each classroom should receive for their creations. Prior to voting on the winner of the contest, the participants developed the following criteria for judging the trash bins:

1. The design addresses the school and/or community environment.
2. The design of the trash bin is well presented.
3. The design on the trash bin is well thought-out.
4. The design is creative.

The participants then developed the following Likert scale for each category:

Poor	Blah	Fair	Great	Excellent
1	2	3	4	5

The class that received the greatest number of points would be the winner. The problem arose when the participants failed to be consistent about what constituted "poor," "blah," "fair," "great," and "excellent." During the initial thirty minutes of judging the bins, they took time to review each bin, read each category, discuss the pros and cons of each entry, vote, and transfer the points to large sheets of paper we had hung on the wall to keep track of the voting. However, after the initial wave of trash bins, they lost their focus and started to put more energy into voting for the class they most wanted to win than judging the bins fairly. They were also distracted by the earlier fight that had occurred between Jason and Blood (described in chapter 3) and were preoccupied with other activities we needed to accomplish before the upcoming assembly. They "took sides" over particular trash bins, yelled out numbers and phrases without much thought ("Ah, that one's a blah"; "No, I like it. Give it a 5"; "No way. I say a 2 or a 3"), and had a difficult time arriving at a consensus about which trash bin was the most creative and best exemplified the theme of the assembly.

I reminded the participants three times to think before they voted, to be fair about the judging, and to give each other a chance to discuss each bin. My reminders were ignored. I was frustrated with the way they were engaging in the activity and handed the magic marker to Rebecca and told her to take over the job of transferring the votes to paper. Then I slumped into a chair. I had reached the saturation point of shared decision making.

The participants continued to engage in a tug-of-war about how to judge the bins and what the criteria were for doing so. At that point, Vonnie took up the challenge of facilitating the judging and was able to refocus the participants, or at least keep them from yelling out random numbers aimed at a variety of trash bins. Shortly thereafter, I breathed a sigh of relief when I heard the school bell ring, indicating that the participants had to return to their homerooms for a short period of time. In retrospect, this provided all of us with a much needed break from each other and from the judging experience.

When we reassembled later that day, the participants were less distracted, I was less frustrated, and the judging process flowed with greater ease. Based on the imaginative and well-decorated trash bins that were completed by the student body, the participants changed the rules about having only one winner and decided that there would be multiple winners, representing three different grade levels.

As it turned out, the assemblies were a great success. During the two events, the participants expressed the need for individuals to stop littering and suggested that the students and staff of the Blair School "work together to keep our school, inside and out, clean and safe for everyone." Although the mayor and the other city officials the participants had invited to the assembly did not attend the event, the participants spoke to the students, staff, and other invited guests about their request that the city of Ellsworth become involved in their efforts to clean up the community by providing more trash receptacles in particular neighborhoods and by including young people in decision-making processes that effected their community. In a letter they wrote to the mayor, they stated: "We hope that the city of Ellsworth will use the students' designs on trash receptacles that we would like to see more of in our community." They also informed the mayor that "Another thing we would like to see is permanent signs in our community informing people that there will be a fine for littering. The city could use the students' designs in creating those signs, too." As Janine stated during the assemblies:

> We know that just putting trash bins throughout the community is not going to solve the problem. But having receptacles placed throughout our neighborhood will be a big help and we hope the city of Ellsworth and the people that represent us will do their part. We see Mayor Steffan on the news speaking about how he and the city want to "Keep Ellsworth Clean." He said that he is always willing to help the people in Ellsworth. We are some of those people and future children are depending on us. The mayor also said that everybody should do their part. That is just what we are doing. But we can't do it alone. We need everyone's help. The city will do its part and we have to do ours. We have to stop littering. (May 7, 1999)

There were other areas in the PAR project in which we wrestled with issues of power, control, and responsibility: who would write to the mayor; what streets we should cover in the neighborhood walk; what photographs we should use in a presentation; who would oversee the sound system during the assembly; who would complete the felt banner that hung on the stage; who would operate the slide projector; and, of course, what kind of bagels we would order for breakfast. Some decisions came easily. The power-sharing approach was effective and we reached consensus without discord. Other decisions required lengthy discussions so that the objections people raised could be worked out by revisiting a particular issue until it was resolved or until people felt comfortable with and accepted the final decision.

The opportunity to participate in decision-making processes and to take responsibility for the decisions made was an educative experience for all of us, but particularly for the participants. By engaging in multiple decision-making processes, mutual inquiry, problem solving, and actively seeking solutions for change, the participants identified and prioritized goals for themselves and for the overall project. Equally important, they learned how to engage in ongoing processes of reflection and action that spurred personal and collective change.

"If They Won't Come to Us, We'll Go to Them"

Following the schoolwide assemblies, we were both excited and exhausted. We felt that the assemblies had been a great success and were confident we had done an effective job informing the teachers and students about the research we had been doing for two years. The performance anxieties had disappeared and a strong sense of accomplishment filled the room that day. The participants were very proud of the work they had done and were eager to continue their efforts to clean up their community. They also demanded that I finally take them to an amusement park so they could "have some time to relax."

It was during this postassembly group session that we began to ponder what the next steps would be and how we would continue with the One STEP program, as well as with other aspects of the PAR project. In an effort to gain a clearer understanding of how the participants felt about the project thus far and how they would like to see the project proceed, I asked them to take a few minutes and answer some questions for me. Knowing that they didn't like to write, I rarely asked them to do so. Yet I wanted to "hear" how they felt and what they thought about particular aspects of the project. I didn't think that asking them to respond to my questions verbally in a large group would be as effective as individual written responses.

I explained to them that there were times when we engaged in large group discussions and some participants simply didn't have the chance—or didn't take the chance—to speak about their feelings, thoughts, experiences, and ideas. Often, we had very animated discussions and we began with one idea and before long we were on to another idea, listening to another story, or raising new questions. Therefore, I asked them to take the time to answer some questions that would help me to think about the past two years and assist me—and us—in framing the next steps of the project.

When asked what they had learned from participating in One STEP, some of the participants said, "I learned that by not littering I help make the earth a lot cleaner" (Melinda). "I learned how to take care of my community and what too much trash can do to the people in my community. And what pollution does to animals" (Janine). "Not to litter any more" (Bill). "That we can make a difference and that even if not everyone listens we could get to that one small group" (Rebecca). "Well, I learned that from being in this program you can do a lot of neat things like have assemblies and do a lot of other great stuff. I also learned that by littering it kills our environment" (Tonesha). "I learned not to litter because it is dirtying our community" (Risha). "Not to put trash on the floor and put it in a trash can" (Monique).

I asked the participants what they wanted to see happen to the One STEP program now that the assemblies were over. All of them wanted to see the program continue. Some of them suggested we travel to other schools in Ellsworth and inform students and teachers about what we were doing. Jo-Anne thought that maybe we should "work with businesspeople" and Tonesha wanted "to form a group of students and teachers in our school to keep the school and community clean." Others wanted to "take the program a step higher. I think that we should show City Hall all of the progress we have made" (Melinda). Melinda's suggestion was supported by Rebecca, who wrote: "I would like for the group to work with city officials so that we could work with them and they can help us clean up the city of Ellsworth." Similarly, other participants wanted to "keep the One STEP going and work with other people like people from City Hall to help the community put trash cans on the corners" (Monique).

As we discussed the participants' desires to make connections with city officials, I asked them if they wanted to arrange a meeting with the mayor and/or with the City Council members that represented their neighborhoods. The participants had noted the fact that no representative from the city had attended the assemblies, even though they had been invited both by written invitation and follow-up telephone calls. Without hesitation, the participants said that they wanted to "go to City Hall. If they don't come to us, we'll just have to go to them."

Over the next few weeks, we made arrangements to speak in front of the monthly City Council meeting. We were allotted ten minutes to describe our project and make our requests to the City Council for their assistance in cleaning up the community. In preparation for the presentation, we revisited the presentation we had made at the assemblies and decided that we wanted to leave most of it intact (except for the dance, skit, and award ceremonies). By this time many of the participants had presented their work three or four times in front of large and small groups. Thus, they felt confident about what they wanted to say, though a bit apprehensive about the setting.

We arrived at City Hall three weeks later with plenty of time in hand to set up our slide show and review our presentation. As we entered the Council Chambers—which none of us had ever been in before—a hush came over the participants. The Council Chambers is an impressive hall with theaterlike chairs for the public and platform seats arranged in a semi-circle for the City Council members. There is a separate platform for the mayor (who was again absent) and the City Clerk. The participants were momentarily stunned by the magnitude of what they were about to do, but quickly regained their composure as we practiced our presentation.

The City Council members arrived sporadically and therefore the session began twenty five minutes later than scheduled. When it did begin, some of the council members appeared to be engaged and interested in the proceedings, which included four different presentations by members of the public. But some of the members seemed to be distracted by other things. They were speaking to one another as people were presenting, leaving their seats, and reading material not related to the presentations. This behavior did not go unnoticed by the participants, who later commented that some of the members were, as Melinda stated, "talking while we were presenting. Did you see that, Ms. Mac? I even looked over at one of them while I was doing my part."

In spite of the mixed responses from the members of the City Council, the participants successfully, and with poise and confidence, presented the information they had gathered over the previous two years regarding the state of the environment. In closing, Tonesha spoke for the group when she requested that the council members consider the following:

1. We would like to create a task force to address the environment. That task force would have representatives from various groups in Ellsworth, including young people like ourselves.
2. We would like to see the city make a commitment to give time, energy, and resources to inform the public about cleaning up the environment. For example, we would like to see public service announcements on television and on the radio, advertisements in the newspaper, billboards, fliers, and letters to city residents.
3. We would like to see more trash receptacles placed in particular locations in Ellsworth—maybe trash receptacles with the designs that many of the Blair School students created on their waste baskets.

The president of the City Council responded enthusiastically to the participants' suggestions, informing them that the city "could absolutely put more trash receptacles in the community." He also informed them that he too would like to develop an informational campaign to address the environment and that he felt the participants themselves should be the ones to develop the public service announcements. He then invited two council members to cochair a committee to work with the participants in addressing their concerns. A number of council members thanked the participants for their efforts and assured them that they were fully supportive of their work and were willing to assist them in any way they could. As we left the Council Chambers, Tonesha remarked, "We did it. We are changing people's lives by this project. Now can we get in that air-conditioned van? It was hot in there."

Two weeks after we had presented our concerns to the City Council, we had our last official group session of the 1998–99 academic year. During our discussion, I asked the participants if they had seen the front page of the city newspaper that week. They told me they hadn't, so I passed out copies of the cover story entitled "City Earns National Award." The article went on to say that Ellsworth had been selected as a first-place winner in a nationwide survey by the U.S. Conference of Mayors assessing the livability of the nation's large cities. Ellsworth's campaign to enhance the quality of life by addressing urban blight (park maintenance, new street signs, planting of trees, flowers, and shrubs) earned it the honor of being chosen as one of the cleanest large cities in the United States. After the participants had read the article, we discussed how they felt about the award, as well as whether they were familiar with the 50 million dollar cleanup campaign that had been going on in Ellsworth for the past three years.

Risha: Why isn't there anything about us in here? They say nothin' about us.

Monique: Thank you! He [the mayor] never showed up for none of our presentations. He didn't even come to the Council on Monday.

Rebecca: Yup.

Alice: So where do you think they spent the fifty million dollars?

[laughter]

Mase: It ain't nowhere. He [the mayor] got it in his back pocket.

Risha: We ain't even got a hundred dollars from them.

Melinda: Remember that City Council person who was talking during our presentation? Is he the one that's talkin' in this article?

Alice: Yeah.

Melinda: This is like, I mean, how come they have fifty million dollars and our community looks like a junkyard?

Alice: What struck me about the article was that [the City Council member] just saw the slides we showed him of the community at the same time that Ellsworth gets voted as one of most livable cities because it's clean.

[laughter]

Mase: I don't know. How did they judge this? I bet they were in Beaconsville and only thought it was Ellsworth.

[laughter]

Mase: The cleanest city award. C'mon.

Alice: Has anyone seen where they put new plants?

Risha: Not near my house! I know that!

Tonesha: Not mine either.

Risha: I ain't seen no new plants.

Vonnie: How about downtown?

Tee: Yeah, I think they decorated [the main street].

Vonnie: They put up a lot of those new fancy street signs.

Monique: The blue ones?

Risha: Oh those little cheap—o things!

Vonnie: It sounds like they were targeting a lot of the business areas . . . because they're probably looking to get new businesses to move in to create more jobs in the city. . . . .

Alice: Well, it will be interesting to talk to the City Council about this when they get back to me. But I haven't heard from them yet.

Melinda: Call them.

Tee: Yeah, call them. We gotta move with this program.

Monique: Yeah, call them. I thought you said we could do it? So why don't we do it?

Alice: All right. Well, which one of you wants to call?

Monique: I'll call.

Tee: I'll call, too.

Rebecca: We'll get too nervous if we have to say something and we don't know what to say, so we should write it out like we did the last time when I called them to remind them to come to the assembly. They didn't come anyway. (June 22, 1999)

Tee and Monique telephoned the president of the City Council and one of the council members who had been appointed as a cochair to collaborate with the participants in addressing the issues we had brought to the council two weeks earlier. This person is also one of two council members who represents the Blair School community. As neither of the council members were available, Tee and Monique left messages on their respective answering machines that said:

Hello _____. My name is Tee [or Monique] and I am a member of One STEP. It has been two weeks since we presented our concerns about the environment to the City Council. We would like to know why we haven't gotten an answer from you. Can you please get back to us as soon as possible? You can call Alice McIntyre at _____. Thank you.

That afternoon, I received a call from the council member who represents the participants' community. She informed me that she had received "a disrespectful message from one of the students you work with about not getting back to her about what the city was going to do about the trash. I wish I had saved the message, Alice. It was really disrespectful." I disagreed with her interpretation of the message, telling her that I was standing right next to Tee—who, I informed her, was a "he" not a "she"—when Tee telephoned her and that I felt the participants' request was a valid one. She then informed me that we "simply don't know how the process works. There are sixteen thousand people before you, you know? I mean you only came two weeks ago. We haven't even had a chance to talk about it. Plus, it is a parks and recreation matter, anyway. It is not the City Council's responsibility." She went on to tell me that the president of the council spoke too soon and that "the city couldn't just put trash bins everywhere and do public announcements without a budget and there was no budget for this."

I listened to her explanations for not responding to the participants, reminding her that it *was* the City Council's responsibility to address the issues the participants had brought before them, and that if they felt it was necessary to bring other departments of the city government into the conversation, that was fine by us. The young people had done their part; now the city had to do theirs. I also reminded her that the president of the City Council had promised the participants that the three areas of concerns they spoke to the council members about would be addressed and therefore, the responsibility was his, hers, and the council's as a whole to make sure that they were. I also informed her that I had spoken with the participants earlier that morning and they expected the City Council to keep their word and help them with their program.

The conversation ended with the council member telling me that she would call the president of the council and arrange a meeting, but I should not "expect anything this summer as the council members are not always available during the summer months." She asked me if I wanted her to write a letter to the participants explaining the procedure for addressing their concerns. In retrospect, I should have said "yes" and had her explain the situation to them herself. But at that moment I simply wanted to get off the telephone. So I assured her that I would pass the message on.

I live one mile from the Blair School and in the same geographical area of Ellsworth as many of the participants. Yet our neighborhoods are distinctly different. According to the 1990 census tract (the latest one available), the section of Ellsworth I live in occupies 3 percent of the city's population—a population that is 91 percent white and includes the mayor of Ellsworth and a state congressman, among other government officials. The majority of people living in this section of Ellsworth own their own homes and work in white-collar professions. Sixty-eight percent of the children living in this neighborhood attend private schools. The problem areas in the neighborhood include burglaries, loud car radios, criminal mischief, and auto and bicycle thefts.

Not even a mile away is the section of Ellsworth where the Blair School and The Courts are located. Seventy-three percent of that section of Ellsworth is populated by African Americans and Latinos/as. The primary occupations of the people living in that area are sales, technical support, and service related. Eighty-nine percent of the children living in this area attend public schools. The concerns in this neighborhood include assaults, homicide, drug activity, stolen vehicle recoveries, prostitution, street and residential robberies, and motor vehicle thefts.

The disparities between the two neighborhoods are stark and no more evident than in their physical layout and upkeep. I am a daily jogger and on most days cover the same four-mile area in my neighborhood. One section of that area is a boardwalk that extends for one mile along the shoreline. It is frequented by many people who live both inside and outside the neighborhood. On any given day, there are people fishing, walking, reading, and biking.

Shortly after my telephone conversation with the council member, I was jogging along the boardwalk when I noticed a number of city trucks digging, moving dirt, and bulldozing the grassy areas that line this section of the walkway. Within the span of two months, there appeared one hundred and ten new street lamps, mounds of mulch, and hundreds of plants, bushes, and small trees. My jogs became less and less enjoyable as I watched the transformation before me. Here was a concerted effort by the city to beautify a section of Ellsworth which was already pristine, well attended to, and safe for walking, jogging, biking, and other activities. Where was the effort to transform the neighborhoods the participants lived in? Where was the decision to channel resources into neighborhoods that would benefit much more than this area would? Where were our trash receptacles?

I spent the month of August telephoning a number of city officials to investigate the cost of the beautification project. I had other questions as well. Was this project funded by the fifty million dollar federal grant Ellsworth had received three years earlier to clean up the city? Were the city officials responsible for the implementation of the new street lamps, plants, and other amenities in this particular section of the city aware of the One

STEP program and the young people's request for the city's assistance in cleaning up *their* section of Ellsworth?

In my efforts to speak with someone who could answer my questions, I was transferred from one person to another, told to call back, told that I would be contacted, and assured that my concerns had been noted and would be passed along.

In September 1999, I finally managed to speak to the secretary to the director of the public facilities office who oversees the upkeep of all the neighborhoods in Ellsworth. She relayed a message to me from the director, instructing me to speak to the education department, as the Blair School was under their jurisdiction. I had spoken to this very secretary on a number of occasions and reminded her that although trash receptacles were needed within the vicinity of the Blair School, we had presented evidence that they were needed elsewhere in the city as well. She then informed me that as an Ellsworth taxpayer I had the right to the information I was seeking, but that I would need to put my request in writing. I sent the director my request that same day. I have yet to hear back from him.

That summer, the participants who were still in the area during their summer break met at the Blair School to begin creating a short video documenting the project thus far. At that gathering, I informed them about my conversation with the City Council person. Tee responded with, "Well, if we don't hear from them, so what. We'll do it anyway. We can just get people involved some other way. And I can't believe she called me a girl!" Melinda chuckled and said, "We did it so far without them so we can do it some more." Risha stated, "Well, that doesn't mean we have to stop trying. We are dedicated." Tonesha shrugged her shoulders and said, "So, if they don't help us, we'll just think of somethin' else to do."

In October 1999, we decided to, as Tonesha had said, "think of somethin' else to do." We invited a congressman from the state who also lives in Ellsworth to the Blair School to listen to our concerns. After an engaging presentation and follow-up discussion, the congressman promised the participants that he would get back to them in two weeks. Tonesha looked right at him and said, "You better or we'll hunt you down."

One month later, we had still not heard from the congressman. Therefore, Tonesha telephoned him at his Ellsworth office. She was told that he was in Washington, D.C. In response, Tonesha asked his secretary to give him a message from the One STEP group, reminding him that he was supposed to get back to the group in two weeks and it was "already a month. Please tell him to call us when he returns."

In December 1999, an organization that is funding the photo-text book the participants are developing invited the young people to present some of their research to other groups who had been awarded funds for a variety of community-based projects. Following that presentation, we were contacted by a number of people who were interested in collaborating with us in the implementation of the One STEP program and in the design of the photo-textbook.

In January 2000, after we returned from the holiday break, we decided to pursue some of those contacts, and "get the message out that we are gonna do this program with or without people's help." The participants made telephone calls and wrote letters to key people at local television and radio stations. In addition, they contacted a number of news organizations in the area. As a result of their efforts, the participants secured an interview with a reporter from a major newspaper. During that interview Monique told her,

> I want to be able to walk outside without my shoes on. 'Cause you know sometimes I ride my bike up to Beaconsville and I watch the white people sittin' in this part that is all grass and they have no shoes on. And like I've always wanted to live in a house where I could walk outside and take my shoes off. You walk outside my house without your shoes on and you step on broken glass, dirty needles, junk. You can get AIDS walkin' around our park. (February 15, 2000)

The participants also told the reporter that they realized "the people who work in City Hall are busy, but they aren't so busy that they can't get back to us about things they already promised us they'd do."[2]

The article describing the participants' project and their disillusionment with government officials appeared in the newspaper the following week. It prompted an immediate response from the president of the City Council and the congressman who had promised to get back to the participants "in two weeks." Within 10 days, there were representatives from various governmental agencies at our weekly group sessions apologizing for what one of them said was simply "an oversight on our part in not getting back to you." The participants accepted their "apologies" and, with confidence and good humor, invited the representatives to join them in organizing a major cleanup day. The aim of the event, which took place in May, was to clean up—and draw public attention to—a section of the community previously identified by the participants during their photography project.

In preparation for the cleanup event, the participants wrote public service announcements that were aired on various radio stations encouraging people to come to the event and inviting them to join the young people in a long-term commitment to keep the community clean. A company in the area donated a dumpster to the group which the participants decided to decorate with a mural symbolizing the One STEP project. In addition, a number of Ellsworth residents, businesses, and community organizations donated equipment, time, and money to the participants' event. Equally important, many of them made a commitment to work with the young people in developing an ongoing cleanup project that would be maintained and sustained by various members of the Ellsworth community.

As of this writing, how that commitment will manifest itself has yet to be realized. Nonetheless, the participants remain hopeful that "the adults will keep their promises. And if they don't, well, we'll just have to do what we did before. Embarrass them and then keep doin' what we're doin'" (Collin).

"I've Become a Litter Freak"

The participants' preoccupation with the environment and their unrelenting struggle to develop strategies for cleaning up their community were part and parcel of the challenges they encountered as they reconciled their own individual behavior with their collective commitment to "make things better around here." Over the course of the project, I have watched the participants throw their trash indiscriminately across a classroom, in the middle of a street, on the sidewalks, in the bathrooms of the university, and in the various cars and vans that we use to drive them from here to there. Initially, when I witnessed a trash-throwing incident, I asked the participant to pick up the item and either throw it in a trash bin or hold onto the item until we found a suitable receptacle. At times, they looked at me in disbelief and confronted me with, "There's no place to throw it away." We would then engage in a discussion about why that might be so. Then I would question them about what they might do with the item in lieu of disposing of it in a trash receptacle.

As the project evolved, and as the participants began to design strategies to clean up the community, our discussions about litter took on new meanings. No longer did I ask them to pick up the item they had carelessly thrown on the ground or on the cafeteria floor. Instead, I began to question them about what their individual and collective actions meant in relationship to the project we were developing. I repeatedly asked them if they thought people would take them seriously about cleaning up the community when they themselves were still littering. My questions evoked a host of contested debates about whether they had to change their behavior in order for the project to be successful. On the one hand, they understood that they needed to change their behavior as that behavior pertained to littering. On the other hand, they were not always in agreement about the extent to which those changes needed to be made. After lengthy discussions, we agreed that they had to be, as Rebecca said, "role models for other people."

Once they saw themselves as role models, the participants took our discussions more seriously and began to take steps to stop their own complicity in the trash problem. Some of them decided to carry plastic bags with them in their knapsacks. Others decided to use their pockets as reservoirs for gum wrappers, candy wrappers, and bottle tops until they could find a trash receptacle. Still others decided that they would ask their friends to carry it. During one of those discussions, Tonesha said to the group, "OK. Let's take a vow. Everyone who is gonna stop littering raise your hand." When all the participants had raised their hands, Tonesha looked at me and said, "See there. We're all gonna stop littering and it is happening today. We promise we won't litter no more."

The participants had good intentions. Yet the conversations, the good intentions, and the vows did not in and of themselves stop them from habitual behavior that is commonplace in their community. On the day we took our neighborhood inventory walk to take photographs of the areas where we wanted the city to put trash receptacles, we stopped at the local McDonald's for lunch. After the participants had finished eating, we left the restaurant to walk back to school. Some of them were still drinking their sodas and eating their ice cream sundaes. As we walked up the main street to the school, I heard some people yelling at Mase, who was walking behind me with a group. As I turned around to see what had happened, I heard the participants yell, "Ms. Mac. Mase threw his straw right in the middle of the street. See it there? And he can't get it 'cause there's too many cars. He'll get killed." I looked into the street, then over at Mase who stood staring at the straw as it lay in the middle of the road. I experienced one of my angrier moments in the project as I stood there with the participants. I turned to Mase, and to the rest of the group, and said, quite loudly,

> What is it that we just did? Did we not just go for a three-mile walk and take pictures of the trash, litter, and debris that covers much of your neighborhood? Have we not talked constantly about how you need to do what you are asking your friends and the community to do? I don't get how you can be so involved in a project to clean the community and then continue to trash it yourselves. (Field notes, February 12, 1999)

Tonesha quickly responded with, "Well, we just saw in our walk that there are no trash receptacles, so what was he supposed to do with it?" I answered her question with a question, "Exactly, what was he supposed to do with it?" Various people said, "He could have held on to it until we found a trash bin or until we got back to school." "He could have put it in his pocket." "He could have asked someone to put it in their bag." "He could have asked you to hold it, Ms. Mac." I agreed with them that he could have done a number of things and that throwing it in the middle of the street was not one of them.

In the midst of the highly charged discussion that ensued, the participants asked me if I had ever littered "in your whole life," to which I responded that I probably had but it was a very long time ago and just because I did, did not justify them littering now. "But we are only teenagers," Tonesha remarked, "and when we get older like you, we'll stop, too." I reminded her that she and the rest of the group had taken vows a few weeks before this incident to "never litter again." She laughed, as did the others, and said, "Oh, yeah. We did. OK. You're right. We're just bein' lazy. And we said we would be role models for other people and we gotta do that. We're gonna get serious about the program now and we know we have to stop littering ourselves."

Our conversation continued in this vein until we returned to school. I left the participants that day with the suggestion that they take some time over the weekend to think about how their actions related to the goals of the One STEP project and to reassess the habits they had developed regarding their trash. I reminded them about the work we had done so far in formulating a set of goals to clean up the community and that if we wanted people to take us seriously, we needed to think about our individual and collective responsibilities for achieving the goals we envisioned for the overall program.

I was somewhat demoralized when I left the participants that day. I recognized my own powerlessness over their habits and behavior and realized that they were the *only* ones who could make the necessary changes to stop littering. I couldn't do it for them, nor would it be productive for me to harp on the subject as we progressed through the process. I had to relinquish the illusion that engaging in the One STEP project alone would change their behavior. Rather, it was up to them to make decisions about their behavior, whether related to littering or to their interpersonal relationships. It was entirely possible for them to be critical of other people's behavior and yet be uncritical of their own. It was also entirely possible for them to change their behavior when they were with me and engaged in project-related activities, and then revert to old behavior once we dispersed.

Shortly after this incident I left the country for three weeks to participate in a community photography project with a group of young children in Belfast, Northern Ireland. Vonnie and Jen continued to meet with the participants and prepare for the assemblies. Upon my return, the participants were both eager to hear about my experiences in Belfast and anxious to tell me that they had become, as Tonesha stated: "litter freaks. I am just not littering anymore. I stopped altogether."

Following Tonesha's declaration about her refusal to litter any more, we held an after-school session to review the upcoming assemblies. As I sat waiting for the participants to get their sodas and snacks, I saw Tonesha drop a napkin. She picked it up and as she did so, a friend of hers, who was not a research participant but came to the session because she was going home with Tonesha afterward, said, "You pick up everything." I looked over at Tonesha's friend and said, "What did you say?" She replied, "She picks up everything and puts it in her pocket until she gets to a trash can. And she yells at me, too, every time I drop something on the floor or outside she tells me, 'Put it in your pocket'." Tonesha and I "high fived" each other. I told her I was very proud of her and she said, "I told you I didn't litter anymore."

One week later, I was walking down a corridor of the school with Risha and Monique. We were dropping off the trash bins to the teachers and students so they could decorate them for the contest we had organized. As we walked by a group of students, one of them looked at Risha, looked over at a piece of paper on the floor, and said, "Hey. Why don't you pick up that paper? You yellin' at everyone at home to pick up their mess. Why don't you do it now? You got the trash bin." I looked over at Risha, who said, "My brother. Don't pay no attention to him." I asked her if she was "yellin' at everybody at home to pick up their mess," and she said, "Yup. I am. But they don't always listen."

As the project evolved, I heard similar stories about the participants' efforts to stop littering and their efforts to help their friends and family members do the same. Monique told us that her mother kept finding little scraps of paper in the washing machine. "I put the stuff in my pocket but then I forget to take it out and it ends up in the wash." Jason said his knapsack was a "trash can itself. I throw the stuff in there but then don't clean it out." In addition, I watched the participants on numerous occasions about to throw something on the floor or on the sidewalk and then stop, look around for a trash bin, ask someone if they had something they could use to throw their litter in, or put the item in their pocket.

These actions may appear insignificant, particularly if judged within the context of the many factors that shape urban life. Yet, as has already been stated in this book, it is the participants' daily practices that form and give meaning to their lives. Thus, it is extremely significant—and hopeful—to see this group of young people reflect on their actions, and in so doing, shape the world of which they are a part.

Concluding Reflections

Through the multiple conversations and activities we engaged in during the PAR project, the participants began to articulate things that were "known" by or in the community but not usually addressed, acknowledged, and/or acted upon in their daily lives. As important, the participants began to understand that they too had and have a responsibility for creating a cleaner, safer, nonviolent community. By engaging in creative activities aimed at better understanding themselves and the community, and by sharing reflections and consolidating the learning that had taken place (Brydon-Miller 1997), they took the first steps toward the actualization of youth-initiated plans that benefited them and their community.

Upon the completion of the second year of the project, I asked the participants to tell me three things about the overall PAR project that had assisted them in thinking differently about themselves, their school, their friends, careers and occupations, and their community. Like their comments about what they had learned about interacting with one another in chapter 3, their responses suggested that by engaging in a reflection-action process that was hands-on, within their grasp, and directly related to their concerns, significant changes could occur both individually and collectively.

It made me be trash free. (Jason)

I learned about my community. I chose community because it is more important than friends or our school. Also, litter concerns our health and the strength we have as young people and it makes me think about littering and just that one little piece of paper can turn into a whole dump yard. (Janine)

Not to litter any more and to help other people to stop littering and bring a bag to throw trash in. (Bill)

I don't litter because I learned that when you throw stuff on the ground you are polluting the earth. (Jo-Anne)

I started thinking differently about littering because I'm litter free. I think differently about working in a group with other people because like two years ago when I was in a group I didn't like it, but now that I am in the One STEP program it's better for me to work in a group. (Tonesha)

Taking pictures of our community and projects like making collages and going on trips helped me think differently about littering. (Blood)

I learned that littering is not good for my community. (Risha)

Three things that overall changed my ideas about certain things are the career development program (it helped me to narrow down what I wanted to do), the walking the neighborhood trip (it helped me to see just how much our community needs), and the program itself helped me to see how much damage I was doing to myself and our community. (Melinda)

As the data reveal, the participants needed consistent reminders and reassurance that this was indeed a collaborative project and that their opinions, thoughts, feelings, ideas, and concerns were the impetus for the over-all process of planning and implementing the program's activities. Because the participants' experiences in educational settings had taught them otherwise, they often doubted themselves and waited for me or members of the research team to direct the project. Each time I reminded them of their agency in the project, I became aware of how easy it is for adults to summarily dismiss young people as key players in setting their own agenda. By overlooking young people in decision-making processes that directly affect them, educators, policymakers, researchers, and a host of other adult figures undermine their sense of agency and their ability to make informed choices in and about their lives.

Participatory action research provided opportunities for the participants to develop and implement action plans based on *their* knowledge, *their* desires, and *their* wishes to improve their community. Although I and the members of the research team collaborated with and participated along-side them, they themselves identified the areas of concern in their community, decided what action to take to address those concerns, and then implemented those decisions in their school and community.

Participatory action research aims to build communities of people who are committed to a systematic learning process where they act deliberately, while remaining "open to surprises and responsive to opportunities" (Mc-Taggart 1997:35–36) for further investigation, reflection, and action. The participants of this project built such a community and in that context remain committed to a learning process that, if engaged, will continue to provide them with challenges, surprises, and a host of new opportunities for self- and collective agency and change.

8

■　　■　　■　　■　　■　　■　　■　　■　　■

Making the Road As We Go

AS MENTIONED IN CHAPTER 7, we began the third year of the project with a working lunch at the local McDonald's. During that lunch, I reminded the participants that we had secured funding for the creation of a photo-text book—a project that we agreed would be a priority for the upcoming year. In addition, we discussed other issues that the participants wanted to address during the year: "go to other schools and show them how to take pictures of the community and teach them what we have learned" (Blood); "explore student interactions" (Melinda); "talk about why we fight people" (Bill); "discuss how we can act with each other when we are angry" (Tonesha); and "learn more about violence" (Risha). Above all, the participants spoke about how committed they were to the One STEP program. As Tonesha stated, "We are determined to keep that project goin'."

The participants were now in three different eighth grade classrooms. Thus, as in previous years, we worked out a new schedule for our group sessions. We also had four new graduate students as members of the research team.

So began the third year of the PAR project—a year and a project—that we continue to create as we go. As of this writing, we are 1) developing a photo-text book; (2) implementing the next phase of the One STEP program; and (3) collaborating with university personnel at developing a shadowing program aimed at exploring the participants' career interests. Along the way, we are also addressing some of the participants' other concerns. In particular, we decided not only to investigate speaking at other schools in Ellsworth so as to inform teachers and students about our work, but the participants also presented their work to a group of university faculty and students at a university in Boston.

As we move through a new phase of the program, we continue to be challenged by residential instability, time constraints, varying forms of participation, and the multiple agendas that crisscross this ongoing process. However, we are buoyed in our efforts to persevere in this PAR project by our trust in one another and by our experiences to date that prove to us that together we can create spaces where young people feel confident about making decisions to improve their realities.

In this final chapter, I examine the implications of PAR with urban youth by focusing on the following questions: What does participating in a PAR project aimed at individual and collective change tell us about urban youth of Color? What does it tell us about ourselves? How can the radical story told herein assist educators, psychologists, and researchers in developing realistic strategies for improving the lives of young people living within multiple contexts of violence? I address these questions by highlighting the key issues that framed, shaped, and influenced this PAR project. In so doing, I hope to generate enthusiasm and curiosity among researchers, educators, and psychologists so that they too will consider using the PAR approach to address a myriad of issues that beset young people living in urban communities.

A Living Story of Hope and Possibility: Engaging in PAR with Urban Youth

I don't want to end this story by cautioning people about the hazards of embarking on a PAR project. Therefore, I will refrain from elaborating on the limitations of PAR as a research approach. Many of those limitations (although I prefer to frame them as challenges) have been outlined in this book. They include the issues of time, scheduling, power, control, trust, race, class, gender, age, ability, interpretation, and representation. These limitations are not unique to PAR. Thus, I argue that, as in other forms of social science research, they can be viewed in two distinct ways: either as insurmountable barriers in the research process and summarily dismissed, or as essential, necessary, and significant variables that are integral aspects of the construction of new forms of knowledge within a research process. Thus, the challenge is not to avoid getting bogged down by the limitations of PAR, but rather to embrace those limitations as important components of a PAR process that will benefit those involved.

Below, I suggest a set of guidelines that can be embraced by practitioners of PAR who are interested in collaborating with urban youth in the development of PAR projects. As suggested in chapter 1, I am not suggesting they are the *only* ones that contribute to framing a PAR project with urban youth. The dynamics of PAR are infinitely complex, unique to specific groups, and difficult to tease apart. However, it is my experience to date that the following guidelines can facilitate a PAR process that promotes mutual inquiry, collective problem solving, and individual and social change among urban youth. Although not exhaustive, they are the most significant factors in laying the groundwork for PAR projects with urban youth.

As suggested in chapter 1, I embed these guidelines within the context of *feminist* participatory action research. Feminist PAR adheres to the belief that researchers need to uncover and understand what causes and sustains all forms of oppression and discrimination, whether based on gender, class, race, culture, age, ethnicity, or ability (Maguire 1987). Equally important, and as revealed in earlier chapters, feminist PAR provides a framework for focusing on specific issues that can sometimes be overlooked in traditional PAR projects: the various dimensions of participation, the composition of the research team, the extent to which investigation, reflection, and action are informed by institutional structures, and the question of who benefits from PAR projects. Lastly, feminist PAR provides a more kaleidoscopic lens of the PAR process by taking into account the status of women, children, and other less visible groups within collaborative processes of action and change.

Guideline One

The starting point for investigating social and educational issues with urban youth is to engage with them *in ongoing processes of critical reflec-*

tion and action that are aimed at better understanding their *realities.* This book's basic premise is that PAR is an approach to "studying" urban youth that affords young people the opportunity to "have their say." As the data reveal, these young people had a lot to say about a lot of things. Yet, how adults frame what urban youth have to say can often be a barrier to fully understanding their concerns. This is particularly true when there are discontinuities across race, gender, educational status, and social class between adults and youth. In addition, professionals (and here I refer mainly to academic researchers) tend to enter urban settings armed with preexisting theories that may not always be relevant to the situation at hand.

One of the strengths of PAR is that many of its practitioners recognize that theory and practice are inseparable and exist within an ongoing dynamic process aimed at social transformation. Thus, theory and practice need to be mediated by the research process itself so that new theories can emerge if necessary—in this case, theories that have their genesis in the life experiences of urban youth. Therefore, the emphasis in a PAR project needs to be on young people's realities, not on what adults want those realities to be or what adults think those realities should be. As the data reveal, the realities for this group of young people are that they are a transitory population; live in an unstable environment; suffer under the weight of discrimination, sexism, and racism; have little opportunity to make informed decisions about their lives; and are often preoccupied with staying safe, being accepted by their peers, and learning how to negotiate the difficult terrain of adolescence. Adults may want those realities to change and may work diligently to do so. But before we can change them, we have to acknowledge that they exist.

Positioning youth as the foci of PAR projects contributes to a way of thinking about young people as researchers, as agents of change, as constructors of knowledge actively involved in the dialectical process of action and reflection aimed at individual and collective change. Positioning the participants of this project as catalytic agents of change provided opportunities for adults to listen to their stories so as to frame research questions around *their* understandings of urban life. Equally important, engaging in a process that focused on the participants' concerns gave them an opportunity to take deliberate action on issues that affect them and their community.

Guideline Two

Urban youth need to have full participation in PAR processes. Vio Grossi suggests that "[t]he idea of participation alone is insufficient" (1980:72). Without a consistent effort to problematize what participation actually means and how it manifests itself in a PAR project, participation "is as likely to lead to social integration as it is to radical change" (1980:72). Thus, a recurring question for us during the PAR project was: What does it mean for this group of inner-city adolescents to *fully* participate in a PAR project?

As the data reveal, there were points of disagreement between and among the members of the research team and the participants about what it meant to "participate" in the overall project. The participants and the members of the research team brought different talents, strengths, desires, and interests to the PAR project—all of which needed to be taken into account when decisions were made and action plans implemented. Similarly, there were many different interpretations of the complex social phenomena that were the foci of the PAR project. Sometimes, I interpreted the participants' actions one way, while they interpreted them in quite another way.

However, the moments of rupture that occurred as we negotiated the differences and confusions that were part of this PAR process were to be expected—even welcomed—for they illuminated issues that needed to be addressed and reexamined. As was evident when Jen and Nicole attempted to control the career exploration program (as described in chapter 6), the participants rebelled and the program almost failed. It was only when a democratic, reciprocal process of reflection and action between the adults and the young people participating in this project was established that the program was rejuvenated to focus on the participants' interests and concerns. A similar process of reflection and action was essential for the subsequent creation of the One STEP program described in chapter 7.

The struggles that occur when people are learning how to negotiate the parameters of participation within a PAR project need not be viewed as reasons to abandon the messiness of collaborative action-based research. Instead, I would argue that those struggles are necessary ingredients in decision-making processes that involve groups of people with multiple agendas. By working through the challenge of what defines "participation" within the PAR project, the participants and the members of the research team learned that we could have different perspectives about particular issues and events but that those differing perspectives did not have to result in termination of the process.

Another issue that warrants attention in terms of participation is how tasks are delegated and performed within a PAR project. Many tasks in this PAR project were burdensome, impractical, or even unfeasible for the participants to fully participate in. For example, the extent to which the participants collaborated in the writing of this book was limited. As mentioned in chapter 6, I described the concepts and themes that I was highlighting in the various chapters to them on an ongoing basis. Then, once I had completed a first draft of the manuscript, I invited them to read it, informing them that I would walk them through the more "academic" aspects of the book. Initially they were willing to do so but when I showed them the first complete draft of the book, they "flipped through it" and told me that "it is way too much stuff. Just show us the stuff we say and the pictures." I did show them the "stuff" they said, along with the photographs I had used to illuminate a variety of stories and themes that were generated throughout the project. Overall, the participants "approved" of the book. Nonetheless, the fact that they neither conducted a detailed analysis of the data with me nor participated in the writing process has implications for the interpretive process as it is presented in this book.

On the other hand, and as the data in this book reveal, the participants fully engaged in the community photography project, the development and implementation of the school assemblies, the creation of the One STEP program, a number of presentations, and the formulation of the photo-text book we are currently developing. Those activities were better suited to the talents and abilities of the young people. Thus it is important for practitioners of PAR, and the young people participating in a PAR project, to be pragmatic and flexible about the meaning of full participation. It is my experience that young people are more than willing to explore the multidimensionality of participation, and with the assistance of adult facilitators, take responsibility for the way that participation will manifest itself in a PAR project.

Guideline Three

Practitioners of PAR who are associated with universities need to engage in ongoing efforts to make links between those institutions and the urban communities with which they work. The sustainability of a PAR project is dependent upon, among other things, the composition of researchers and participants. In this particular project, we worked within the context of an urban school and a private university. Thus the issue became: how do we participate with urban youth in processes of change within the context of institutional structures that both facilitate and constrain a process that is "unruly, anarchic, and ad-hoc to those of us who are schooled in the neat, well-defined, and preset methodolog[ies]" (Tandon 1982:85) that dominate social science research?

On some days I felt profoundly challenged by the institutional structures associated with this PAR project. In part, those challenges grew out of the clash of personalities, agendas, desires, and goals that overlapped and interconnected within the overall project. A greater part of those challenges emerged because of the institutions to which the project was linked. The Blair School is a public institution that has its own set of rules, regulations, and procedures which are maintained, sustained, and enforced in conjunction with the Ellsworth school system. There is a clearly defined schedule in place at the Blair School which we worked around and with. Most of the time, the schedule we worked out for the project was "fixed" in the sense that the teachers and staff knew that we were arriving at a specified time each week and the participants needed to be available for our group sessions. Nonetheless, there were times when teachers scheduled field trips, outside speakers, or assemblies during our meeting times, which resulted in changes in the schedule or partial representation of the participants at those particular meetings. Schedule changes also needed to be made during the weeks when the students were required to take standardized tests. There were also early release days, report card conferences, teacher absences (which often resulted in the students being reassigned to another teacher who was not always amenable to having the participants leave the class), fire drills, snow days, and other last-minute changes to the school day that disrupted the PAR process.

Having been a classroom teacher for many years, I am familiar with the structure and the day-to-day life of a public school. Therefore I was prepared for surprises and more often than not was able to work through the scheduling glitches. Nevertheless, engaging in PAR in a public school can be a challenging experience. Thus, it is important that practitioners of PAR accept and work within the daily realities that exist in many public schools in the United States if they are to be successful in developing long-term collaborative relationships with all involved.

The other institution that played a pivotal role in this PAR project was the university where I am employed. The university is classified as a comprehensive university, meaning that it awards baccalaureate and master's degrees but not doctoral degrees. As noted in chapter 2, that can be somewhat problematic for faculty and students who want to engage in long-term PAR projects. It is more difficult to attract students in credentialling programs at the master's level to participate in a long-term research experience than it is to attract doctoral students who, unlike the former group, are required to engage in extended research experiences. In addition, if and when universities require students to do research, PAR is not usually the type of research that is supported, encouraged, and/or funded. There is an institutional inertia in many universities about actually implementing policies that support what some academics perceive as unconventional research approaches.

Redesigning university programs and school curricula to include the tenets of PAR is one way to attract students to PAR—both of which require university support. With that type of support, I have developed courses that provide opportunities for students to participate in learning about and engaging in the project described in this book. I feel very fortunate that I have had the opportunity to work with so many eager, interested, curious, and committed graduate students in this PAR project.

Unfortunately, that is not always the case in other universities. In many institutions of higher learning, there is a tendency to require master's students in education programs, for example, to take one or two courses in educational research, believing that once completed, the students understand the relationship between education and research. Meanwhile, the majority of those introductory courses focus on traditional research paradigms and require students to peruse a number of studies on a particular topic so that they can more effectively distinguish "good" research from "bad." I fully support the notion that students should be able to make judgments about educational research. What I find disturbing is that there is little room for dispelling the notion that an introduction to educational research course is the only way to accomplish that goal, particularly since there is very little, if any, attention paid to PAR in those courses.

Instead of requiring students to take one or two courses in educational research, I would argue that we should teach research courses that ask the questions, "What can you see, hear, feel? How can you relate it to your personal experience? What are the common themes or problems among us? Why do they exist? What can we do about them?" (Barnd, as cited in Jackson, Conchelos, and Vigoda 1980:48). Furthermore, I strongly believe that credentialling programs in education and psychology need to include opportunities for students to engage in some type of school-community work outside the boundaries of the classroom or the school psychologist's office. I think it is essential, particularly in areas located near or in inner cities, that university faculty advocate for some types of structured immersion experience so that students spend time in urban schools and communities, which would provide them and us with greater opportunities to link our theory and practice, reflection and action, talking and doing.

Another issue that needs to be considered, and was addressed in chapter 1, is the extent to which faculty members can and will invest in a PAR project. As the data in this book reveal, it takes time to engage in a long-term PAR project. It also requires that practitioners of PAR remain available, active, committed, and supportive of the pace and the direction of the overall process. For untenured faculty members in particular, that type of commitment appears overwhelming when one looks at the landscape ahead: full teaching loads, committee work, student advising, publications, presentations at conferences, service to the academic community, and a host of other responsibilities that are integral to working in a university. I am not suggesting that those practices be eliminated. What I am suggesting is that universities do a better job of providing support for PAR processes, which means reevaluating the time academics invest in other aspects of university life. It is my experience that universities need to provide faculty—and students—with the time and resources to enter, stick with, and accompany communities who are engaged in the very struggles we spend much of our time theorizing about in our classrooms.

Fals-Borda asks the question: "Can we conceive of a university in diaspora that may be judged more upon its comprehensive social effects than for its physical qualities" (1980:37)? I believe we can, if faculty members and administrators can commit themselves to carving out spaces in universities where we can engage in PAR-type processes of social change. That requires faculty members who are associated with universities to think about how much time we can and will invest in a long-term PAR project. For, as Jackson and his colleagues argue, "When professionals strike political alliances [with community groups] new demands are made upon their time and energies [and] they are, in a very real sense, accountable to the 'struggle'" (1980:54).

Guideline Four

Urban youth need committed adults who will accompany them in processes of change. The ultimate aim of PAR is that the participants themselves sustain a PAR project without the assistance of outside researchers (see, for example, Fals-Borda 1987; Maguire 1987; Park, Brydon-Miller, Hall, and Jackson 1993). I am in full agreement that participants own, and benefit from, the PAR projects they are involved in. Yet it is my experience that urban youth need adults to accompany them in that process. The young people described in this book illuminate how adults can do just that. They clearly show adults how we can participate *with* young people as they negotiate the difficult terrain of urban adolescence. The accounts by and of this particular group of young people also reveal the multiple responsibilities that psychologists, researchers, institutions, the adolescents themselves, and society at large have in creating safe communities where urban youth can succeed and thrive. In addition, this PAR project provided young people with opportunities to tell adults what they expect from us, what we should do, how we should be, and why it is important that we accompany them in processes of just social change. It also provided participating adults with a challenging and highly provocative way to envision how we can engage in individual and social processes of change.

   Another area of concern related to the commitment of adults to PAR projects is the extent to which outside funding practices affect the possibilities and life expectancy of PAR projects. With the help of two staff members who work in the development office at the university where I teach, Jen and I have written over fifteen grant applications for the PAR project in Ellsworth. We also spend a great deal of time seeking funds for an ongoing project I am participating in in Belfast, Northern Ireland. Thus, we have become quite adept at the grant-writing process and have become sensitive to the subtle shifts in the way a PAR project needs to be presented so as to "make it to the first round." We have successfully made the first round on three occasions, only to be rejected in the final analysis. We have been rejected outright in seven others. We have a few grants pending.[1]

During the course of this project, the participants have been interviewed by reporters, had their pictures printed in a number of local newspapers, been spoken about on various local radio stations, presented their work to funding agencies, city officials, parents, teachers, students, and anyone else who will listen to their plea for creating a cleaner, safer community. The participants do so with humor, anxiety, enthusiasm, self-doubt, and a great deal of realism—the latter quality being the most difficult for me to accept. They have had a good deal of publicity, yet have had little concrete support from funding organizations who tell me—and them—how "wonderful it is that young people are so involved in their community." One representative of a funding agency told the participants that she was "incredibly impressed" with them, their questions, their presentation, and their focus. Three months later we received a form letter telling us that we were not eligible for funding.

Seeing young people involved in their community *is* wonderful. But it doesn't *stay* wonderful unless young people are accompanied by adults who support, encourage, and cheer them on as they negotiate the art of activism. In terms of funding, that means a modification of policies and procedures in the way many funding agencies support PAR projects. As Maclure (1990) suggests,

> The yardsticks by which standard social science research projects are normally selected for funding (and for which agency personnel are usually trained to adjudicate) are the general relevance of topics, the clarity of project objectives, the rigor of design and methodology, and the expertise of professional researchers. In terms of participatory research, however, the criteria for selection may not be so clear-cut. While the tenets of clarity and rigor should be retained, standards used to assess conventional research proposals are not likely to illuminate all the relative merits of prospective PR projects. (1990:12)

Thus, if we are to carve out spaces in social science research for people to engage in research projects that emphasize participation, investigation, and action—without the safety net of having a finished product prior to implementation—it is essential that funding organizations rethink the way they review and assess PAR projects.

Implications of PAR in the Development of Pedagogy

The four guidelines outlined above have implications for the development of PAR projects with urban youth. Equally important, engaging in PAR has implications for pedagogy as well. For Paulo Freire (1970, 1973), pedagogy should transform the individual and/or collective consciousness by providing a context for people to become active participants in the creation of their own knowledge and the critical examination of their realities. The PAR project described in this book represents a learning-teaching process that exemplifies Freire's idea of a dialogic educational experience where pedagogy is based on open inquiry, shared knowledge creation, and critically stimulating communication between participants and researchers.

A similar type of relationship can occur in educational institutions—institutions that often rely heavily on system maintenance rather than social transformation. As the data reveal, the participants are accustomed to an educational system that uses various forms of social coercion to maintain discipline and order. Thus, it took them time to adjust to working within a very different paradigm—one that required risk taking, active participation, and the possibility of both change and failure. This PAR project was not about *us* transmitting knowledge to *them*—a teaching paradigm all too common in educational systems in the United States. This was about us constructing knowledge together so that the participants would have the opportunity to make informed choices about their lives.

I have been an educator for over twenty years and although I have witnessed, and continue to witness, "politically relevant teaching" (Beauboeuf-Lafontant 1999:702), those sites of possibility are the exception rather than the rule. This is the case with all types of schools: public, private, elementary, middle and high school, as well as institutions of higher education. In far too many classrooms there is a silencing of discussions about the relationship between schooling and social justice, between the construction of knowledge and the formulation of social policies, between people's lived experiences and their engagement in various forms of public life. Instead, there is a strong focus on aligning oneself with the norms of a particular school, the norms of U.S. society, and the norms of a cultural ideology that may not be relevant for all students.

The underlying premise of PAR is that we problematize ideologies that promote injustice. By teaching in a way that reflects the tenets of PAR we can critique ideologies, disrupt hegemonic practices that consciously or unconsciously maintain systems of privilege and oppression, and take what we are doing "out in the field" into our classrooms. For it is in those sites of struggle and possibility that we can truly promote a "radical revisioning of the institution of education and its lingering ties to social injustice" (Beauboeuf-Lafontant 1999:717).

What's Been Left Out

Stewart suggests that as we study people's lives, we "look for what's been left out, analyze [our] role or position, [and] identify agency in the context of social constraint" (1994:12). There is much that was "left out" of this book. For example, we have spent little time discussing the role of religion in the lives of the participants in this PAR project. Some of them are regular churchgoers; others have never been to a church service. We also have yet to explore—in depth—the participants' relationships with their parents and caregivers, siblings, and extended families. Nor have we examined how those relationships intersect with the major themes addressed in this project: violence, "becoming somebody," and "the trashy way the community looks." Another area that we have not spent time investigating is the academic standings of the participants or their relationship with teachers and other young people attending the Blair School who are not participants in the PAR project. These dimensions of the participants' lives have been left out for a variety of reasons: the participants don't feel it is necessary to talk about them; I feel that delving into another area of study would require more resources than we can bring to bear; the topic simply does not generate sustained attention by the participants; and, of course, the lack of time.

However, what has been "left in" for us and what is presented in this book convinces me that by creating spaces for urban youth to narrate and renarrate their stories so as to act on them, we contributed to further understanding the impact of urban life on young people. Equally important, the PAR process provided insight into the power of creativity and personal expression in the construction of knowledge, which is often "left out" of the field of education, psychology, and social science research. The participants' investment in this PAR project, their determination to create new knowledge and take risks in their own lives, invites the rest of us "to carve out 'spaces,' to inspire a sense of the 'not yet,' to reinvent schools and communities that are engaging for young people who have seen more devastation, felt more pain, and witnessed more violence than anyone should" (Fine 1998b:214–15).

Concluding Reflections

Two weeks before the final draft of this manuscript was due on the editor's desk, I asked the participants what they would say to other girls and boys their age who wanted to address issues they felt were problematic in their communities. Here is what some of them said:

Melinda: First, you have to be willing to participate. You have to have the urge to want to do something good for your community. You have to be determined and like what you are doing.

Tonesha: We're very serious, so you have to be very serious about what you are trying to do. You have to always listen. The key is listening because if you don't listen, you won't know what you are doing and that will throw you off. And if you really want to be in a participatory project, you will have to know how to work in a group of kids. I like working in groups now. . . . .

Tee: They need cooperation and participation.

Blood: And friendship. I'd tell them about friendship.

Tee: And fun. It's fun doing this.

Janine: I'd say participation, too.

Monique: And listening. They have to listen to each other.

Mase: We could tell them how good it feels to clean up your community. . . . .

Risha: They can't have no attitudes. They need to follow rules and they need to have patience 'cause you do have to wait on some things. And they have to work as a group so that they can get things accomplished.

I also asked the participants what young people need from adults in order to address issues that concern them.

> *Tonesha:* Oh, I'll go first on this one. I'm really upset with some adults. I mean I'm really caught up in this one! See, if adults wanted to work with us, that would be great because they are more focused than us kids[
>
> *Melinda:* Not necessarily. It's not to say that they're not more focused but they have a smaller viewpoint than younger kids.
>
> *Tonesha:* Yeah, that's true, too. They gotta listen to what we got to say. Help us wherever we need help. 'Cause adults don't listen to us and what we have to say. You listen to us. You listen to us all the time and all the adults in this project listen to us, too. . . . .
>
> *Blood:* They need to take us seriously.
>
> *Tee:* Yeah, understand what we are sayin' and take us seriously.
>
> *Alice:* How do you know when adults are taking you seriously?
>
> *Tee:* They take time with us, like you have been doin' and pay attention to us. And they stay with us, like you, through the rough and smooth.
>
> *Mase:* They are older than us so they should at least give us[
>
> *Monique:* Advice.
>
> *Mase:* Yeah, and be role models.
>
> *Risha:* Well, they need to set examples because if they are gonna do some stuff that they don't have no business doin', then they can't be goin' around tellin' us "don't do this," "don't do that." They should get more involved with the community and listen more 'cause some people are just blowin' stuff off. They could give us what we askin' for. They don't have even have to give it all. They just have to at least call us back. Just let us know that they ain't messin' with our heads and stuff, tryin' to get us all hyped up and then they do nothin'. (November 30, 1999)

The message the participants are sending to young people is clear: participate, learn to work in groups, listen to each other, have fun, and "don't have an attitude." Their message to adults is also very clear: listen, take young people seriously, and stop "messin' with our heads." Somewhere between the message to young people and that to adults is a space of hope and possibility, where both groups have multiple opportunities to create new ways of teaching, learning, doing, and being. It is my hope that those of us in the latter category seize those opportunities and in so doing, contribute to developing collaborative relationships with urban youth that assist them in, as Tonesha once said, "feelin' smackin' good about ourselves and the work we are doin' in our community."

■ ■ ■ ■ ■ ■ ■ ■ ■

Appendix A

Transcription Code

[unint.]	unintelligible.
[ct]	crosstalk, defined as two or more persons in the sessions talking over a speaker or amongst themselves while a speaker is talking.
[	interruptions and or overlapping speech.
,	comma indicates end of a clause or phrase.
.	period indicates end of a sentence.
. . . .	four periods indicate omission between speakers.
. . .	three spaced ellipses indicate omission within or between sentences.
?	question mark *within* the transcript indicates a question either by intonation or syntax. Question mark *preceding* a line of text indicates an unidentifiable participant.

Demonstrative expressions are included in square brackets. For example [laughter].

■　　■　　■　　■　　■　　■　　■　　■　　■

Appendix B

Community Resource Inventory—Youth

Name
Address
Phone number or how you can be reached
Age　　Grade
Living with: Parents　　Caregivers　　Friends　　Other
Language spoken most often at home
Racial/ethnic background

1. What are some of your skills? What do you like to do? Check below and
add more if we left some out.

math	sports	sewing
dance	photography	drama
science	being a friend	cooking
child care	singing	hairdresser
writing	mechanics	carpentry
playing an instrument	caring for the elderly	
caring for the sick	housecleaning	

2. What skills are you willing to share with the school community and/or the neighborhood? This includes, but is not limited to, the above skills, plus ones like:

your humor	your compassion
your ability to listen	your ability to play with children

3. What are some skills or things you would like to learn?

4. When you think about your skills, what three things do you think you do best?

5. Which of your skills would you like to volunteer to the school and the community?

6. Do you belong to any community, youth, church, or school organizations? If so, which one(s)?

7. What are some community and school activities happening in your neighborhood that you know about?

8. How do you find out about what is happening in your community (e.g., parents, friends, newspaper, teacher, etc.)?

9. What does community mean to you?

10. What are your concerns about your neighborhood? What bothers you the most about your neighborhood? Circle as many as you want. Add more if we left some out.

drugs	crime	nowhere to go	no jobs
gangs	litter	traffic	vacant lots
education	graffiti	poor housing	
public transportation		nowhere to play sports	

11. What do you think you could do to help your community?

12. Do you have employment experience?

13. What was/is it?

14. What kind of work would you like to do in the future?

15. Who do you like to spend time with?

16. Do you like helping other people? If yes, how?

17. What are some improvements you'd like to see in your neighborhood?

18. Is there anything else you would like to add?

Notes

Notes to the Introduction

1. Except for two members of the research team, Jen and Nicole, all names and places have been changed. Each participant chose her or his own pseudonym, which was used throughout the research project.

2. Although there are multiple theoretical perspectives that inform PAR, there are some principles and guidelines that characterize many PAR projects (see chapter 1). Many of these underlying principles also guide feminist PAR projects. Yet there are particular dimensions that distinguish feminist PAR from traditional PAR, which I discuss more fully in chapter 1. In order to maintain consistency, I use the term participatory action research (PAR) throughout the book. For further discussions of the relationship between feminism and PAR, see Maguire 1987, 1996; McIntyre and Lykes 1998; and Wolf 1996.

3. While writing this book I was torn between how much of the existing scholarship on violence, education, urban communities, and urban youth should frame the manuscript. Although it is important to have a working knowledge of the above literature, it was the participants themselves rather than existing scholarship, who ultimately framed this PAR project. Thus I have cited numerous researchers and scholars in the footnotes and throughout the manuscript, reserving the greater part of the book for the participants' narratives.

Notes to Chapter 1

1. The transcription code can be found in Appendix A.

Notes to Chapter 2

1. Participating with master's students in PAR raises a number of questions for consideration. Who should or can participate in PAR projects and for what reasons? Is it an effective strategy to have a research team consisting of students who cannot always remain with the project for more than one semester or one year? How does the fact that I am an advisor for many of the team members who participated in the project, and that I grade various aspects of their participation in the project, effect their involvement? These and related questions were not easily answered yet were ever-present in the research process and problematized at length by me and the members of the research team.

2. Collective representations of the community via the use of collages were adapted from Lykes's work in Latin America (see Lykes 1994). In addition, see McIntyre 1997, for a further discussion of the use of collages as a research tool.

3. For further discussions about the use of storytelling, see Lykes 1996, and Zipes 1995.

4. Although extensive research has been conducted over the past few decades on adolescent friendships, that research has looked exclusively at white middle-class populations. As Way argues, "Our knowledge of friendships among adolescents is limited greatly . . . by the fact that few research projects have explored friendships among urban, poor, or working-class adolescents" (1996:173).

Notes to Chapter 3

1. For further discussions about the effects of interpersonal and systemic violence on children and families living in violent, low-income urban communities, see, for example, Barrett 1993; Bell and Jenkins 1991; Black and Krishnakumar 1998; Chasin 1998; Garbarino 1995a; Hill, Soriano, Chen, and LaFromboise 1994; Ladd and Cairns 1996; Limber and Nation 1998; McCord 1997; Prothrow-Stith 1991; Wandersman and Nation 1998; Wang and Gordon, 1994. In addition, see, for example, Berman, Kurtines, Silverman, and Serafina 1996; Garbarino 1993a; Horn and Trickett 1998; Osofsky, Wewers, Hann, and Fick 1993; and Werner and Weist 1996, for discussions about the relationship between violence and Post-Traumatic Stress Syndrome; Rutter 1983; Steinberg, Lamborn, Dornbusch, and Darling 1992; and Werner 1992, for discussions about the impact of violence on inner-city youth and academic success; and Black and Krishnakumar 1998; Garbarino 1999, 1995b; Garmezy 1991, 1993; Hetherington and Blechman 1996; Masten and Coatsworth 1998; and Rak and Patterson 1996, for the way families and communities contribute to resiliency in and among youth living in violence-prone communities.

2. The insights gleaned from research on violence has contributed to the development of various intervention and prevention programs, particularly aimed at inner-city students, teachers, and other school personnel, about the effects of violence on youth, families, schools, and communities. Many of these programs are attempts to effectively bridge the gap between urban students' daily lives and ex-

periences and what is happening in their classrooms and schools (see, for example, Bigelow, Christensen, Karp, Miner, and Peterson 1994; Burt, Resnick, and Novick 1998; Garbarino 1993b; Kivel and Creighton 1997; and *Teaching Tolerance*). Although many of these programs have the potential to alter our understandings of violence and its effects on young people, a recent report suggests that most of the nation's schools do not utilize violence prevention programs and the ones that do are by and large ineffective (Drug Strategies 1998). The report posits that the majority of violence-prevention programs in urban (and suburban) schools are not integrated into the curriculum but are used episodically throughout various grade levels. In addition, schools tend to address issues of violence only *after* a crisis has occurred.

3. Ignacio Martín-Baró, a Salvadoran social psychologist, was assassinated in El Salvador on November 16, 1989. He and M. Brinton Lykes (1994, 1997), two psychologists who focus on the effects of state-sponsored violence and war on native communities, argue that Western psychological theories that view violence and the accompanying trauma as intrapsychic phenomena share "the problem inherent in the medical model, of abstracting sociohistorical realities and insisting on locating disorders in the individual" (Martín-Baró 1994:124). Thus, they speak of psychosocial trauma as dialectical, socially produced, and "chronic when the factors that bring it about remain intact" (Martín-Baró 1994:125). Even though Martín-Baró was referring to communities of people living within the context of state-sponsored violence, his words ring true for many people in the United States who live in environments characterized by types of violence that are chronic, pervasive, and allowed to remain intact.

Notes to Chapter 5

1. Michelle Fine argues that many students attending urban high schools in this country do not necessarily drop out of school as much as they are "coerced to leave" or discharged from school "by choice" (1992b:105).

Notes to Chapter 7

1. I explained the PAR project to interested teachers and other members of the school staff at various moments in the research project. They were supportive, encouraging, and agreed with my request that the participants' involvement in the PAR project not be dependent on their academic standing or their behavior in school. I also requested that the participants' engagement in the project not be perceived as a reward for their behavior while they were in school or be used as a bargaining chip with them. At the same time, the participants were expected to complete the work they missed while they attended the group sessions. If this became a problem, the participants, teachers, and I agreed that we would discuss the situation and develop a plan to address their academic responsibilities. There were occasions when some of the participants did not complete their assignments or when they used the project as an excuse for not completing their work. Due to the

relationships we developed over the course of the project, the teachers and I addressed the problem with the particular participant, who was quick to remedy the situation.

2. See "Cleaning Up [Ellsworth]: Kids Take Matters into Their Own Hands for Nice Play Areas," *The Connecticut Post,* February 27, 2000, p. A16.

Notes to Chapter 8

1. Currently, we are fortunate to be funded, albeit in a limited way, by a few private foundations who trust me/us and the work we are doing and do not ask or expect us to distort or magnify phenomena so as to enhance their visibility. Nor do I feel any pressure from them to color my interpretations of the data or to present the participants' experiences in ways that are not authentic.

References

ABC News (1985?). *Eye of the Storm.* [Film]. ABC Media Concepts, Mount Kisco, N.Y.: Center for Humanities.

Alder, C., and D. Sandor (1990). Youth Researching Youth. *Youth Studies* 9(4):38–42.

Anyon, J. (1997). *Ghetto Schooling: A Political Economy of Urban Educational Reform.* New York: Teachers College Press.

Artiles, A. J., and S. C. Trent (1994). Over Representation of Minority Students in Special Education: A Continuing Debate. *Journal of Special Education* 27(4):410–37.

Atweh, B., C. Christensen, and L. Dornan (1998). Students as Action Researchers. In B. Atweh, S. Kemmis, and P. Weeks (eds.), *Action Research in Practice: Partnerships for Social Justice in Education* (pp. 114–38). London: Routledge.

Back, L. (1996). *New Ethnicities and Urban Culture: Racisms and Multiculture in Young Lives.* New York: St. Martin's Press.

Barrett, R. K. (1993). Urban Adolescent Homicidal Violence: An Emerging Public Health Concern. *International Migration Review* 27(1):67–75.

Beauboeuf-Lafontant, T. (1999). A Movement against and beyond Boundaries: "Politically Relevant Teaching" among African American Teachers. *Teachers College Record* 100(4):702–23.

Behar, R., and D. A. Gordon (eds.). (1995). *Women Writing Culture.* Berkeley: University of California Press.

Bell, C. C., and E. J. Jenkins (1991). Traumatic Stress and Children. *Journal of Health Care for the Poor and Underserved* 2(1):175–88.

Bell, L. (1993). *Rethinking Ethics in the Midst of Violence: A Feminist Approach to Freedom*. Lanham, Md.: Rowman and Littlefield.

Berliner, D. C., and B. J. Biddle (1995). *The Manufactured Crisis: Myths, Fraud, and the Attack on America's Public Schools*. Reading, Mass.: Addison-Wesley.

Berman, S. L., W. M. Kurtines, W. K. Silverman, and L. T. Serafina (1996). The Impact of Exposure to Crime and Violence on Urban Youth. *American Journal of Orthopsychiatry 66*(3):329–36.

Bigelow, B., L. Christensen, S. Karp, B. Miner, and B. Peterson (1994). *Rethinking Our Classrooms: Teaching for Equity and Justice*. Milwaukee: Rethinking Schools Limited.

Black, M. M., and A. Krishnakumar (1998). Children in Low-Income, Urban Settings: Interventions to Promote Mental Health and Well-Being. *American Psychologist 53*(6):635–46.

Bryceson, D., and K. Mustafa (1982). Participatory Research: Redefining the Relationship between Theory and Practice. In Y. Kassam and K. Mustafa (eds.), *Participatory Research: An Emerging Alternative Methodology in Social Science Research* (pp. 87–109). New Delhi: Society for Participatory Research in Asia.

Brydon-Miller, B. (1993). Breaking Down Barriers: Accessibility Self-Advocacy in the Disabled Community. In P. Park, M. Brydon-Miller, B. Hall, and T. Jackson (eds.), *Voices of Change: Participatory Research in the United States and Canada* (pp. 125–44). Toronto: Ontario Institute for Studies in Education.

Brydon-Miller, M. (1997). Participatory Action Research: Psychology and Social Change. *Journal of Social Issues 53*(4):657–66.

Burt, M. R., G. Resnick, and E. R. Novick (1998*). Building Supportive Communities for At-Risk Adolescents: It Takes More Than Services*. Washington, D.C.: American Psychological Association.

Charmaz, K. (1990). "Discovering" Chronic Illness: Using Grounded Theory. *Social Science Medicine 30*(11):1161–172.

Chasin, B. (1998). *Inequality and Violence in the United States: Casualties of Capitalism*. Amherst, N.Y. Humanity Books.

Chataway, C. J. (1997). An Examination of the Constraints on Mutual Inquiry in a Participatory Action Research Project. *Journal of Social Issues 53*(4): 747–766.

Children's Defense Fund (1999). *The State of America's Children: Yearbook 1999*. Washington, D.C.: Children's Defense Fund.

Collins, P. H. (1998). *Fighting Words: Black Women and the Search for Justice*. Minneapolis: University of Minnesota Press.

Collins, P. H. (1991). *Black Feminist Thought: Knowledge, Consciousness, and the Politics of Empowerment*. New York: Routledge.

Collins, P. H. (1990). Women's Studies: Reform or Transformation? *Sojourner: The Women's Forum 10*:18–20.

Connell, N. (1999). Public Education. In F. Schultz (ed.), *Education 99/00: Annual Editions* (26th ed., pp. 151–52). Guilford, Conn.: Dushkin.

Council of the Great City Schools (1994). *Critical Education Trends: A Poll of America's Urban Schools.* Washington, D.C.: Council of Great City Schools.

Cushman, E. (1998). *The Struggle and the Tools: Oral and Literate Strategies in an Inner City Community.* Albany: SUNY Press.

Darling-Hammond, L. (1995). Inequality and Access to Knowledge. In J. Banks (ed.), *Handbook of Research on Multicultural Education* (pp. 465–83). New York: Macmillan.

Darling-Hammond, L., and E. Sclan (1996). Who Teaches and Why: Dilemmas of Building a Profession for the Twenty-First Century Schools. In J. Sikula, T. Butter, and E. Guyton (eds.), *Handbook of Research on Teacher Education* (pp. 67–101). New York: Macmillan.

de Wit, T., and V. Gianotten (1980). Rural Training in Traditional Communities of Peru. In F. Dubell, T. Erasmie, and J. de Vries (eds.), *Research for the People—Research by the People: Selected Papers from the International Forum on Participatory Research in Ljubljana, Yugoslavia* (pp. 131–42). Linkoping, Sweden: Linkoping University and Amersfoort, Netherlands: S. V. E. The Netherlands Study and Development Center for Adult Education.

Dill, B. T., M. B. Zinn, and S. Patton (1999). Race, Family Values, and Welfare Reform. In L. Kushnick and J. Jennings (eds.), *A New Introduction to Poverty: The Role of Race, Power, and Politics* (pp. 263–86). New York: New York University Press.

Drug Strategies (1998). *Safe Schools, Safe Students: A Guide to Violence Prevention Programs.* Washington, D.C.: William T. Grant Foundation.

Education Week (1998). *Quality Counts: The Urban Challenge, Public Education in the Fifty States, 17*(17).

Elikann, P. (1999). *Superpredators: The Demonization of Our Children by the Law.* New York: Plenum Press.

Ewald, W. (1996). *I Dreamed I Had a Girl in My Pocket: The Story of an Indian Village.* New York: Double Take Books.

Ewald, W. (1985). *Portraits and Dreams: Photographs and Stories by Children of the Appalachians.* New York: Writers and Readers Publishing.

Fals-Borda, O. (1997). Participatory Action Research in Columbia: Some Personal Reflections. In R. McTaggart (ed.), *Participatory Action Research: International Contexts and Consequences* (pp. 107–12). Albany: SUNY Press.

Fals-Borda, O. (1987). The Application of Participatory Action-Research in Latin America. *International Sociology 2*(4):329–47.

Fals-Borda, O. (1985). *Knowledge and People's Power.* New Delhi: Indian Social Institutes.

Fals-Borda, O. (1980). Science and the Common People. In F. Dubell, T. Erasmie, and J. de Vries (eds.), *Research for the People—Research by the People: Selected Papers from the International Forum on Participatory Research in Ljubljana, Yugoslavia* (pp. 13–40). Linkoping, Sweden: Linkoping University and Amersfoort, Netherlands: S. V. E. The Netherlands Study and Development Center for Adult Education.

Fals-Borda, O., and M. A. Rahman (eds.). (1991). *Action and Knowledge: Breaking the Monopoly with Participatory Action-Research.* New York: Apex Press.

Fine, M. (1998a). Pilgrimages to Power: Research, Evaluation, and Public Policy Dilemmas. Paper Presented at American Psychological Association, San Francisco, Calif.

Fine, M. (1998b). Greener Pastures. In W. C. Ayers and J. L. Miller (eds.), *A Light in Dark Times: Maxine Greene and the Unfinished Conversation* (pp. 209–19). New York: Teachers College Press.

Fine, M. (1992a). Passions, Politics, and Power: Feminist Research Possibilities. In M. Fine (ed.), *Disruptive Voices: The Possibilities of Feminist Research* (pp. 205–31). Ann Arbor: University of Michigan Press.

Fine, M. (1992b). "The Public" in Public Schools: The Social Construction/Constriction of Moral Communities. In M. Fine (ed.), *Disruptive Voices: The Possibilities of Feminist Research* (pp. 101-114). Ann Arbor: University of Michigan Press.

Fine, M. (1991). *Framing Dropouts: Notes on the Politics of an Urban High School.* Albany: SUNY Press.

Fine, M., and L. Weis (1998a). Writing the "Wrongs" of Fieldwork: Confronting Our Own Research/Writing Dilemmas in Urban Ethnographies. In G. Shacklock and J. Smyth (eds.), *Being Reflexive in Critical Educational and Social Research* (pp. 13–35). London: Farmer Press.

Fine, M., and L. Weis (1998b). Crime Stories: A Critical Look through Race, Ethnicity, and Gender. *Qualitative Studies in Education* 11(3):435–59.

Finnegan, W. (1998). *Cold New World: Growing Up in a Harder Country.* New York: Random House.

Fordham, S. (1996). *Blacked Out: Dilemmas of Race, Identity, and Success at Capital High School.* Chicago: University of Chicago Press.

Forester, J., J. Pitt, and J. Welsh (1993). *Profiles of Participatory Action Researchers.* Ithaca: Einaudi Center for International Studies and Department of City and Regional Planning, Cornell University.

Franklin, K. L., and N. McGirr (eds.). (1995). *Out of the Dump: Writings and Photographs by Children of Guatemala.* New York: Lothrop, Lee, and Shepard.

Franz, C. E., and A. J. Stewart (eds.). (1994). *Women Creating Lives: Identities, Resilience, and Resistance.* Boulder: Westview Press.

Freire, P. (1994). *Pedagogy of Hope: Reliving Pedagogy of the Oppressed.* Trans. R. Barr. New York: Continuum.

Freire, P. (1985). *The Politics of Education: Culture, Power, and Liberation* Trans. D. Macedo. South Hadley, Mass.: Bergin and Harvey.

Freire, P. (1973). *Education for Critical Consciousness* Trans. M. B. Ramos. New York: Seabury Press.

Freire, P. (1970). *Pedagogy of the Oppressed* Trans. M. B. Ramos. New York: Seabury Press.

Garbarino, J. (1999). *Lost Boys: Why Our Sons Turn Violent and How We Can Save Them.* New York: Free Press.

Garbarino, J. (1995a). The American War Zone: What Children Can Tell Us about Living with Violence. *Developmental and Behavioral Pediatrics 16*(6): 431–35.

Garbarino, J. (1995b). *Raising Children in a Socially Toxic Environment.* San Francisco: Jossey-Bass.

Garbarino, J. (1993a). Children's Responses to Community Violence: What Do We Know? *Infant Mental Health Journal 14*(2):103—15.

Garbarino, J. (1993b). *Let's Talk about Living in a World of Violence.* Chicago: Erikson Institute.

Garmezy, N. (1993). Children of Poverty: Resilience despite Risk. *Psychiatry 56*(1):127–36.

Garmezy, N. (1991). Resiliency and Vulnerability to Adverse Developmental Outcomes Associated with Poverty. *American Behavioral Scientist 34*(4):416–30.

Garrod, A., J. V. Ward, T. L. Robinson, and R. Kilkenny (1999). Preface. In A. Garrod, J. V. Ward, T. L. Robinson, and R. Kilkenny (eds.), *Souls Looking Back: Life Stories of Growing Up Black* (pp. xiii–xvi). New York: Routledge.

Gaventa, J. (1988). Participatory Research in North America. *Convergence 24*(2/3):19-28.

Gaventa, J., and B. D. Horton (1981). A Citizen's Research Project in Appalachia, USA. *Convergence 14*(3):30–43.

George, A. (1996). Methodological Issues in the Ethnographic Study of Sexuality: Experiences from Bombay. In K. de Koning and M. Martin (eds.), *Participatory Research in Health: Issues and Experiences* (pp. 119–29). London: Zed Books.

Gilens, M. (1999). *Why Americans Hate Welfare: Race, Media, and the Politics of Antipoverty Policy.* Chicago: University of Chicago Press.

Grant, C. A., and C. A. Zozakiewicz (1995). Student Teachers, Cooperating Teachers, and Supervisors: Interrupting the Multicultural Silences of Student Teaching. In J. Larkin and C. Sleeter (eds.), *Developing Multicultural Teacher Education Curricula* (pp. 259–78). Albany: SUNY Press.

Grundy, S. (1997). Participatory Educational Research in Australia: The First Wave—1976 to 1986. In R. McTaggart (ed.), *Participatory Action Research: International Contexts and Consequences* (pp. 125–49). Albany: SUNY Press.

Haberman, M. (1995). The Dimensions of Excellence in Programs Preparing Teachers for Urban Poverty Schools. *Peabody Journal of Education 70*(2): 24–43.

Hacker, A. (1995). *Two Nations: Black and White, Separate, Hostile, Unequal.* New York: Ballantine Books.

Hall, B. (1993). Introduction. In P. Park, M. Brydon-Miller, B. Hall, and T. Jackson (eds.), *Voices of Change: Participatory Research in the United States and Canada* (pp. xiii–xxii). Toronto: Ontario Institute for Studies in Education.

Hall, B. (1981). Participatory Research, Popular Knowledge and Power: A Personal Reflection. *Convergence 14*(3):6–17.

Hall, B. (1977). *Creating Knowledge: Breaking the Monopoly.* Toronto: Participatory Research Project of the International Council of Adult Educators.

Heaney, T. W. (1993). If you Can't Beat 'em, Join 'em: The Professionalization of Participatory Research. In P. Park, M. Brydon-Miller, B. Hall, and T. Jackson (eds.), *Voices of Change: Participatory Research in the United States and Canada* (pp. 41–46). Toronto: Ontario Institute for Studies in Education.

Heide, K. M. (1999). *Young Killers: The Challenge of Juvenile Homicide.* Thousand Oaks, Calif.: Sage.

Henig, J. R., R. C. Hula, M. Orr, and D. S. Pedescleaux (1999). *The Color of School Reform: Race, Politics, and the Challenges of Urban Education.* Princeton: Princeton University Press.

Hetherington, E. M., and E. A. Blechman (1996). *Stress, Coping, and Resiliency in Children and Families.* Mahwah, N.J.: Lawrence Erlbaum.

Hill, H. M., F. I. Soriano, S. A. Chen, and T. D. LaFromboise (1994). Sociocultural Factors in the Etiology and Prevention of Violence among Ethnic Minority Youth. In L. D. Eron, J. H. Gentry, and P. Schlegel (eds.), *Reason to Hope: A Psychological Perspective on Violence and Hope* (pp. 59–97). Washington, D.C.: American Psychological Association.

hooks, b. (1984). *Feminist Theory: From Margin to Center.* Boston: South End Press.

Horn, J. L., and P. K. Trickett (1998). Community Violence and Child Development: A Review of the Research. In P. K. Trickett & C. J. Schellenbach (eds.), *Violence against Children in the Family and the Community* (pp. 103–38). Washington, D.C.: American Psychological Association.

Horton, B. (1981). On the Potential of Participatory Research: An Evaluation of a Regional Experiment. Paper presented at the Annual Meeting of the Society for the Study of Social Problems. Toronto.

Hubbard, J. (1996). *Lives Turned Upside Down: Homeless Children in Their Own Words and Photographs.* New York: Simon and Schuster.

Hubbard, J. (1991). *Shooting Back: A Photographic View of Life by Homeless Children.* San Francisco: Chronicle Books.

Hughes, L. (1951). *Montage of a Dream Deferred.* New York: Holt.

Jackson, T., G. Conchelos, and A. Vigoda (1980). The Dynamics of Participation in Participatory Research. In F. Dubell, T. Erasmie, and J. de Vries (eds.), *Research for the People—Research by the People. Selected Papers from the International Forum on Participatory Research in Ljubljana, Yugoslavia* (pp. 41–60). Linkoping, Sweden: Linkoping University and Amersfoort, Netherlands: S. V. E. The Netherlands Study and Development Center for Adult Education.

Kanhare, V. P. (1980). The Struggle in Dhulia: A Women's Movement in India. In F. Dubell, T. Erasmie, and J. de Vries (eds.), *Research for the People—Research by the People. Selected Papers from the International Forum on Participatory Research in Ljubljana, Yugoslavia* (pp. 110–17). Linkoping, Sweden: Linkoping University and Amersfoort, Netherlands: S. V. E. The Netherlands Study and Development Center for Adult Education.

Kassam, Y. (1980). The Issue of Methodology in Participatory Research. In F. Dubell, T. Erasmie, and J. de Vries (eds.), *Research for the People—Research by the People. Selected Papers from the International Forum on Participatory Research in Ljubljana, Yugoslavia* (pp. 61–68). Linkoping, Sweden: Linkoping University and Amersfoort, Netherlands: S. V. E. The Netherlands Study and Development Center for Adult Education.

Kelley, R. D. G. (1997). *Yo' Mama's Disfunktional: Fighting the Culture Wars in Urban America*. Boston: Beacon Press.

Kelley, R. D. G. (1994). *Race Rebels: Culture, Politics, and the Black Working Class*. New York: Free Press.

Khanna, R. (1996). Participatory Action Research (PAR) in Women's Health: SARTHI, India. In K. de Koning and M. Martin (eds.), *Participatory Research in Health: Issues and Experiences* (pp. 62–71). London: Zed Books.

Kivel, P., and A. Creighton (1997). *Making the Peace: A Fifteen-Session Violence Prevention Curriculum for Young People*. Alameda, Calif.: Hunter House.

Kohl, H. (1995). *Should We Burn Babar? Essays on Children's Literature and the Power of Stories*. New York: New Press.

Kozol, J. (1995). *Amazing Grace: The Lives of Children and the Conscience of a Nation*. New York: Crown.

Kozol, J. (1991). *Savage Inequalities: Children in America's Schools*. New York: Crown.

Kraai, Z., B. MacKenzie, and F. Youngman (1982). The Use of Popular Theatre for Adult Education: Botswana and Its Relation to the Concept of Participatory Research. In Y. Kassam and K. Mustafa (eds.), *Participatory Research: An Emerging Alternative in Social Science Research* (pp. 154–78). New Delhi: Society for Participatory Research in Asia.

Kretzmann, J. P., and J. L. McKnight (1997). *A Guide to Capacity Inventories: Mobilizing the Community Skills of Local Residents*. Evanston, Ill.: Center for Urban Affairs and Policy Research Neighborhood Innovations Network.

Kretzmann, J. P., and J. L. McKnight (1993). *Building Communities from the Inside Out: A Path toward Finding and Mobilizing a Community's Assets*. Evanston, Ill.: Center for Urban Affairs and Policy Research Neighborhood Innovations Network.

Ladd, G. W., & Cairns, E. (1996). Children: Ethnic and Political Violence. *Child Development 67*(1):14–18.

Lakes, R. D. (1996). *Youth Development and Critical Education: The Promise of Democratic Action*. Albany: SUNY Press.

Lather, P. (1997). Working the Ruins of Feminist Ethnography: Economies of Responsibility and Possibility. Paper presented at American Educational Research Association. Chicago.

Leadbeater, B. J. R., and N. Way (1996). Introduction. In B. J. R. Leadbeater and N. Way (eds.), *Urban Girls: Resisting Stereotypes, Creating Identities* (pp. 1–12). New York: New York University Press.

Limber, S. P., and M. A. Nation (1998). Violence within the Neighborhood and Community. In P. K. Trickett and C. J. Schellenbach (eds.), *Violence against Children in the Family and the Community* (pp. 171–94). Washington, D.C.: American Psychological Association.

Lipman, P. (1998). *Race, Class, and Power in School Restructuring*. Albany: SUNY Press.

Luke, C. (1996). *Feminism and Pedagogies of Everyday Life*. Albany: SUNY Press.

Luke, C., and J. Gore (1992). *Feminisms and Critical Pedagogy*. New York: Routledge.

Lykes, M. B. (2000). Creative Arts and Photography in Participatory Action Research in Guatemala. In P. Reason and H. Bradbury (eds.), *Handbook of Action Research: Toward Research/Practice* (pp. 363–371). Thousand Oaks, CA: Sage.

Lykes, M. B., with A. Caba Mateo, J. Chávez Anay, A. Laynez Caba, U. Ruiz, and J. W. Williams, (1999). Telling Stories—Rethreading Lives: Community Education, Women's Development and Social Change among the Maya Ixil. *International Journal of Leadership in Education: Theory and Practice* 2(3): 207–227.

Lykes, M. B. (1997). Activist Participatory Research among the Maya of Guatemala: Constructing Meanings from Situated Knowledge. *Journal of Social Issues* 53(4):725–46.

Lykes, M. B. (1996). Meaning Making in a Context of Genocide and Silencing. In M. B. Lykes, A. Banuazizi, R. Liem, and M. Morris (eds.), *Myths about the Powerless: Contesting Social Inequalities* (pp. 159–78). Philadelphia: Temple University Press.

Lykes, M. B. (1994). Terror, Silencing and Children: International, Multidisciplinary Collaboration with Guatemalan Maya Communities. *Social Science Medicine* 38(4):543–52.

Lykes, M. B. (1989). Dialogue with Guatemalan Indian Women: Critical Perspectives on Constructing Collaborative Research. In R. Unger (ed.), *Representations: Social Constructions of Gender* (pp. 167–85). Amityville, N.Y.: Baywood.

MacLeod, J. (1995). *Ain't No Makin' It: Aspirations and Attainment in a Low-Income Neighborhood*. Boulder: Westview Press.

Maclure, R. (1990). The Challenge of Participatory Research and Its Implications for Funding Agencies. *International Journal of Sociology and Social Policy* 10(13):1–21.

Maguire, P. (1996). Proposing a More Feminist Participatory Research: Knowing and Being Embraced Openly. In K. de Koning and M. Martin (eds.), *Partici-*

patory Research in Health: Issues and Experiences (pp. 27–39). London: Zed Books.

Maguire, P. (1993). Challenges, Contradictions, and Celebrations: Attempting Participatory Research as a Doctoral Student. In P. Park, M. B. Miller, B. Hall, and T. Jackson (eds.), *Voices of Change: Participatory Research in the United States and Canada* (pp. 157–76). Toronto: Ontario Institute for Studies in Education.

Maguire, P. (1987). *Doing Participatory Research: A Feminist Approach.* Amherst: Center for International Education, University of Massachusetts.

Marecek, J., M. Fine, and L. Kidder (1997). Working between Worlds: Qualitative Methods and Social Psychology. *Journal of Social Issues* 53(4):631–44.

Martín-Baró, I. (1994). War and the Psychosocial Trauma of Salvadoran Children. Trans. A. Wallace. In A. Aron and S. Corne (eds.), *Writings for a Liberation Psychology: Ignacio Martín-Baró* (pp. 122–35). Cambridge: Harvard University Press.

Martín-Baró, I. (1988). From the Dirty War to the Psychological War: The Case of El Salvador. In A. Aaron (ed.), *Flight, Exile, and Return* (pp. 2–22). San Francisco: Committee for Health and Human Rights.

Masten, A. S., and J. D. Coatsworth (1998). The Development of Competence in Favorable and Unfavorable Environments: Lessons from Research on Successful Children. *American Psychologist* 53(2):205–20.

Mbilinyi, M. (1982). The Unity of Struggles and Research: The Case of Peasant Women in West Bagamoyo, Tanzania. In M. Mies (ed.), *Fighting on Two Fronts: Women's Struggles and Research* (pp. 102–42). The Hague: Institute of Social Sciences.

McCord, J. E. (ed.). (1997). *Violence and Children in the Inner City.* New York: Cambridge University Press.

McIntyre, A. (1997). *Making Meaning of Whiteness: Exploring Racial Identity with White Teachers.* Albany: SUNY Press.

McIntyre, A., and M. B. Lykes (1998). Who's the Boss? Confronting Whiteness and Power Differences within a Feminist Mentoring Relationship in Participatory Action Research. *Feminism and Psychology* 8(4):427–44.

McQuillan, P. J. (1998). *Educational Opportunity in an Urban American High School.* Albany: SUNY Press.

McTaggart, R. (1997). Guiding Principles for Participatory Action Research. In R. McTaggart (ed.), *Participatory Action Research: International Contexts and Consequences* (pp. 25–43). Albany: SUNY Press.

Mduma, E. K. (1982). Appropriate Technology for Grain Storage in a Bwakira Chini Village. In Y. Kassam and K. Mustafa (eds.), *Participatory Research: An Emerging Alternative in Social Science Research* (pp. 198–213). New Delhi: Society for Participatory Research in Asia.

Minh-Ha, T. T. (1989). *Woman, Native, Other: Writing Postcoloniality and Feminism.* Bloomington: Indiana University Press.

National Center for Educational Statistics (1999). *Teacher Quality: A Report on the Preparation and Qualifications of Public School Teachers.* (NCES 1999–080). Washington, D.C.: U.S. Department of Education.

National Center for Educational Statistics (1997). *The Condition of Education.* (NCES 1997–388). Washington, D.C.: U.S. Department of Education.

National Commission on Teaching and America's Future (1996). *What Matters Most: Teaching for America's Future.* New York: National Commission on Teaching and America's Future.

Newman, K. S. (1999). *No Shame in My Game: The Working Poor in the Inner City.* New York: Alfred Knopf and The Russell Sage Foundation.

Newman, K. S., and C. Ellis (1999). "There's No Shame in My Game": Status and Stigma among Harlem's Working Poor. In M. Lamont (ed.), *The Cultural Territories of Race: Black and White Boundaries* (pp. 151–81). Chicago: University of Chicago Press.

Nieto, S. (1999). *The Light in Their Eyes: Creating Multicultural Learning Communities.* New York: Teachers College Press.

Nieto, S. (1996). *Affirming Diversity: The Sociopolitical Context of Multicultural Education* (2d ed.). New York: Longman.

Oakes, J. (1990). *Multiplying Inequalities: The Effects of Race, Social Class, and Tracking on Opportunities to Learn Mathematics and Science.* Santa Monica, Calif.: RAND Corporation.

Orona, C. (1990). Temporality and Identity Loss Due to Alzheimer's Disease. *Social Science Medicine* 30(11):1247–256.

Osofsky, J. D., S. Wewers, D. M. Hann, and A. C. Fick (1993). Chronic Community Violence: What Is Happening to Our Children? *Psychiatry* 56(1):36–45.

Park, P. (1993). What Is Participatory Research? A Theoretical and Methodological Perspective. In P. Park, M. Brydon-Miller, B. Hall, and T. Jackson (eds.), *Voices of Change: Participatory Research in the United States and Canada* (pp. 1–20). Toronto: Ontario Institute for Studies in Education.

Park, P., M. Brydon-Miller, B. Hall, and T. Jackson (eds.). (1993). *Voices of Change: Participatory Research in the United States and Canada.* Toronto: Ontario Institute for Studies in Education.

Pastor, J., J. McCormick, and M. Fine (1996). Makin' Home: An Urban Girl Thing. In B. J. R. Leadbeater and N. Way (eds.), *Urban Girls: Resisting Stereotypes, Creating Identities* (pp. 15–34). New York: New York University Press.

Pessar, P. (1997). Dominicans: Forging an Ethnic Community in New York. In M. Seller and L. Weis (eds.), *Beyond Black and White: New Faces and Voices in U.S. Schools* (pp. 131–50). Albany: SUNY Press.

Polakow, V. (1999). Savage Distributions: Welfare Myths and Daily Lives. In L. Kushnick and J. Jennings (eds.), *A New Introduction to Poverty: The Role of Race, Power, and Politics* (pp. 241–62). New York: New York University Press.

Ponder, W. S. (1994). *Educational Apartheid in a Pluralistic Society: Reform,*

Access, Equity and Admissions in America. Chapel Hill, N.C.: Professional Press.

Pope, J. (1999). Women in the Welfare Rights Struggle. In L. Kushnick and J. Jennings (eds.), *A New Introduction to Poverty: The Role of Race, Power, and Politics* (pp. 287–304). New York: New York University Press.

Preston-Whyte, E., and L. Dalrymple (1996). Participation and Action: Reflection on Community-Based AIDS Intervention in South Africa. In K. de Koning and M. Martin (eds.), *Participatory Research in Health: Issues and Experiences* (pp. 108–18). London: Zed Books.

Prothrow-Stith, D. (1991). *Deadly Consequences.* New York: HarperCollins.

Rak, C. F., and L. E. Patterson (1996). Promoting Resilience in At-Risk Children. *Journal of Counseling and Development* 74(March/April):368–73.

Reay, D. (1996). Dealing with Difficult Differences: Reflexivity and Social Class in Feminist Research. *Feminism and Psychology* 6(3):443–56.

Rosaldo, R. (1989). *Culture and Truth: The Remaking of Social Analysis.* Boston: Beacon Press.

Ruby, J. (1991). Speaking for, Speaking about, Speaking with, or Speaking alongside: An Anthropological and Documentary Dilemma. *Visual Anthropology Review* 7(2):50–67.

Rutter, M. (1983). Stress, Coping, and Development: Some Issues and Some Questions. In N. Garmezy and M. Rutter (eds.), *Stress, Coping and Development in Children* (pp. 1–42). New York: McGraw-Hill.

Selener, D. (1997). *Participatory Action Research and Social Change.* Ithaca: Cornell Participatory Action Research Network.

Shapiro, H. S., and D. E. Purpel (eds.). (1998). *Critical Social Issues in American Education: Transformation in a Postmodern World* (2d ed.). Mahwah, N.J.: Lawrence Erlbaum.

Solis, J. (1995). The Status of Latino Children and Youth: Challenges and Prospects. In R. E. Zambrana (ed.), *Understanding Latino Families: Scholarship, Policy, and Practice* (pp. 62–84). Thousand Oaks, Calif.: Sage.

Spelman, E. (1988). *Inessential Women: Problems of Exclusion in Feminist Thought.* Boston: Beacon Press.

Steinberg, L., S. D. Lamborn, S. M. Dornbusch, and N. Darling (1992). Impact of Parenting Practices on Adolescent Achievement: Authoritative Parenting, School Involvement, and Encouragement to Success. *Child Development* 63(5):1266–88.

Stewart, A. J. (1994). Toward a Feminist Strategy for Studying Women's Lives. In C. E. Franz and A. J. Stewart (eds.), *Women Creating Lives: Identities, Resilience and Resistance* (pp. 11–36). Boulder: Westview.

Strauss, A., and J. Corbin (1998). *Basics of Qualitative Research: Techniques and Procedures for Developing Grounded Theory* (2d ed.). Thousand Oaks, Calif.: Sage.

Strauss, A., and J. Corbin (1990). *Basics of Qualitative Research: Grounded Theory Procedures and Techniques.* Newbury Park, Calif.: Sage.

Sullivan, M. L. (1989). *"Getting Paid": Youth Crime and Work in the Inner City.* Ithaca: Cornell University Press.

Swantz, M. (1982a). Research as Education for Development: A Tanzanian Case. In B. Hall, A. Gillette, and R. Tandon, (eds.), *Creating Knowledge: A Monopoly* (pp. 113–26). New Delhi: Society for Participatory Research in Asia.

Swantz, M. (1982b). Participatory Research as an Instrument for Training: The Youth Development Project in the Coast Region of Tanzania. In Y. Kassam and K. Mustafa (eds.), *Participatory Research: an Emerging Alternative Methodology in Social Science Research* (pp. 117–38). New Delhi: Society for Participatory Research in Asia.

Tandon, R. (1996). The Historical Roots and Contemporary Tendencies in Participatory Research: Implications for Health Care. In K. de Koning and M. Martin (eds.), *Participatory Research in Health: Issues and Experiences* (pp. 19–26). London: Zed Books.

Tandon, R. (1982). Discussant Response to Paper 3. In Y. Kassam and K. Mustafa (eds.), *Participatory Research: An Emerging Alternative Methodology in Social Science Research* (pp. 83–86). New Delhi: Society for Participatory Research in Asia.

Tandon, R. (1981). Participatory Research in the Empowerment of People. *Convergence 14*(3):20–27.

Tarpley, N. (1995). On Giving Testimony, or the Process of Becoming. In N. Tarpley (ed.), *Testimony: Young African Americans on Self-discovery and Black Identity* (pp. 1–10). Boston: Beacon Press.

Teaching Tolerance magazine. Montgomery, Ala.: Southern Poverty Law Center.

Tellez, K., P. S. Hlebowitsh, M. Cohen, and P. Norwood (1995). Social Service Field Experiences and Teacher Education. In J. M. Larkin and C. Sleeter (eds.), *Developing Multicultural Teacher Education Curricula* (pp. 65–78). Albany: SUNY Press.

Townshend, B. L., D. D. Thomas, J. P. Witty, and R. S. Lee (1996). Diversity and School Restructuring: Creating Partnerships in a World of Difference. *Teacher Education and Special Education 19*(2):102–8.

Vio Grossi, F. (1980). The Socio-Political Implications of Participatory Research. In F. Dubell, T. Erasmie, and J. de Vries (eds.), *Research for the People—Research by the People: Selected Papers from the International Forum on Participatory Research in Ljubljana, Yugoslavia* (pp. 69–80). Linkoping, Sweden: Linkoping University and Amersfoort, Netherlands: S. V. E. The Netherlands Study and Development Center for Adult Education.

Wandersman, A., and M. Nation (1998). Urban Neighborhoods and Mental Health: Psychological Contributions to Understanding Toxicity, Resilience, and Interventions. *American Psychologist 53*(6):647–56.

Wang, C. (1999). Photovoice: A Participatory Action Research Strategy Applied to Women's Health. *Journal of Women's Health 8*(2):185–92.

Wang, C. (October 1995). Methodology for Community Photography: Participatory Needs Assessment and the Critical Image. Unpublished manuscript.

Wang, C., K. Wu, W. Zhan, and K. Carovano (1998). Photovoice as a Participatory Health Promotion Strategy. *Health Promotion International 13*(1):75–86.

Wang, M. C., and E. W. Gordon (eds.). (1994). *Educational Resilience in Inner-City America: Challenges and Prospects*. Hillsdale, N.J.: Lawrence Earlbaum.

Way, N. (1998). *Everyday Courage: The Lives and Stories of Urban Teenagers*. New York: New York University Press.

Way, N. (1996). Between Experiences of Betrayal and Desire: Close Friendships among Urban Adolescents. In B. J. R. Leadbeater and N. Way (eds.), *Urban Girls: Resisting Stereotypes, Creating Identities* (pp. 173–92). New York: New York University Press.

Webster's College Dictionary (1996). New York: Random House.

Werner, B. S., and M. D. Weist (1996). Urban Youth as Witnesses to Violence: Beginning Assessment and Treatment Efforts. *Journal of Youth and Adolescence 25*(3):361–375.

Werner, E. E. (1992). The Children of Kauai: Resiliency and Recovery in Adolescence and Adulthood. *Journal of Adolescent Health 13*:262–68.

Wolf, D. L. (1996). Situating Feminist Dilemmas in Fieldwork. In D. L. Wolf (ed.), *Feminist Dilemmas in Fieldwork* (pp. 1–55). Boulder: Westview Press.

Wolf, D. L. (ed.). (1996). *Feminist Dilemmas in Fieldwork*. Boulder: Westview Press.

Wu, K., M. Burris, V. Li, Y. Wang, W. Zhan, Y. Xian, K. Yang, and C. Wang (eds.). (1995). *Visual Voices: One Hundred Photographs of Village China by the Women of Yunnan Province*. Yunnan, China: Yunnan People's Publishing House.

Zeichner, K., and S. Melnick (1997). The Role of Community Field Experiences in Preparing Teachers for Cultural Diversity. In K. Zeichner, S. Melnick, and M. L. Gomez (eds.), *Currents of Reform in Preservice Education* (pp. 176–96). New York: Teachers College Press.

Ziller, R. C., H. Vern, and C. Camacho de Santoya (1988). The Psychological Niche of Children of Poverty and Affluence through Auto-photography. *Children's Environment Quarterly 5*(2):34–39.

Zipes, J. (1995). *Creative Storytelling: Building Community, Changing Lives*. London: Routledge.

Index